Bill Wyman's
CHELSEA

Bill Wyman's
CHELSEA
FROM MEDIEVAL VILLAGE TO CULTURAL CAPITAL

UNICORN

Pavilion Road

Contents

MISCELLANY

*Discover Chelsea's remarkable transformation
from village to cultural hotspot*

ITINERARIES

*Follow four walking tours
highlighting the best of Chelsea*

CHELSEA STREETS A TO Z

*Street-by-street guide to the
curiosities of Chelsea*

Welcome

ON A GREY, COLD WINTER'S DAY on the 8th of December 1962, I went with my drummer friend to a pub in Chelsea called the Wetherby Arms. It sat on the corner of the King's Road and Slaidburn Street. It was here that my life would change forever, taking a turn that I could have never believed imaginable. I had with me my bass and my three amps; and in that pub, I met Mick, Keith and Brian. It has been said I brought electricity to the Rollin' Stones. I joined the band that day. The boys shared a flat down the road at 102 Edith Grove and it was here we would meet up for rehearsals, along with Charlie Watts, who joined the band a month later. We were now called the Rolling Stones, without the apostrophe. My journey as a Rolling Stone started in Chelsea.

It's no wonder Chelsea holds such a warm place in my heart. My love for the neighbourhood continued to grow throughout the 1960s, when I began to go on shopping sprees at the fashionable boutiques in the King's Road, buying Edwardian velvet jackets from Dandy Fashions, Moroccan clothes and jewellery at the Chelsea Antique Market, and visiting the Chelsea Drugstore. During these escapades, I would inevitably cross paths with the many celebrities who also shopped and ate

The Rolling Stones in 1967, Bill Wyman seated centre

there. I was part of this exciting new era, when music, fashion, art, film and theatre were all changing.

The late 1960s and the 1970s took the band away from England, playing our music to audiences around the world. We settled in the south of France in 1971 in tax exile (but that is another story altogether). Then, in the spring of 1982, I decided to return to England to live; Chelsea was my first choice. The Stones had an office there and I bought my own office down the road from the band's.

I have lived in many flats across the borough over the years. But once I stopped rolling with the Stones, I settled down to start a family and have been living in the same house for more than 27 years with my wife and daughters, who have gone to local schools in the area.

Chelsea has always felt like a wonderful little village to me, with the myriad of shops, restaurants, unique fixtures and sights that adorn its streets. I enjoy quiet strolls along the Embankment Gardens beside the wonderful River Thames. This village has held me in happy times and rough times, for which I am forever grateful. I hope this book is a worthy gift to say thank you.

My life opened up the first time I set foot in Chelsea. May this book open up your life to Chelsea, the village I call my home.

Bill Wyman

The Rolling Stones Exhibitionism retrospective show at the Saatchi Gallery, 2016

How to Use This Book

This is a book about Chelsea, about its streets, its buildings and the people who made it one of Britain's most vibrant and culturally relevant destinations. The book is divided into three parts: Miscellany, Itineraries and Chelsea Streets A to Z.

MISCELLANY

A brief history of Chelsea, its great lost houses, its bridges and riverside walks, beautiful architecture and ironmongery; including door knockers and coal hole covers, and an exploration of the Chelsea Physic Gardens. It offers historical context and a fair amount of whimsy. Start at the beginning and enjoy.

ITINERARIES

There are four itineraries: Historic Chelsea, Literary Chelsea, Artistic Chelsea, and Music & Fashion in Chelsea. Each is designed to be followed as a walking tour that pulls in relevant locations, houses where famous people lived and all the most important sights of Chelsea. There is a map for each itinerary, and plotted on each are the route and numbered points of interest related to locations mentioned in the main text. You can also follow the text. They are designed to be walked in a few hours. Take your time, stop for a coffee, pop into a shop, learn and enjoy the culture and heritage of Chelsea.

CHELSEA STREETS A-Z

This is the core of the book. There is an entry for almost every street and mews in Chelsea. Along each road, I've highlighted the houses, buildings, artworks, shops, pubs and galleries that have shaped Chelsea. It could be the home of an author, a fascinating piece of architecture, an artwork in a public garden or one of the star attractions of Chelsea. I've also delved into the life of some of Chelsea's remarkable (or notorious) residents and some of the more curious events to have happened in the borough.

In Chelsea Streets A to Z, I've also added icons that highlight an area of interest:

 **H** – History   **L** – Literature   **A** – Art   **M** – Music & Fashion

MISCELLANY

A Riverside Village

THE NAME 'CHELSEA' is thought to derive from the Anglo-Saxon 'Chelcehithe', meaning 'a landing place for chalk', or from 'Chesil', meaning 'gravel bank'.

In 1857, a magnificent Bronze-Age shield was found in the River Thames, at the site where Battersea Bridge now stands. The Battersea Shield dates back to the Iron Age, sometime between 350 and 50 BC. It is not a complete shield, but rather the metal cover that is attached to a wooden shield's front. The polished bronze shield with red enamel inlays was thrown or placed in the river, where weapons were offered as sacrifices in the Bronze and Iron Ages. It is now on display at the British Museum.

Half a mile down the river, below where the Chelsea Bridge is now, is where, in 54 BC, Julius Caesar was said to have first crossed the Thames. Ancient Britons used the ford, over a shoal of gravel, at low tide, which was no more than 90cm (3ft) deep. Excavations were undertaken when the bridge was built, and human bones and large numbers of discarded weapons

Top: Bronze-Age shield

Bottom: Engraving after J. Maurer, *Chelsea: viewed from the Surrey bank with boats on the river*, 1755

Opposite: Houseboats at Chelsea Reach

were unearthed. It led archaeologists to believe that the river crossing was the site of a battle between ancient Britons and the invading Romans.

Chelsea began life as a little Saxon village on the Thames. Early records from 785 and 816 AD mention religious assemblies at Chelsea attended by King Offa, who had a residence in the village at the time. King Alfred also held important assemblies here in the 800s AD and drove the early Viking invaders away from the area. Early records reveal that Chelsea was the site of a royal manor or palace, or home to a large church or minster, around that time.

In 980 AD, the Vikings were back, having sailed up the Thames. They occupied London until 1014, when King Ethelred (The Unready) and the Norseman Olaf recaptured the city.

Little is known of Chelsea in the Dark Ages, apart from the building of All Saints Church (Chelsea Old Church) around 1300. It was probably built on the site of an earlier Saxon church.

The Old Church, Chelsea, looking along the bank with luxuriant trees in the centre, boats on the river, 1792

Thomas More's Chelsea

BY THE EARLY 1500s, Monmouth House and Shrewsbury House had already been established here, but it was the arrival of Sir Thomas More (1478–1535) that first put Chelsea on the map. He was appointed under-treasurer to Henry VIII in 1520, and in around 1525 he purchased twenty-three acres of land in Chelsea and built himself a large home by the river, which would later be called Beaufort House. The household was extensive, including three married daughters, their husbands and their children. More received numerous distinguished visitors to his home, including the artist Hans Holbein, who later painted More's portrait.

King Henry VIII also loved visiting Thomas More at his house, and the two men would discuss worldly affairs. More became Lord Chancellor in 1529 after the death of Cardinal Wolsey. The following year, Henry wanted to divorce Catherine of Aragon, which Thomas More had strong reservations about. He resigned the chancellorship in 1532 and retired to Chelsea. More was later opposed to the dissolution of the monasteries and Henry assuming the title of Supreme Governor of the Church in England. His reluctance to accept the king's decisions caused him, in 1534, to be arrested at Chelsea and taken to the Tower, where he was later tried for treason and beheaded in 1535.

Just off the Chelsea Embankment Gardens, outside Chelsea Old Church, is a statue of Thomas More in the little St Thomas

Statue of Sir Thomas More outside Chelsea Old Church

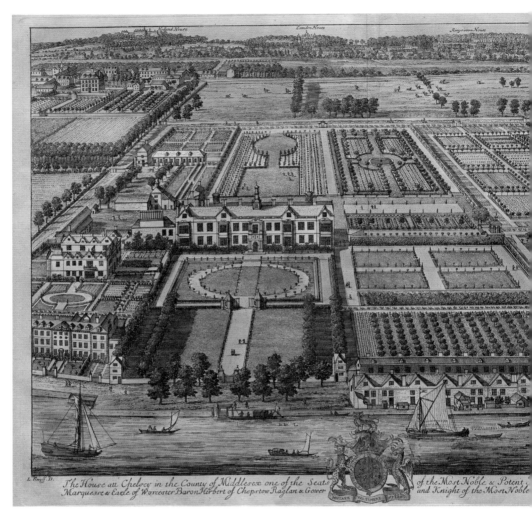

The House att Chelsey in the County of Middlesex one of the Seats
Marquesse & Earle of Worcester Baron Herbert of Chepstow Raglan & Gower

*of the Most Noble & Potent ;
and Knight of the Most Noble*

More Gardens. The figure is by Leslie Cubitt Bevis and was erected here
in July 1969.

Thomas More's house was later occupied by several aristocratic
owners, including Sir Robert Cecil, in 1597. By 1627, King Charles I
had granted it to George Villiers, 1st Duke of Buckingham. His family
continued to live there after he died, until the state seized the house in
the 1650s during the Civil War.

In 1682, with Charles II on the throne, the house came into the
ownership of Henry Somerset, Marquess of Worcester (1629–1700).
When he gained the title 1st Duke of Beaufort, the house was named
Beaufort House, and was at the time the most important mansion in
Chelsea. The Duke lived there until his death, and the Beauforts finally
moved out in 1736.

Left: Johannes Kip, *Beaufort House, Chelsea*, 1707–9

Right: Godfrey Kneller, *Henry Somerset (1629–1699), 1st Duke of Beaufort, KG, PC*

A year later, the new Lord of Chelsea Manor, Sir Hans Sloane, demolished the house, and its site and grounds were added to those of Sloane's manor house. His property included most of the frontage of the Thames at Chelsea and stretched northwards as far as the King's Road. The estate was laid out in gardens and orchards. A farmhouse, barns and stables were constructed on the original 1630 Lindsey House site. Later, the Moravian Burial Ground was here.

To the southwest of Beaufort House was the smaller gabled Gorges House, built *c.* 1600 for Sir Arthur Gorges and his wife Elizabeth. She was the daughter of the Earl of Lincoln, who had briefly occupied the grand mansion of Sir Thomas More. Gorges later inherited the main property on the death of his father-in-law. Gorges House was sold *c.* 1664 to a schoolmaster called Josias Priest, who sold it on to Sir William Milman in 1697. A number of cottages called Milman's Row were built across the site of Gorges House in 1726 but were eventually replaced in 1952 by council housing.

King Charles II was a frequent visitor to Chelsea, and in 1681 he responded to the need to look after soldiers injured in the Civil War. He issued a Royal Warrant authorising the building of the Royal Hospital in Chelsea. To the present day, a member of the royal family attends Founders' Day every June to 'receive' the Chelsea Pensioners.

A Village Transformed

THE EARLY HEART of the village of Chelsea was formed beside the river on either side of the Chelsea Old Church, where the wharves, old inns, shops and houses were loved by the artists, poets and writers who lived there.

It is hard to believe that by the 1950s the river was so filthy that it could not support marine life. Tremendous efforts were made to clean up the river in the 1960s and 1970s, and although salmon have not yet returned in any numbers, numerous fish species and eels have been recorded. I have observed cormorants diving beside the Albert Bridge and surfacing with small eels.

The development of the King's Road in the nineteenth century and the building of St Luke's Church in Sydney Street in 1824 were the causes of the gradual move of the village northwards.

Cheyne Walk and Cadogan Pier, 1860

In 1901, at the express wish of Queen Victoria, the area was given royal borough status by King Edward VII. Although this title does not carry any particular rights or privileges, it is seen as an honour and a matter of civic pride.

Over the years, various newspapers have been published for Chelsea residents, but few have had staying power. The *Chelsea News* was published from 1860 to 1867. It became the *Westminster and Chelsea News* in 1885, and its descendant, the *Chelsea News*, has been published since 1972.

John Varley, *View along the Thames towards Chelsea Old Church*, 1810–15

The *Kensington and Chelsea Times* has been printed since 1983.

Today, Chelsea is a thriving and highly desired residential district as well as an upmarket shopping and dining destination. Yet it is still one of London's most iconic urban villages. Young royals often visit, and with Prince William and the Duchess of Cambridge living in Kensington Palace, Kate is often seen shopping on the King's Road.

St Luke's Church, Sydney Street

Thriving café culture on Pavilion Road

The Great Houses of Chelsea

THE FIRST CHELSEA MANOR HOUSE was located at the northern end of what is now Lawrence Street. Sir Reginald Bray owned the manor from 1485 to 1503, and was succeeded by his nephew Sir Edmund, Lord Bray. He surrendered the property in 1510 to Sir William Sandys, who, in 1543, exchanged the house and manor with Henry VIII for property in Hampshire. The house faced the river where the Cadogan Pier is today.

In 1583, it came into the possession of goldsmith Thomas Lawrence, after whom Lawrence Street was named. He died in 1593 and was buried in a chapel in the Old Church, which was then called the Lawrence Chapel. The state seized Manor House in 1653.

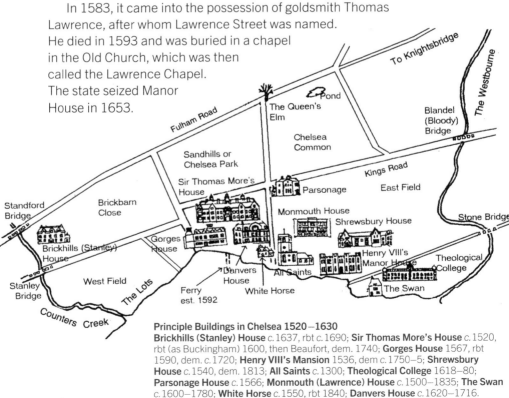

Principle Buildings in Chelsea 1520–1630
Brickhills (Stanley) House c.1637, rbt c.1690; **Sir Thomas More's House** c.1520, rbt (as Buckingham) 1600, then Beaufort, dem. 1740; **Gorges House** 1567, rbt 1590, dem. c.1720; **Henry VIII's Mansion** 1536, dem c.1750–5; **Shrewsbury House** c.1540, dem. 1813; **All Saints** c.1300; **Theological College** 1618–80; **Parsonage House** c.1566; **Monmouth (Lawrence) House** c.1500–1835; **The Swan** c.1600–1780; **White Horse** c.1550, rbt 1840; **Danvers House** c.1620–1716.

HENRY VIII'S MANOR HOUSE

Henry VIII's manor house was to the east side of what is today Oakley Street, in the vicinity of Nos.19–26 Cheyne Walk. Henry gave the place to his last wife, Catherine Parr, as a wedding present. The young Edward VI and Elizabeth I lived here with Catherine for part of their childhoods, with occasional visits from Jane Grey, then a girl of eleven. Following Henry's death in 1547, Catherine Parr continued to live there with her former suitor, Thomas Seymour, who she married. Further residents included Anne of Cleves, another of Henry's discarded wives, who died there in 1557. Later, residents included the widows of the Lord Protector Somerset, who was executed in 1552, and the Duke of Northumberland, who was executed for his plan to put Jane Grey on the throne. The house was then given to Lord Howard of Effingham, the hero of the defeat of the Spanish Armada. Queen Elizabeth I often dined with him there.

The old Chelsea Manor House, *c.* 1880

Sometime later, it passed into the possession of the Duke of Hamilton (*see Upper Cheyne Row in A-Z*). After the Restoration, the house and manor passed into the possession of Lord Cheyne, from whom the name of Cheyne Walk is derived.

SIR THOMAS MORE'S MANOR HOUSE

Part of the grounds of Sir Thomas More's old house at Chelsea was purchased by Sir John Danvers (1588–1655) in 1622. He was a courtier of King James I and Charles I, and well-travelled. He supported the Parliamentary cause during the Civil War and was one of the signatories of King Charles I's death warrant. The house had grounds that stretched back to the King's Road. Grand though Danvers House was, it was in such a bad state in 1696 that it was condemned. It was demolished in 1720, parts of the garden were leased, and Danvers Street was constructed across it. Later, some of the new houses on the western side of the street were demolished to make way for Crosby House.

MONMOUTH HOUSE

The manor house that Sir Hans Sloane took possession of in 1742 was where he lived until he died in 1753. He intended his remarkable collection of antiquities and natural history specimens should be housed at Chelsea, and it was eventually to form one of the founding collections of the British Museum in Bloomsbury. The house and grounds went on the market when development along the Chelsea riverfront was an attractive proposition. This house was demolished in 1755.

The site was taken over by several houses, one of which was occupied by the widow of James, Duke of Monmouth. This became known as Monmouth House. The Duchess of Monmouth had begun life as Anne Scott and was Countess of Buccleuch in her own right. In 1663, she was married to James, an illegitimate son of Charles II, when he was only fourteen years old; that same year, he was made Duke of Monmouth. Over the years, he developed aspirations to assume the throne. Charles II had no legitimate male heir, and his brother, who became James II, was not popular in England, partly because he was Catholic. Monmouth was persuaded to take his chance upon the death of Charles II and led the so-called Monmouth Rebellion in 1685. For his part in this uprising, he was executed at the Tower.

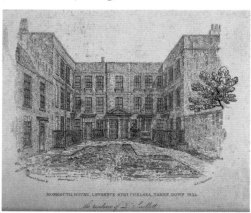

R.B. Schnebbelie, *Monmouth House*, c.1849

We know that in 1716, Princess Caroline of Ansbach, the future queen (wife of George II), visited the duchess at Chelsea, and the parish registers record that six shillings were paid to the bell-ringers at the church on that occasion. The duchess died in 1732, and the next tenant of note in Monmouth House was the novelist Tobias Smollett (1721–71), who came with his wife and child in 1749, but had left by 1763. Contemporary with Smollett in part of the property was Nicholas Sprimont, who ran the Chelsea Porcelain Works adjacent. In 1815, all or part of Monmouth House was occupied by a boarding school, though the house seems to have been entirely demolished in 1835.

Stephen Slaughter, *Sir Hans Sloane, BT*, 1736

Next to Monmouth House was Duke's House, and a little lower down towards the river was Lawrence House. In 2002, another house called Manor House was identified, built in 1780 by Thomas Richardson, facing east along present-day St Leonard's Terrace. It was demolished in 1870.

Chelsea's Noble and Notable Families

SIR HANS SLOANE

Sir Hans Sloane (1660–1753) was elected to the Royal College of Physicians in 1687. That year, he went to the West Indies for fifteen months and brought back 800 species of plants, many of which he donated to the Physic Garden at Chelsea. Two years earlier, he had been elected a Fellow of the Royal Society at the age of twenty-five, and became its

Statue of Sir Hans Sloane in the Physic Garden

president (following Isaac Newton) in 1727. He developed a great affection for the Physic Garden. When he bought the manor of Chelsea in 1712, he ensured that the Society of Apothecaries had a freehold of the site as long as the Garden produced new species each year.

He amassed a vast library of 50,000 books and more than 3,000 volumes of manuscripts, 347 volumes of drawings and illuminated books, 32,000 coins and many natural specimens. Upon his retirement in 1742, he moved all of these to Chelsea, where he lived in the manor house built for Henry VIII. Sloane had directed that on his death (which occurred in 1753, when he was ninety-two), his entire collection should be offered to the country at a nominal price and kept together at Chelsea. This was not to be, as the government was finally persuaded to buy the collection at the price specified. It was housed at Montagu House in Bloomsbury, where it became one of the keystones of the British Museum. A statue was erected at the museum in his honour.

THE CADOGAN FAMILY

Much of Chelsea, and many of its street names, reflect developments put in hand by the Cadogan family, whose manor of Chelsea made up about half of the Chelsea parish. The Cadogan name first appears locally upon the death of Sir Hans Sloane in 1753.

Sloane's property was divided between his two daughters, Sarah, who had married George Stanley of Paultons in Hampshire (hence Paultons Square), and Elizabeth, the

Solomon Joseph Solomon, *George Henry (1840–1915), 5th Earl of Cadogan, KG, JP, First Mayor of Chelsea (1900–1901)*, c. 1900

wife of Baron Cadogan of Oakley (hence Oakley Street). Eventually, the Cadogan family owned about three-quarters of the manor (around 270 acres at the time). At the same time, the balance was retained by Sloane's great nephew, also named Hans, a holding which later became the Sloane-Stanley estate.

The Cadogan estate developed some of the finest streets in Chelsea. The 5th Earl Cadogan (1840–1915), the first Mayor of Chelsea, made a significant contribution to Chelsea's fabric, for it was during his time as head of the estate that Cadogan Square and the redevelopment of the Hans Town area occurred. In 1902, the estate sold a twenty-acre site comprising the more significant part of the old Chelsea Common. Very soon after that, the remodelling of Sloane Square commenced with the construction of the large building on the south side of Sloane Square. Amos Faulkner designed it for the developer William Willett (1856–1915), whose main claim to fame was to persuade the government to adopt the annual system of changing the clocks by one hour to save daylight time.

When the 7th Earl Cadogan succeeded to the title in 1933, he inherited 100 acres of Chelsea and substantial death duties. He had the choice of selling Chelsea to pay for these and concentrate on the family home of Culford, but he wisely chose to keep Chelsea, and the Cadogans have continued to have a substantial influence in Chelsea since. He was the Mayor of Chelsea when he died in 1997.

THOMAS CARLYLE

Thomas Carlyle (1795–1881) was a literary giant of his era, renowned for what became a classic book on the history of the French Revolution,

published in 1837. Thomas and his wife Jane took up residence at No.5 (now No.24) Cheyne Row on 10 June 1834, and remained there until he died in 1881. At his Cheyne Row residence, he was host to many forward thinkers of the time, including William Makepeace Thackeray, Charles Darwin, John Stuart Mill, Robert Owen and his great friend Charles Dickens. In 1872, Carlyle had the rare distinction of having a square named after him while he was still alive, when Oakley Square became Carlyle Square.

His house in Cheyne Row was bought by a group of admirers in 1895 and was eventually presented to the National Trust. Joseph Boehm's statue of Thomas Carlyle in the Embankment Gardens was unveiled in October 1882 at a ceremony attended by

Statue of Thomas Carlyle in the Embankment Garden

Robert Browning. The inscription below the figure states: 'Thomas Carlyle B: Dec: 4, 1795 at Ecclefechan Dumfriesshire D: Feb: 5, 1881 at Great Cheyne Row Chelsea'.

Thomas Carlyle's interesting description of Chelsea when he moved there in 1834 was as follows: 'A singular heterogeneous kind of spot, very dirty and confused in some places, quite beautiful in others, abounding in antiquities and traces of great men'.

DR JOHN SAMUEL PHENE

Of all Chelsea's eccentrics, Dr John Samuel Phene (1823–1912) is one of the most celebrated. He was a short, dapper man with a Van Dyke beard, and was a traveller, a collector, a scholar, a poet, a property developer and a recluse (who nevertheless seems to have had many friends). An innovator in architecture and planning, he pioneered the now-accepted theory that trees purify the air in towns, and convinced Victorian developers to have the streets lined with trees.

Dr John Samuel Phene

Dr Phene's house on the corner of Oakley Street and Upper Cheyne Row, later demolished

The woman to whom he was engaged died of rheumatic fever many years before he built the extraordinary chateau on the corner of Oakley Street and Upper Cheyne Row. It was built on the grounds of the crumbling eighteenth-century mansion Cheyne House, and was surrounded by a large, overgrown garden with many rare and interesting trees. Work began in 1901 when he was seventy-eight, and it was a home of two halves. The Oakley Street side was all staid Victoriana, whilst the highly decorated edifice facing Upper Cheyne Row was covered in gargoyles, beasts, birds, gods and goddesses, dragons and serpents, all picked out in scarlet and gold. The wording above the doorway read 'Renaissance Du Chateau de Savenay'.

Dr Phene never actually lived in the house, but he and his friends seem to have spent time in it, long enough to have created, among other features, a mortuary for cats within its walls. Sources differ as to whether the house was built in the style of a French chateau or an Italian palazzo, but in any case it was a celebration of Dr Phene's rich and varied ancestry. He is said to have avoided completing the building because of a dispute over the rates with the Chelsea Vestry, which is a dull enough explanation to be plausible, but perhaps he just never got around to finishing it. The house would later become No.2 Upper Cheyne Row.

Dr Phene also designed many conventional houses on Oakley Street, where he later lived in a place that wasn't exactly conventional in appearance. He later married his cousin Margaretta and built Margaretta Terrace, which he named in honour of her. Some claim the marriage soon failed, while others maintain that it lasted for some time before Margaretta left and went to live in Paris.

Another story told about Dr Phene is that Queen Victoria came to see the new houses he was building off Oakley Street and was pleased enough with them to say he could name the new street after her, but he declined as he had already promised the name to his wife. If this is true, it sounds quite a daring thing to do. He may have made up for the slight by writing a long narrative poem entitled 'Victoria Queen of Albion – an idyll of the world's advance in her life and reign', published in 1897.

Dr Phene would sit alone in his eerie monumental garden, safeguarded by a secret lock of his own design, dwarfed by the vast statues in a tangle of undergrowth. He died in 1912, aged eighty-nine. After his death, the building continued to stand empty, and gave rise to myths and rumours from the time of its construction to its demolition in 1917 (or in 1924, as some references state).

Phene Street, below Margaretta Street, runs east from Oakley Street and was named after him, as was the Phene Arms public house there.

It is shameful that this great and far-seeing man has not been honoured by a blue plaque in Oakley Street, where he lived.

The Chelsea Bun

THE WORLD-FAMOUS CHELSEA BUN is a spicy, cinnamon-flavoured pastry synonymous with the London borough. The Chelsea Bun first appeared in the early 1700s at the Bun House, a building near the Ranelagh Pleasure Gardens (now part of the grounds of Royal Hospital Chelsea). It was owned by four generations of the Hand family. The premises had a colonnaded front, which protected the people who queued outside. It was often visited by members of the royal family of the time, including King George II, Queen Caroline and the princesses, and by Queen Charlotte, consort of George III. Author Jonathan Swift is also supposed to have been partial to a Chelsea Bun. Thanks to its regal patronage, the bakery became informally known as the Royal Bun House. It survived until the 1830s, and the building was demolished c. 1840 when Belgravia was developed.

Trade card of Richard Hand

The Chelsea Bun House, 1810

The Chelsea Bun, however, remains a favourite in the city. The popularity of the Chelsea Bun is being spearheaded by Partridges, a local grocer and purveyor of fine foods. They launched the World Chelsea Bun Awards in 2019 with an aim to revive the baking of Chelsea Buns in the area and around the world. If you fancy a Chelsea Bun, you'll find Partridges at 2–5 Duke of York Square or have go at making your own with the recipe on the back flap!

Julia Page,
Partridges Chelsea Bun

The River Thames

CHELSEA WAS A VILLAGE that relied on the River Thames. It was the scene of local trades, and because it was within easy reach of the city, wealthy London citizens often chose the area to build their country homes. Crossing the river was always challenging, and no bridges existed until 1771.

A horse ferry at Chelsea is referred to in a manuscript of 1292/93, noting the expense for a 'passage of the Thames at Cenlee'. It is again mentioned in 1592 as one of the horse ferries that crossed the Thames from the south bank, and docked where Danvers Street is today. Horses or mules would walk a treadmill that powered the boat. The Crown owned the ferry, but it was sold by King James I to the Earl of Lincoln in 1603. It can be seen in prints from 1699 and 1738.

There were still no bridges across the Thames between Westminster and Putney until as late as 1766, and travellers would still need to cross the river using the Chelsea horse ferry if they wished to continue their journeys south.

BATTERSEA BRIDGE

In 1766, an Act of Parliament to build the first Battersea Bridge was spearheaded by Earl Spencer, who owned the horse ferry and manorial land on the other side of the river in Battersea. It was in his interest to encourage travel to the south bank to foster development.

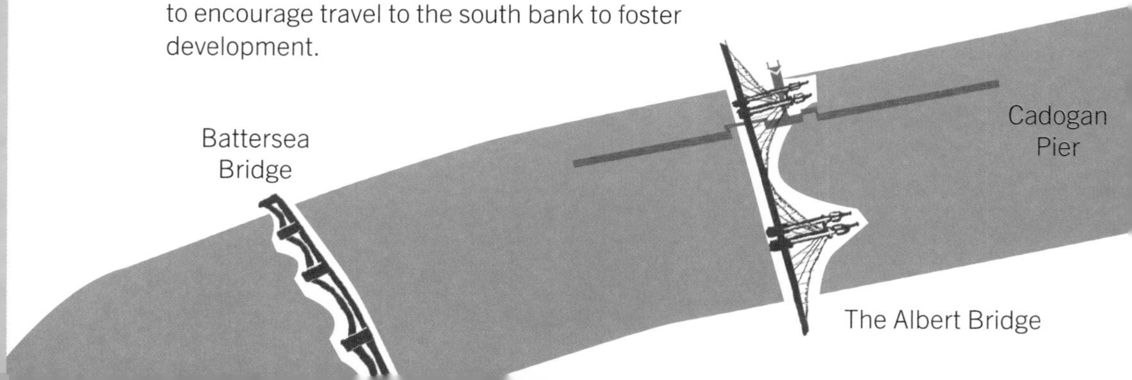

Battersea
Bridge

Cadogan
Pier

The Albert Bridge

View of the West End of London with the Thames and Vauxhall Bridge and Victoria Bridge in the centre, Battersea Park to Vauxhall Gardens on the south bank, and the area from Chelsea to Pimlico via the King's Road and Cheyne Walk, reaching to the Oratory and Hyde Park, on the north bank; April 1859

The bridge was opened to pedestrians in 1771 and carriage traffic the following year, thereby making the old horse ferry redundant.

It was built entirely of wood by Henry Holland and needed constant maintenance. In 1799, it became the first wooden bridge across the Thames to be lit by oil lamps. In later years, these would be replaced by gas lamps.

It was a picturesque structure and much-loved by local painters such as J.M.W Turner and James Abbott McNeill Whistler, whose painting

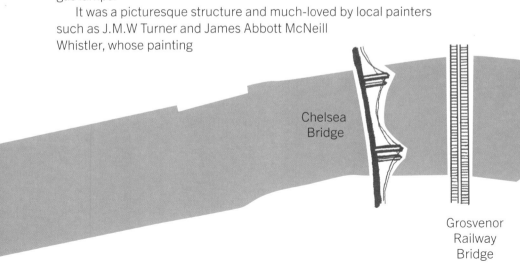

Chelsea Bridge

Grosvenor Railway Bridge

James Abbott McNeill Whistler, *Nocturne: Blue and Gold – Old Battersea Bridge*, c. 1872–5

Nocturne: Blue and Gold can be seen at Tate Britain in Pimlico. However, the bridge had quite narrow spans, which made it a problem for the boats wishing to navigate under it.

It was decided to bring the bridge up to a better standard in 1873, and six years later, the Metropolitan Board of Works took it over. By 1883, it had been restricted to foot passengers only. It was later closed and dismantled, to the disappointment of the local residents. Sir Joseph and Edward Bazalgette constructed its replacement, and the Earl of Rosebery opened the present bridge in July 1890. There is a small plaque there that states 'Battersea Bridge 1890 Structure No.4'.

For a while, Chelsea resisted the spread of London's electric tram system, but in 1911 a short line crossed Battersea Bridge, running north up part of Beaufort Street to terminate at the King's Road. However, the route (the No.34) closed in 1950 after a shipping accident weakened the bridge's structure.

The climactic sequence of Guy Ritchie's 1998 movie *Lock, Stock and Two Smoking Barrels* was filmed on the bridge.

THE ALBERT BRIDGE

The Albert Bridge was designed and built by Rowland Mason Ordish in 1873 as a toll bridge. The opening ceremony in 1874 for this structure was a quiet affair, with just a hundred people assembled at a wooden barrier at the Chelsea end, guarded by two policemen.

The Albert Bridge was a commercial failure. After six years of mismanagement it became publicly owned and the tolls lifted (although the toll booths on the Chelsea side still exist). The bridge was also structurally unsound, with local residents dubbing it the 'Trembling Lady'

The Albert Bridge

because it vibrated when crowds walked across it. Consequently, the Greater London Council employed civil engineer Sir Joseph Bazalgette to strengthen the bridge between 1884 and 1887. A sign can still be seen on the toll booth that states: 'All troops must break step when marching over this bridge'.

Given its structural idiosyncrasies, it was clearly not suitable for the advent of the car. In the 1950s, London County Council wanted to demolish the bridge, but a campaign, led by John Betjeman, saved it. He wrote: 'Shining with electric lights to show the way to Festival Gardens or grey and airy against the London sky, it is one of the beauties of the London river.'

Two piers were added in 1973 by the Greater London Council, transforming the Albert Bridge into a beam bridge. It was rewired and repainted in 1992. The unusual colour scheme is to improve visibility. Today, 4,000 bulbs light up the Grade II listed structure. When lit up at night, my young daughters would always call it the 'Fairy Bridge'.

CHELSEA BRIDGE

Chelsea Bridge is located where a ford crossed the Thames at a time when the river was much broader and shallower. The eighteenth-century historian William Maitland noted that, at times, the river here was only about 1.09m (3ft 7in.) deep. In July 1948, Joe Simms, aged fifty-one, claimed to have walked across the river with his head above water.

The first Chelsea Bridge was designed and built by Thomas Page in 1851. It opened in March 1858 as a toll bridge, but the tolls were soon discontinued. The bridge needed constant strengthening, and there was no opposition from the Chelsea Society when it was demolished and replaced in the mid-1930s. The current Chelsea Bridge was designed by G.Topham Forrest and E.P.Wheeler, and was, for some reason, opened by the Prime Minister of Canada in May 1937.

The decorative lighting on Chelsea Bridge

Chelsea New Bridge connects Chelsea with Battersea Park on the east side. It has beautiful light standards featuring galleons in full sail above two individual heraldic shields, with light fittings on either side.

CADOGAN PIER

Cadogan Pier is located immediately east of the Albert Bridge on Cheyne Walk. It was erected in 1841 by Earl Cadogan and designed by Nathaniel Handford. It was rebuilt around 1875 following the completion

Walter Greaves, *Old Swan and Royal Barge*, 1860s–70s

of the Albert Bridge. The pier was extended in 2004 and has numerous residential moorings that increase yearly.

RIVER WESTBOURNE

The River Westbourne once formed the eastern boundary of Chelsea. Various tributaries rise in West Hampstead, joining up at Kilburn. The river flows below ground to Paddington, Bayswater Road and Hyde Park, and then crosses beneath the road at Knightsbridge, very near the Harvey Nichols department store. It then meanders east of Cadogan Place to Sloane Square by the Blandel Bridge (nicknamed the 'Bloody Bridge'), where it crosses above the District Line tracks and out to the Thames, west of Chelsea Bridge. Some parts remained open until c. 1856, but it is now entirely underground as the Ranelagh Sewer. The outfall is sometimes visible at low tide.

CHELSEA CREEK

Chelsea Creek was the old boundary between Chelsea and Fulham, and one of the last Chelsea riversides to be swept away by modern development. The creek was the outlet of the stream known initially by several names, including Billingswell Ditch and Counters Creek. In 1828, a project was instigated by the 2nd Earl of Kensington to canalise Counters Creek, but by the mid-1830s the scheme was deemed a 'total failure'.

As recently as 1952, the inlet was described as being 'still visible as a stagnant ditch'. In the 1980s, the area around Chelsea Creek was chosen for an expensive development, when twenty acres of coal yards were bought to create Chelsea Harbour.

CHELSEA REACH

From earliest times, the muddy foreshore of Chelsea Reach had been a scene of boats and wharves. Before the Embankment was constructed, the area was busy, as seen in the photographs of James Hedderley and the paintings of Walter Greaves and his brother Harry. Their father owned a boatyard here and ferried the artist J.M.W. Turner to wherever he wanted to go. The Chelsea Yacht and Boat Company, founded here in 1935 by Charles Fleming, was mainly for boat repairs, although some mooring space was kept. During the Second World War, the firm became contractors to the admiralty, and naval launches and barges were built there. Vessels built here joined in the evacuation of soldiers from Dunkirk in 1940, and other vessels were used in the Normandy invasion of 1944. Gradually, the houseboat moorings began to dominate due to the shortage of regular housing. After Fleming's death, the Chelsea Yacht and Boat Company was taken over by the father of Chelsea footballer Peter Osgood, and later by Peter himself until he died in 2006, aged fifty-nine.

DOGGETT'S COAT & BADGE WAGER

For those not wealthy enough to live in the area, the Thames at Chelsea was a fine place for Londoners to come to on a day out. In 1666, the Old Swan stood east of the Physic Garden. The pub marks the finishing line for the annual Doggett Coat and Badge Wager, the oldest rowing event in the world. Irish actor Thomas Doggett instituted the race in 1715 in

honour of King George I's accession to the throne a year earlier. Every year, six Thames watermen race against the tide from London Bridge to Cadogan Pier in Chelsea, a distance of 7,400 metres. The winner receives a scarlet coat with silver buttons and a large silver badge on the left arm.

Edward Francis Burney, *View at Chelsea of the Annual Sculling Race for Doggett's Coat and Badg*, undated

COAL HOLE COVERS

or manhole covers as they are often referred to — are seen in every street in Chelsea. They were manufactured by a number of companies established both in Chelsea and other parts of London. They display a large variety of attractive designs that add interest to many dull pavements. The following are the most common manufacturers of the covers I've photographed around Chelsea.

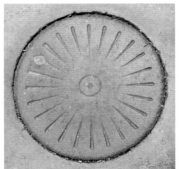

Jas Bartle (Western Iron Works, Notting Hill, London)

J.W. Carpenter (188–90 Earl's Court Road, London)

Durey Castings (Hawley Road, Dartford, Kent)

Green & London (121 King's Road, Chelsea)

C.L. Hacking (259 King's Road, Chelsea)

Hayward Brothers (187–9 Union Street, Borough, London)

T. Hyatt (9 Farringdon Road, London)

R.H. & J. Pearson (Notting Hill Gate, London)

A. Smellie (Westminster)

A.D. Woodrow (London)

A Brief History of Chelsea Old Church and Rectory

THE FIRST MENTION of a church at Chelsea is found in a papal taxation document of 1290 from Pope Nicholas IV, when it was named as Chelchurche of All Saints. However, it is likely that a church existed here in 1157, which could itself have been built on the site of an earlier Saxon church.

The church will be forever associated with Sir Thomas More, who rebuilt the south-east chapel in 1528 for his own private worship and his tomb. Two Renaissance capitals on the arch leading into the original Italian chancel were probably designed by Hans Holbein the Younger, a close friend of More. Henry VIII was secretly married to Jane Seymour in the Lawrence Chapel a few days before the official marriage ceremony.

By 1667, the church was too small for the growing population of noble families. Local families were often finding themselves excluded from worship. It was for this reason that the church was altered in 1670. The tower was replaced, the windows enlarged, new pews installed, and an extension made. A new roof was paid for by Lady Jane Cheyne, whose monument, designed by Gian Lorenzo Bernini, is here. At that time, the new tower was the highest brick-built edifice in the country. Inside

The exterior and stained glass details of Chelsea Old Church

are the only chained books remaining in a London church.

At the north side of the burial ground was a workhouse consisting of several buildings, some of which had children spinning silk (*see Mulberry Walk in A-Z*). A charity school for forty boys was built in 1706, paid for by lawyer and antiquarian William Petyt (1636–1707) (*see Petyt Place in A-Z*).

There are numerous seventeenth- and eighteenth-century monuments here, including the tomb of the celebrated scientist Sir Hans Sloane (1660–1753), which is on the embankment south of the church. It is a magnificent monument of stone supporting a central vase of marble. On the south side of the monument is inscribed: 'In the memory of Sir Hans Sloane, Bart. President of the

The Hans Sloane memorial

Royal Society and of the College of Physicians; who, in the year of our Lord 1753, the 92nd year of his age, without the least pain of body, and with a conscious serenity of mind, ended a virtuous and beneficial life. This monument was erected by his two daughters Elizabeth Cadogan and Sarah Stanley'. On the north side it is inscribed: 'Here lies interred Elizabeth Lady Sloane, wife of Sir Hans Sloane, Bart. Who departed this life in the year of our Lord 1724, and the 67th of her age'. On the east side is a heraldic shield.

A direct hit to the church during the Blitz, April 1941

DISASTER STRIKES

In April 1941, 450 German bombers combined to blitz London. Eighteen hospitals and thirteen churches were hit, one of which was Chelsea Old Church, which was reduced to a shell. The tower of the Old Church had come down, and bricks and rubble blocked the streets.

The Thomas More tomb was in pieces; the Bray Tomb, protected by its arch, remained... yet, rising out of all this ruin, there – almost incredibly – stood the More Chapel, the pillars with the Holbein capitals still supporting the arch, intact. After the bombing, the building was boarded up except for the More Chapel, which was repaired sufficiently to enable worship to continue there.

In 1949, the great author Sydney R. Jones wrote: 'Hitler's chivalrous knights shattered Chelsea Old Church and the memorials of Sir Thomas More, Holbein, and the Duchess of Northumberland, progenitress [parent or ancestor] of the Earl of Leicester and Sir Philip Sidney. At the same time the Huns murdered many of my neighbours'.

A booklet was published in 1957 in aid of the rebuilding fund. It told the story of that night when Old Church Street was devastated, killing all but one of the fire-watchers and injuring many more.

The plaque, placed there in 2004, reads: 'AFS London In Memory of Auxiliary Firewoman Yvonne Green who died near this site killed by enemy action on duty with four others as Firewatchers at Chelsea Old Church on the night of 16th/17th April 1941. All five names are remembered together on a memorial stone in the entrance of Chelsea Old Church'.

The church was rebuilt in 1954–58 and restored to its original appearance. The monuments that survived the bombing were restored, including a memorial to Thomas Lawrence (1516–98), after whose family Lawrence Street is named, and one of the grandest monuments, that of Sir Robert Stanley.

A sundial dated 1692 was restored to the upper side of the rebuilt tower, beside the clock, and is engraved 'Ut Vita Finis Ita 1692 Remade 1957' ('As the life is, so is its end'). Both the clock and sundial have Roman numerals.

The clock and sundial on the south elevation of the church

CHELSEA RECTORY

Chelsea Rectory, with its two acres of garden on the eastern corner of Old Church Street, was built *c.* 1725 and extended while still in church hands. The garden, one of the largest in central London, was originally about fourteen acres. Rectors have included William Cadogan, who was happy to have John Wesley in his pulpit. In 1824, St Luke's in Sydney Street was consecrated as the new parish church, but the first vicar, the Hon. Rev. Gerald Wellesley, brother of the Duke of Wellington, continued to live in the Rectory. Other rectors included Charles Kingsley, father of two notable authors, Charles and Henry Kingsley. It was here that the younger Charles, author of *The Water Babies*, was brought up in the 1830s. It was an immensely valuable site and was sold into private hands in the 1980s.

Chelsea historian Reginald Blunt (1857–1944) was brought up in the Rectory, where his father, the Rev. Gerald Blunt, was rector. He remembered meeting the great Thomas Carlyle and recalled Chelsea when it was just a riverside village.

Chelsea Rectory, *c.* 1900

Distressed by the rapid physical changes in Chelsea in the 1920s, Blunt formed the Chelsea Society to protect its architecture and nature. For many years, he was the Society's secretary and moving spirit. He had the good fortune to have a flat in Carlyle Mansions with a view of the sweep of the river, but he must have been devastated when the German bombing destroyed his beloved Old Church and much of the property near him. He died in 1944 before the church was rebuilt.

Today, the house is one of the largest and most expensive properties in London, with two new wings and a massive ballroom. Only Buckingham Palace and Witanhurst have larger gardens in London.

A Tour of the Chelsea Embankment

THE IDEA OF BUILDING an embankment on the Chelsea side of
the Thames between Vauxhall and Battersea Bridges was first made
by the Commissioners of Woods and Forests in 1839. However, very
little happened for years following this, owing to the cost of building
the bridge at Chelsea. Still, in 1871 the Metropolitan Board of Works
finally embarked on the massive construction project between the Royal
Hospital and Battersea Bridge.

The scheme demanded the removal of all houses and wharves that
backed on to the river. In 1873, Lombard Street and Duke Street were
swept away, together with a part of Lawrence Street. The old Adam & Eve
public house was also lost. Lombard Street was an extension of Cheyne
Walk, and was entered through the arch of a building called Arch House,
otherwise known as Alldin's Coal Wharf. The Embankment construction
was not popular with the local artistic community, who enjoyed the
pleasant riverside here.

The Duke and Duchess of Edinburgh opened the Chelsea

Embankment on
9 May 1874.
Although unpopular
with many Chelsea
residents, it brought
improvements to
sanitation, as well as
putting an end
to tidal floods that
would lap the gardens
and doorsteps on
Cheyne Walk.

James McNeill Whistler, *The 'Adam and Eve' Old Chelsea,* 1878–79
Opposite: Chelsea Embankment at sunset

Many statues and monuments in the Embankment Gardens are in honour of famous Chelsea residents. Walking from west to east are the following:

STONE LAMP

There is a highly decorated stone lamp standard on the north pavement, with figures of boys in green climbing it. There is another identical one east of the Albert Bridge on the south side with the same inscription: 'Chelsea Embankment opened May 1874 Lieut, Col, Sir James Macnaughten Hogg KCB MP Chairman of the Metropolitan Board of Works Sir Joseph William Bazalgette CB Engineer'.

Just east of Chelsea Old Church is the beautiful memorial to Thomas More, mentioned earlier.

DRINKING FOUNTAIN

On the pavement on the north side is a large stone drinking fountain, erected in 1880. An inscription reads: 'In affectionate remembrance of the late George Sparkes of Bromley in Kent formerly Judge at Madras in the East India Company's Civil Service a great and good man gifted with every refined feeling and much esteemed by all who knew him died 30th January 1878 in his 68th year erected by his widow A.D.1880'. On the reverse is the same inscription in Latin.

The fountain was restored between March and April 2016 to provide clean water for passers-by. It has troughs at its base for horses and pets, and taps above for their owners or passing walkers. The old plaques were refurbished and a new plaque was added to the fountain base to commemorate the formal reopening: 'The restoration of the fountain was undertaken by Transport for London and the Royal Borough of Kensington and Chelsea. The completion of the works was marked in a ceremony led by the Worshipful The Mayor of the Royal Borough, Councillor Robert Freeman on 18th May 2016'.

BIRD BATH DEDICATED TO MARGARET DAMER DAWSON

Farther east is a monument dated 1933 dedicated to the memory of Margaret Damer Dawson, co-founder of the Women's Police Service in Chelsea. It is in the form of a bird bath and decorated around the upper rim as follows: 'He playeth best who loves best all things both great and small'. On one side of the base is inscribed 'Police Worker Margaret Damer Dawson OBE'.

I took a photo of the monument in 2002 when just the base existed, along with a rusted metal central stem. The base was inscribed with the dates 1931 and 1933 in Roman numerals and the name of the sculptor C. Pibworth (Charles James Pibworth, 1878–1958), who was living at 14a Cheyne Row at the time.

Whilst walking through the Embankment Gardens in early September 2016, I saw that the bird bath was again missing (possibly destroyed by vandals) and, once again, just the base remained.

BRONZE STATUE OF THOMAS CARLYLE

A little further east is the wonderful bronze statue of Thomas Carlyle by Sir Joseph Edgar Boehm, unveiled on 26 October 1882 to commemorate the great essayist and historian. He is depicted here sitting on his study chair with a pile of reference books. England's great poet Robert Browning (1812–89) attended the unveiling.

ATALANTA

On the pavement on the south side of the Embankment, a little west of the Albert Bridge, is a bronze statue of a naked woman named *Atalanta* by Francis Derwent Wood. It was erected in 1929 and is inscribed: 'F. Derwent Wood R.A. 1871 Sculptor 1926. This example of his work is placed here in his memory by members of the Chelsea Arts Club and other friends'.

BOY WITH A DOLPHIN

Where Oakley Street joins the Embankment, on the site where the Pier Hotel once stood, stands a bronze statue titled *Boy with a Dolphin*. David Wynn created it, and the plaque below states: 'This Sculpture is exhibited by Wates Limited 13th October 1975'.

PAVEMENT PLAQUES

On the riverside, just east of the Cadogan Pier, in front of the green decorated lamp standard, is a blue metal plaque set into the pavement that reads as follows: 'The Royal Borough of Kensington & Chelsea Directorate Of Highways And Traffic Restored 1992'.

Beside a seat nearby is a further blue metal plaque set into the pavement that reads as follows: 'Seat Donated By Heritage Of London Trust The Royal Borough of Kensington & Chelsea 1992'.

THE BOY DAVID

Heading past Oakley Street, in the Embankment Gardens themselves, is a fibreglass statuette on a pink granite column of a boy with a sword, titled *The Boy David*. It is by Edward Bainbridge Copnall, after Francis Derwent Wood, whose model of the figure stood here until it was stolen in 1969. This replacement was erected in May 1971. At the base on four sides are plaques that read:

Plaque 1: 'This bronze fibreglass statue was sculptured by E. Bainbridge Copnall 1902–1973 and set in the granite column which the sculptor donated to the Royal Borough of Kensington and Chelsea'.

Plaque 2: 'The Machine Gun Corps Old Comrades' Association lives on a century later continued to remember the brave men who fought with the Machine Gun Corps from 1915 to 1922'.

Plaque 3: 'The Boy David by Bainbridge Copnall MBE PPRBS. A memorial to the members of the Machine Gun Corps who served in World War One'.

Plaque 4: 'The original Boy David statue sculptured in bronze by Francis Derwent Wood was the model for the Machine Gun Corps memorial, which stands at Hyde Park Corner and was presented to the Borough of Chelsea in 1963, which was later stolen. This bronze fibreglass replacement was erected by the Royal Borough of Kensington and Chelsea and the Old Comrades Association of the Machine Gun Corps'.

DANTE ROSSETTI BUST

Opposite No.16 Cheyne Walk (a house once owned by Dante Gabriel Rossetti) is a large stone drinking fountain sculpted by Ford Madox Brown with the bust of the poet, who died in 1882. It was unveiled in 1887 by the artist William Holman Hunt (1827–1910). There is a new plaque on the ground below as follows: 'This plaque commemorates the completion of the refurbishment of this memorial fountain by Transport for London and the Royal Borough of Kensington and Chelsea and the formal opening by the Worshipful The Mayor of the Royal Borough of Kensington and Chelsea, Councillor Robert Freeman, and Dana Skelley OBE, Director of Asset Management, Transport for London, 18th May 2016'.

ON THE EMBANKMENT

In the Gardens themselves, opposite the entrance from Cheyne Gardens, is the base of a broken or destroyed monument with the top missing, which states as follows: 'This garden was replanted by the Chelsea Borough Council and many fellow workers and friends of Jacqueline Theodore Cockburn 1804–1941 in her memory & honour.'

Another monument among the gardens is in honour of the English classical composer Vaughan Williams (1872–1958). The plaque

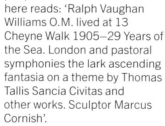

here reads: 'Ralph Vaughan Williams O.M. lived at 13 Cheyne Walk 1905–29 Years of the Sea. London and pastoral symphonies the lark ascending fantasia on a theme by Thomas Tallis Sancia Civitas and other works. Sculptor Marcus Cornish'.

The Embankment Gardens are a pleasant sight throughout the year, with large, well-attended circular flowerbeds. There are also numerous seats throughout the gardens,

some with dedications to the memory of local parishioners. Some chairs are decorated with leaf designs, while others have a winged sphinx on each end and one central. One located towards the Battersea Bridge has been prettily defaced, with the central sphinx face and breasts painted pink and red.

Other items of interest along the riverfront include decorated

street lamps along the Embankment wall, the standing-shaped metal posts with the Kensington & Chelsea insignia, and the signpost east of the Albert Bridge with various directions to walk.

Travelling further east is a row of significant historical and attractive houses with highly decorated entrances:

Nos.1–2: Earlier known as The Clock House, which was built in 1879, this house is now named Dawliffe Hall. Although all references to Dawliffe Hall give the address as No.1, it is numbered No.2 at the entrance.

No.5: The Old Ferry House.

No.6: Sun House, which has a crude

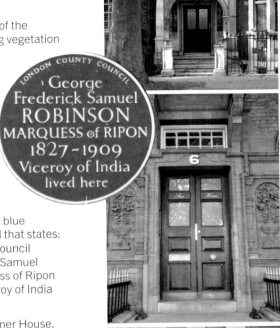

white plaque east of the entrance, featuring vegetation and a swan.

No.7: This property has a decorated entrance and ceiling with the word 'Salve' inset.

No.9: Turner's Reach House, with a large green clock jutting from the building and a blue plaque on the wall that states: 'London County Council George Frederick Samuel Robinson Marquess of Ripon 1827–1909 Viceroy of India lived here'.

No.13: Garden Corner House, with a decorative door.

No.14: Star House, also with a decorative door.

No.15: Delahay House, with a decorated entrance and tiled floor.

No.17: This is the beautiful, highly decorated Swan House.

No.22: This building is another with a highly decorated entrance, with vegetation and angels over the door, and a very old black-and-white battered street sign that states: 'Chelsea Embankment S.W.3'.

Explore the Chelsea Physic Garden

The gates to the Physic Garden

ALONG THE EMBANKMENT towards Chelsea Bridge is the Physic Garden. The handsome iron gates at the entrance are decorated with the sign of Apollo and a dragon. On either side of the gate are slightly faded stone plaques. The western one states: 'The Botanic Garden of the Society of Apothecaries of London A.D. 1673'. The eastern one reads: 'Granted to the Society in Perpetuity by Hans Sloane Bart. A.D. 1727'.

The Physic Garden is the second-oldest botanical garden in Britain. (The earliest is the University of Oxford Botanic Garden, founded in 1621.) It is dedicated to the conservation of plants and is home to around 100 different types of trees. This plot of land was leased in 1673 by Sir Charles Cheyne, then Lord of the Manor of Chelsea, to the Society of Apothecaries to form a Botanical and Physic Garden, the word 'physic' referring to the science of healing.

It came under the patronage of Sir Hans Sloane, who studied there as a young man and became a successful physician. He had bought the Chelsea Manor estate from the Cheyne family in 1712, and gave the freehold of the garden to the Society of Apothecaries

Statue of Hans Sloane

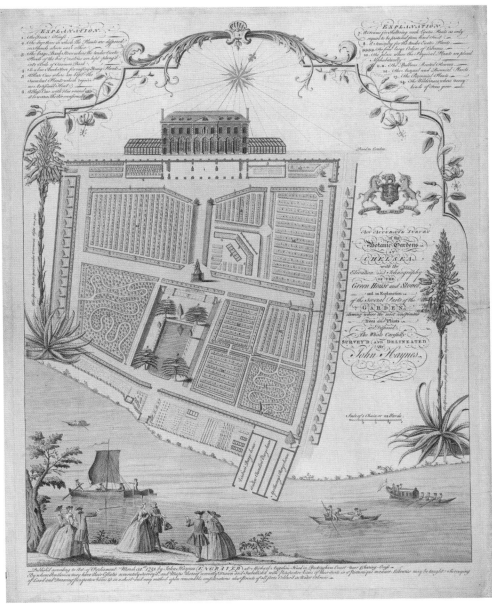

The Physic Garden, Chelsea: a plan view. Engraving by John Haynes, 1751

ten years later. In return, the Society commissioned a large statue of him in 1757. It is a replica of the original figure from 1733 that was made by John Michael Rysbrack, installed in 1737, and moved to the British Museum in 1983. The plaque below is in Latin and dated in Roman numerals 'MDCCXXXIII' (1733).

The Physic Garden

In 1732, the cotton plant seeds from these gardens were sent to America, beginning the great cotton industry there. Parts of this garden were lost with the 1874 construction of the Embankment.

It was rumoured that the Society of Apothecaries were to sell off their land at Chelsea for development, but a protest meeting was held at Chelsea Town Hall and resistance was formulated. The government was enticed to give financial help, but only if students from the Royal College of Science at South Kensington used the Garden. In 1983, the Garden became a registered charity, and today thrives as a world-famous centre for cultivating and studying plants and their use in treating disease. There is also a pleasant shop and café on site.

The Chelsea Physic Garden welcomed the Queen Mother as their patron in 1984, and in 2002 the enjoyable task was passed on to the Prince of Wales. The elaborate main gates on the Embankment (previously mentioned) are only ever opened for his visits.

The Physic Garden, Chelsea: a view showing the pair of cedar trees, and the statue of Sloane in the centre of the garden. Lithograph by H. Warren after J. Fuge

The Greenhouse at the Physic Garden

The garden's official address is 66 Royal Hospital Road, and is open to the public via an entrance through a small door in Swan Walk. Beside this small entrance is a stone plaque set into the wall that states, in Latin, 'Hortus Botanicus Societatis Pharmaceuticae Lond: 1686', which is fairly obviously translated. North of the entrance, above the Swan Court road sign, is a squared blue plaque that reads:

Plaque by the entrance to the garden

'Royal Borough of Kensington and Chelsea. The Chelsea Physic Garden was established by the Worshipful Society of Apothecaries of London in 1673 and is the oldest Botanic Garden, after Oxford, in England. A statue of Sir Hans Sloane, an early benefactor, sculpted by Michael Rysbrach, stands in the centre. In 1899, responsibility for the garden passed to the Trustees of the London Parochial Charities'.

Chelsea
Door
Knockers

JUST ABOUT EVERY FRONT DOOR in Chelsea features a door knocker. They are mostly brass and come in a variety of designs – some strange, others very amusing. They often represent a variety of animals and marine creatures together with the odd heraldic or historical design. Most are a delight, as I found while photographing the streets of Chelsea. Here is a small selection from the 429 photos of door knockers that I took during my research.

The Royal Chelsea Hospital

CHELSEA COLLEGE WAS FOUNDED by Dr Matthew Sutcliffe, the Dean of Exeter. King James I was one of its foremost patrons, and supported it with grants and timber from the Windsor forest. He laid the first stone of the new edifice on 8 May 1609. It was incorporated a year later, in May 1610, and the King ordered it be called 'King James's Colledge at Chelsey'. The building commenced on a site of six acres called Thames Shot, but the project never received the funding it was promised and very little was built. The project finally sank into insignificance when,

The Royal Hospital and gardens with the central obelisk in the foreground

Chelsea pensioners relax in the gardens of the hospital

in 1636, Charles I refused to help.

In 1651, the building was taken over by the state and used as a prison. Because the college was on the Crown Estate, it reverted to the ownership of Charles II, who promised that the newly formed Royal Society should use it. Nevertheless, it was once again used as a prison for Dutch and Swedish prisoners in 1665, the year of the Great Plague of London. Over the years the College building deteriorated and the site was finally sold.

The current Royal Chelsea Hospital was founded in 1682 by Charles II, at the instigation of Nell Gwyn, as a retirement place for old soldiers. Further financial help came from William Sancroft, Archbishop of Canterbury. Sir Christopher Wren (1632–1723) designed most of the buildings, and his work can be seen at its finest in the Figure Court and the Chapel. King Charles II laid the foundation stone, and the Hospital finally opened in 1692. Robert Adam and Sir John Soane later made alterations and additions.

Today, it houses around 500 army pensioners who, on special occasions, wear the traditional uniform of Marlborough's time. In honour of Charles II, they parade in these scarlet frock coats on Oak Apple Day (29 May). A statue of Charles II stands in the open square facing the Thames, and is decorated with oak leaves and branches in memory of his escape after the Battle of Worcester in 1651, when he hid in an oak tree. The pensioners wear dark blue overcoats in the winter. The chapel and the old dining hall contain about 100 flags taken in various battles.

The Royal Hospital Gardens, which stretch down to the Thames Embankment, display several cannons, some of which were captured from the French at the Battle of Waterloo. The central obelisk was erected in 1843 in memory of the men of the 24th Regiment who were killed at the Battle of Chillianwala during the Second Anglo-Sikh War in 1849.

The Old Dining Hall

The Hospital's museum originated with a display in the Great Hall in 1866, but was later moved to the Secretary's Block in 1960. It now contains a striking model of the Royal Hospital as it would have appeared in 1742. The entrance hall is dedicated to the Duke of Wellington, and some exhibits relate to him. There are also more than 2,000 medals, mostly bequeathed to the Hospital by former inmates or unclaimed on their deaths. There is also a reconstruction of a typical living quarter of a pensioner. The Infirmary was mostly destroyed by a landmine in 1941 but was rebuilt in 1961. The Chapel, the Great Hall and the museum are now open to the public.

To the north is the extensive Burton Court, which is used for sporting occasions and cricket matches to this day.

RANELAGH GARDENS

Richard Jones, the 1st Earl of Ranelagh, became Paymaster General of the Royal Hospital in 1685 and built himself a handsome house on the grounds. Jones then created walks, pools, orchards, an aviary, a bathing house and statues. However, in 1702 he was found guilty of gross fraud and dismissed from his post. After his death, his daughter entertained

Thomas Bowles, *A view of the Royal Hospital at Chelsea & the Rotunda in Ranelaigh Gardens*, after 1751

'Finding Our Way: An NHS Tribute Garden', RHS Chelsea Flower Show 2021

King George I here, engaging Handel and a fifty-strong orchestra for a performance of his *Water Music* on a flotilla of boats ferrying the guests from the river to her garden.

By 1741, the house and grounds were in the hands of a company headed by Sir William Robinson, who decided to convert the premises to a rival to Vauxhall Gardens. The grounds were laid out in spectacular fashion, with the sensational centrepiece being the famous Rotunda. It opened in April 1742, and the Prince and Princess of Wales, the Duke of Cumberland, and much nobility attended. Entertainment included music, opera, gambling, dancing and masquerades. It lost its popularity towards the end of the century, and by 1826 the gardens were closed and the site was sold to the Royal Hospital.

Perhaps the most famous event held here annually is the Royal Horticultural Society's Chelsea Flower Show, originally staged in 1888 at the Inner Temple Gardens in the City of London. Its popularity necessitated it to be moved to the more extensive grounds here, and in 1912 the Society organised the first Chelsea event, which was called the Royal International Horticultural Exhibition. This was followed a year later by the very first Chelsea Flower Show.

Chelsea Common and the Cremorne Estate

WHAT USED TO BE Chelsea Common is bounded today by Fulham Road, Sydney Street, Cale Street, Elystan Place and Draycott Avenue. James Hamilton's map of 1664 shows the parish poorhouse on its western extremity, a pond and gravel pits on the northwest (Pond Place today is a reminder), and a total extent of about thirty-seven acres. Although the Lord of the Manor owned the common, residents had the right to graze animals and gather wood there. However, in 1790, the Cadogan family obtained an Act of Parliament enabling them to enclose the land and develop low-grade houses on the site.

CHELSEA PARK

Lord Wharton's Chelsea Park is shown on Hamilton's map of 1677, and the area is easy to pick out on modern maps. It lay between Fulham Road and the King's Road, with its western boundary at Park Walk by the kink in the King's Road, and its eastern boundary at Old Church Street.

CHELSEA PARK GARDENS

Chelsea Park Gardens was on land owned by Sir Thomas More. It was called Sandhills and later named Wharton Park. In 1718, the name Chelsea Park was given to it when it was bought as a mulberry garden for silk production. Two thousand trees were planted, but the scheme soon foundered. A few of the trees from this failed venture remain.

The area was developed in the 1830s and called Camera Square. The change of name to Chelsea Park Gardens was approved in 1915, subject to the proviso that the central portion of the area be laid out as a garden. Earlier properties were demolished for the construction of the houses built between 1914 and 1923, which tended to be in the Arts and Crafts style.

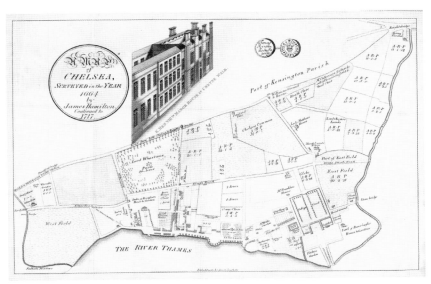

Map of Chelsea, surveyed in 1664 by James Hamilton, continued to 1717

Artist Sir Alfred Munnings (1878–1959) lived at No.96 from 1920 until his death. He painted horses, which made him a rich man. He was mainly in vogue between the First and Second World Wars, and was President of the Royal Academy between 1944 and 1949.

THE CREMORNE ESTATE

The Cremorne Estate covers a large area between the King's Road and Cheyne Walk, encompassing a myriad of streets, including Anchor, Brunel House, Chelsea Farm Studios, Lacland, Purcell and West Field, amongst others. More familiar streets within this estate are as follows:

Ann Lane is probably named after Mary Ann, the wife of the builder of nearby Riley Street. It is a quiet residential location close to the many fashionable amenities of the King's Road.

Apollo Place was built on Stephen Riley's land and was probably named after a local public house. It is located on the site of an original mews, a cul-de-sac off Riley Street, and contains five properties used for residential and commercial purposes. During the Second World War, a high-explosive bomb fell directly on to the mews, damaging some properties.

Bowling Green, with Bowling Green House, is here.

Moravian Place is where the Moravian Protestant community was established in Chelsea in the 1750s. Its burial ground adjoins this road.

Munro Terrace is known for being where The Rolling Stones offices were located (at No.2) from the mid-1970s to December 1990. The street has a pre-1965 'Chelsea' road sign.

Riley Street is named after the land leased by Stephen Riley, an upholsterer who later married its owner, Mary Ann Jones. There's a building here with a plaque dated 1890.

CREMORNE GARDENS

Balloon ascents at Cremorne Gardens

A pretty garden area situated on the riverside at the eastern entrance from the Chelsea Embankment to Lots Road.

Initially, the area was known as Chelsea Farm. Cremorne House was built in 1740 for the Duke of Huntingdon, whose widow founded the Huntingdon Connexion, a splinter group of Wesleyan Methodists. Irish landowner and politician Thomas Dawson (1725–1813), later the 1st Viscount Cremorne, bought the property in 1778. Upon his wife's death, the estate was bought by Baron de Beaufain, Charles Random de Berenger, who claimed to be a Prussian nobleman but was in fact a fraudster. He established a sporting club for men and women called Cremorne Stadium in 1832, but it was not a great success and subsequently closed in 1843.

In 1845, under the promotion of Thomas Bartlett Simpson, the Gardens were converted to a pleasure garden. It delighted the masses, many of whom arrived by steamboat, but was the bane of the more select residents of Chelsea. The grounds consisted of twelve acres between the river and the King's Road. It included space for a large orchestra surrounded by a dancing platform. The painter James Whistler was a frequent visitor with Walter and Henry Greaves. Together with the public, they enjoyed gardens, grottos, mazes, a theatre, concerts, circus performers, supper rooms and evening fireworks.

THE CREMORNE POLKA.

C. H. R. MARRIOTT.

Cremorne Gardens pleasure grounds

Ballooning was among the most significant attractions at the Gardens. In 1874, balloonist Vincent De Groof, known as 'The Flying Man', attempted to descend from a balloon 1,524m (5,000ft) in the air in a contraption with wings 1.12m (37ft) wide. As the balloon drifted 91m (300ft) above St Luke's Church, De Groof attempted an emergency landing, but crashed to his death on Sydney Street.

Another remarkable event occurred in 1861, when Madame Genevieve (Selina Young), known as the 'Female Blondin', attempted to cross the Thames from Battersea to the Cremorne Gardens on a tightrope. When she was halfway across the river, someone cut the guy ropes supporting the tightrope in order to steal the attached lead weights. As the tightrope gave way, she managed to swing herself down to the river, where she was rescued by boat.

Afternoons at Cremorne Gardens were a popular family outing, but after dark, drink and rowdiness gave it a bad name. Consequently, in 1877 its application for a licence renewal was refused. The estate was sold for building upon and the trees were sold off for timber. This allowed the Ashburnham Park Nursery, which belonged to horticulturist James Wimsett, to expand. The nursery was later sold as a school site in 1907. Most of the old site is now the Lots Road Power Station and the terraces around it.

Cremorne Gardens inner gate

ITINERARIES

HISTORIC CHELSEA

THE HISTORY OF CHELSEA reflects the history of London in that both city and borough exist in this location as a consequence of geography. Moreover, Chelsea's history is inextricably linked with the Thames. Even the name 'Chelsea' is thought to come from the Anglo-Saxon 'Chelcehithe', meaning a 'landing place for chalk', or from the word 'Chesil', meaning 'gravel bank'.

It is the Thames that provided a water source and a means of travel to early settlers. It is also at Chelsea where people could ford the great river. Early Britons would have waited for low tide and crossed a gravel shoal situated there. As recently as the eighteenth century, the river at Chelsea Bridge was still only around 90cm (3ft) deep. Historians also believe it was where, in 54 BC, Julius Caesar would have crossed the Thames. Large amounts of Roman and ancient British artefacts were found in the riverbed when the Chelsea Bridge was built, the most significant of which is the Battersea Shield, a beautiful bronze and enamel shield now on display in the British Museum.

Records from 785 and 816 AD show Chelsea as a small Saxon village, but it was still significant enough that King Offa attended a religious ceremony here and King Alfred held assemblies here, driving Vikings from the area.

Several centuries later, Sir Thomas Moore (1478–1535), judge, lawyer and statesman to Henry VIII, boosted the village's popularity. In 1525, More bought up twenty-three acres of land and built a substantial house in the area. It was one fit for frequent visits by the king, who would travel along the Thames by barge to visit More.

As transport moved from boats to horse-drawn carriages, Charles II developed the 'King's Road' as a private route between Whitehall and Hampton Court. He also set up the Royal Hospital in Chelsea to look after soldiers injured during the Civil War, an institution later to be home to the borough's most famous residents, the venerated Chelsea Pensioners.

Chelsea remained primarily agricultural until as late as the early nineteenth century, with a settlement no bigger than a small village around the riverside Chelsea Old Church. However, by the late 1800s, Chelsea was being developed at pace, turning itself away from the river.

The area became a popular haunt of artists, writers and poets, who would paint and write about life along the river, visiting the old inns and living in riverside homes. The bewildering number of famous names who made Chelsea their home can be seen in our other itineraries, but for our historical walk we'll concentrate on the most significant locations that tell the story of the borough, the city and the Thames. It is fitting, then, that we start our journey through time at Battersea Bridge. It won't be entirely chronological, but it will be full of fascinating places to visit.

Let's start on a whim, right in the middle of Battersea Bridge, and gaze back at Chelsea. To the west, you'll see houseboats on the Thames and, beyond, the great brick towers of the World's End estate. To the east of Battersea Bridge you'll see the leafy Chelsea Embankment, the tower of Chelsea Old Church (the oldest building in Chelsea) and Cheyne Walk, home to some of the borough's most influential residents.

The next bridge along the Thames is Albert Bridge. Beyond that, in the direction of our walk, are the Chelsea Embankment Gardens, the Physic Garden, the National Army Museum and the Royal Hospital, where we'll finish again on the Thames.

As you look down into the Thames, imagine the countless artefacts from throughout history still likely buried here, dating back to ancient Britain, through the Roman era, all the way up to modern day. Among those recovered is the magnificent Battersea Shield, a bronze metal facing with twenty-seven red glass studs.

The first Battersea Bridge ❶ was completed in 1771, making the horse ferry that was previously sited there redundant. It was a simple wooden structure and featured in artworks by J.M.W. Turner and James Abbott McNeill Whistler, including *Nocturne: Blue and Gold* which can be seen at Tate Britain.

Attractive though the bridge was to paint, it wasn't particularly safe, with its narrow spans proving tricky for watermen. The Battersea Bridge that you stand on now was opened in 1890.

Walk towards Chelsea and right on to Cheyne Walk. ❷ This handsome road of houses takes its name from William Lord Cheyne (1657–1728), and is built on the site of Henry VIII's palace gardens. Ownership transferred from the Cheyne family to the Sloane family in 1712, paving the way for the broader redevelopment of Chelsea, the architecture of which still defines the borough today.

You're now standing on the Chelsea Embankment, ❸ which was opened by the Duke and Duchess of Edinburgh on 9 May 1874. Coal wharves, houses and the Adam & Eve public house were demolished to make way for the Embankment, built to stop floods along Cheyne Walk.

The first road you'll reach along the Embankment is Danvers Street, ❹ named after Sir John Danvers, who bought part of the grounds of Sir Thomas More's property in 1622. Despite being a courtier of King James I and Charles I, Danvers supported the Parliamentary cause during the Civil War and was one of the signatories of King Charles I's death warrant. His house was demolished in 1720, and Danvers Street was built across the land.

No.20 Danvers Street is Fleming House ❺ and the former home of Alexander Fleming (1881–1955), the discoverer of penicillin, who lived here from 1929 until his death.

On the other side of Old Church Street is St Thomas

More Gardens, ❻ which features a statue of Thomas More by Leslie Cubitt Bevis. More played a huge role in popularising the region, buying up land in 1525, including the area where you now stand. His Beaufort House was where Beaufort Street is now, directly opposite Battersea Bridge.

More became Lord Chancellor to Henry VIII in 1529, and was one of his closest aides. Henry VIII would often visit More's house to discuss the affairs of the day. More would later resign from his post in opposition to the dissolution of the monasteries, brought about by Henry's divorce from Catherine of Aragon. This led him to be tried for treason and beheaded in 1535. His head remained on a pike for a month until his daughter retrieved it.

Behind the gardens is Chelsea Old Church, ❼ one of the oldest buildings in Chelsea. The first mention of a church here was in 1290. More rebuilt one of the chapels at the church, and you'll see monuments to him inside, along with dozens more, including of the novelist Henry James. A parachute mine largely destroyed

the church on 14 April 1941. The More chapel was the least affected. The church was restored and reconsecrated in 1958.

The nearby Old Church Street is likely to be one of the oldest streets in Chelsea.

Turn left on to Cheyne Walk and then on to Lawrence Street. On the corner here is the Carlyle Mansions, ❽ built in 1886. Famous former residents include Henry James, Somerset Maugham, Charlie Watts, Ian Fleming and historian Reginald Blunt.

Follow Lawrence Street to Justice Walk. Here you'll find Judge's House ❾ and Justice House. The street's name relates to Sir John Fielding (1721–80), a magistrate who, with his half-brother, the novelist Henry Fielding, formed the first professional police force, the Bow Street Runners.

The Court House saw hundreds of trials, including many people accused of highway robberies. It was a short walk for convicts to the prison ships moored on the Thames and a life in the British penal colonies. The building is the only surviving courthouse jail in London.

Opposite: The statue of Thomas Moore outside Chelsea Old Church

Lawrence Street is named after Sir Thomas Lawrence, a goldsmith who lived in Chelsea Manor House, now located at the northern end of the street. He is buried in a chapel in Chelsea Old Church.

From here, turn left on to Cheyne Walk, which takes its name from William Lord Cheyne (1657–1728). The houses here have long been among the capital's most desirable.

No.46 Cheyne Walk ❿ started life as the Cheyne Hospital for Children; the Three Tuns public house and a bowling green were also among these three houses.

The houses between No.43 ⓫ and No.45 were built in the early eighteenth century, on the site of the home of the 4th Earl of Shrewsbury, who was Privy Councillor to Henry VIII. The 6th Earl was the fourth (and most unhappy) husband of the infamous Bess of Hardwick, and left the house to her upon his death.

No.37 Cheyne Walk ⓬ was the Magpie and Stump public house, built on land that was granted by Henry VIII. In 1803, conspirators met there to discuss their plot to kill George III and steal the Crown Jewels.

You're now at Oakley Street and the Albert Bridge. ⓭ Turn left onto Oakley Street and head up the road to No.56. This was the home of Antarctic explorer Robert Falcon Scott (1868–1912), ⓮ who lived here between 1904 and 1908 whilst writing the account of his 1904 expedition to the Antarctic. There's a blue plaque here to commemorate him.

Head back towards Cheyne Walk and turn left. Between houses at No.23 and No.24 ⓯ you'll see a large blue plaque that reads: 'King Henry VIII's Manor House stood here until 1753, when it was demolished after the death of its last occupant, Sir Hans Sloane. Nos. 19 to 26 Cheyne Walk were built on its site in 1759–65.

The old manor house garden still lies beyond the end wall of Cheyne Mews and contains some mulberry trees said to have been planted by Queen Elizabeth I.'

No.18 ⓰ was formerly a well-known coffee house called Don Saltero. Sir Hans Sloane began donating unwanted objects to the owner, former servant James Salter, who displayed them in Don Saltero's Coffee House and Curiosity Museum, which was sited here. Sloane used to drink coffee with Sir Isaac Newton here, surrounded by taxidermy animals.

No.16 Cheyne Walk ⓱ is the former home of Dante Gabriel Rossetti and the poet Algernon Charles Swinburne. Rossetti kept a menagerie of animals in

Thomas Shepherd, *Cheyne Walk in 1850, depicting Don Saltero's Hotel and Tavern*

his back garden, including a kangaroo and a brown bear. His wombat was much loved by his friend Lewis Carroll, who is said to have based his dormouse character in *Alice's Adventures in Wonderland* on it.

No. 14 was the home of philosopher Bertrand Russell (1872–1970), **18** who wrote *The Principles of Mathematics* here.

The composer Ralph Vaughan Williams (1872–1958) **19** lived at No. 13 between 1905 and 1929. There's a statue in his honour in the Embankment Gardens.

No. 10 was the former home of British prime minister David Lloyd George. **20**

Among the older buildings of Cheyne Walk are Nos. 3–6, which were built in 1718. No. 6 **21** used to be Dr Dominicetti's Fumigatory Steam Baths, which were said to treat anything from asthma to leprosy. Patients included the Duke of York and Sir John Fielding.

No. 4 **22** counts artists William Dyce (1846–7) and Daniel Maclise (1861–70) among its former residents. However,

the most famous was George Eliot (born Mary Ann Evans) (1819–80), author of *Middlemarch*.

George Eliot (born Mary Ann Evans)

No. 3 was the home of Admiral William Henry Smith (1788–1865), **23** a vice president of the Royal Society and a founder of the Royal Geographical Society. A later resident was Keith Richards of The Rolling Stones.

Follow Royal Hospital Road east to the Chelsea Physic Garden, **24** first opened in 1673. It's well worth the modest charge to enter the second-oldest botanical garden in Britain. Sir Charles Cheyne, then Lord of the Manor of Chelsea, leased the land to the Society of Apothecaries. They formed the Botanical and Physic Garden, the word 'physic' referring to the science of healing. Sir Hans Sloane (1660–1753), a member

of the Royal College of Physicians, donated 800 species of plants to the Physic Garden after a fifteen-month journey around the West Indies. Later, he granted the Society of Apothecaries freehold of the site as long as they produced a new species every year.

Physician Elizabeth Blackwell (1688–1758), who lived on Swan Walk in Chelsea, drew more than 500 beautiful depictions of plants in the Physic Garden, published in 1737 as *The Curious Herbal*. She would become the first woman on the Medical Register of the General Medical Council.

Botanical illustrarions by Elizabeth Blackwell

Continue along Royal Hospital Road to the National Army Museum. **25** This fascinating museum charts the history of the British Army from the Civil Wars in the seventeenth century to the modern day, analysing its impact on society.

A little farther along is the Royal Hospital Chelsea, **26** home to around 300 Chelsea Pensioners. It was built during the reign of King Charles II, who issued a Royal Warrant for a hospital to care for those 'broken by age or war'. Sir Christopher Wren designed and erected the building in the wide open spaces of Chelsea. The first Chelsea Pensioners were admitted in 1692. Chelsea Pensioners wear the distinctive scarlet frock coats and tricorne hats,

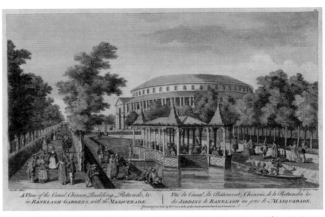

Charles Grignion, *A View of the Canal, Chinese Building, Rotundo and Church in Ranelagh Gardens with the Masquerade*, undated

but are only allowed to do so within two miles of the Royal Hospital.

The Royal Horticultural Society's Chelsea Flower Show has been held on the South Grounds since 1913.

The Royal Hospital Gardens display several

cannons, some captured from the French at the Battle of Waterloo. Guided tours are available if booked in advance.

The Ranelagh Gardens **27** were first laid out by Richard Jones, the 1st Earl of Ranelagh, Paymaster General of the Royal

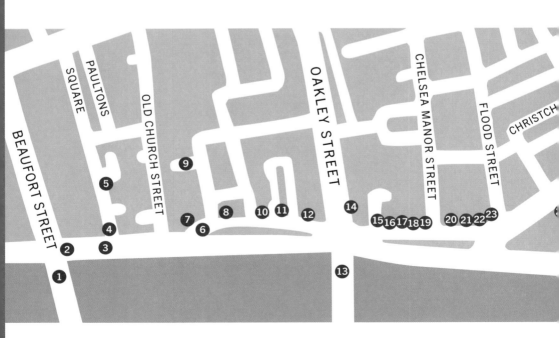

Hospital. In 1702, he was dismissed from his post for fraud. His daughter later entertained King George I here, engaging George Frideric Handel and a fifty-strong orchestra to perform *Water Music* on a flotilla of boats ferrying the guests from the river to her garden.

The Ranelagh Pleasure Gardens stood here between 1742 and 1826. It had a vast rotunda in the middle, which once hosted Mozart. John Gibson, the designer of several royal parks, laid out the current gardens, which is now the site of the Chelsea Flower Show.

Walk around the gardens, down towards the Thames and Chelsea Bridge, 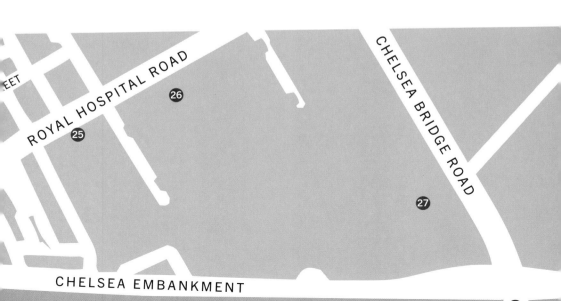 28 and the very origins of the village of Chelsea.

End again on a whim and walk to the middle of the bridge. Our starting point, Battersea Bridge, can be seen beyond the Albert Bridge in the near distance. The first Chelsea Bridge was opened in 1858 but required constant expensive maintenance. The current bridge was opened in 1937 by the Prime Minister of Canada.

It is here that Julius Caesar was said to have crossed the Thames in 54 BC. Look again into the water. Archaeologists believe that this was the site of a battle, maybe between ancient Britons and the invading Romans, such is the quantity of discarded weapons discovered when the bridge was built.

Imagine the river being a mere 3-feet deep, with a gravel bank exposed at low tide. This spot became one of the most important places to cross the Thames. Thanks to a quirk of geography, life congregated around this spot. A village grew as more and more people headed here from the countryside. London expanded, and Chelsea became a borough around the place you now stand.

ROYAL HOSPITAL ROAD

CHELSEA BRIDGE ROAD

26

25

27

CHELSEA EMBANKMENT

28

LITERARY CHELSEA

Whenever I walk in a London street,
I'm ever so careful to watch my feet;
And I keep in the squares,
And the masses of bears,
Who wait at the corners all ready to eat
The sillies who tread on the lines of the street
Go back to their lairs,
And I say to them, 'Bears,
Just look how I'm walking in all the squares!'

A.A. Milne, 'Lines and Squares' from *When We Were Very Young*
written at No. 11 Mallord Street, Chelsea

POETS, NOVELISTS, JOURNALISTS and playwrights have all made their home in Chelsea. A bewildering number, in fact. Within the confines of the Borough of Kensington and Chelsea, we see the former homes of Oscar Wilde, Jonathan Swift, George Eliot, John Galsworthy, Elizabeth Gaskell, Dylan Thomas, Samuel Beckett, poet laureate Sir John Betjeman, Charles Kingsley, Bram Stoker and Ian Fleming, among many others. Some were even in the same house. Writer and painter Wyndham Lewis lived at No.21 Chenye Walk two decades after Henry James died in the house (before him, the painter James Whistler lived there).

Carlye Mansions was home to Ian Fleming, Somerset Maugham, espionage novelist Erskine Childers, Henry James and T.S. Eliot (the last two at the same time). The two were certainly fond of each other, with Eliot describing James as the 'most intelligent man of his generation'. No wonder the flats were monikered 'Writers' Block'.

Many great works were written in Chelsea. Jerome K. Jerome, for example, wrote his humorous classic *Three Men in a Boat* (1888) whilst living in the area. Most notably, A.A. Milne wrote *When We Were Very Young* for his son Christopher Robin, who was born at 11 Mallord Street. The family moved next door to No.13 in 1925, which is where Milne wrote *Now We Are Six*, *Winnie-the-Pooh* and *House at Pooh Corner*.

Chelsea wasn't merely home to writers, but became the setting for scenes in great literature. Charles Dickens wrote about Cadogan Place in his novel *Nicholas Nickleby*. Henry James used the same street as the home for Fanny and Robert Assingham in *The Golden Bowl*. John Le Carré stated that the home of his recurring intelligence officer George Smiley was at No.9 Beaufort Street. The BBC used the location in the 1997 adaptation of *Tinker Tailor Soldier Spy*.

According to fellow writer William Boyd, Ian Fleming, when looking for inspiration for the Chelsea home of James Bond, decided upon No.25 Wellington Square, the former flat of Fleming's friend Desmond MacCarthy.

We start our itinerary at Cadogan Place, ❶ opposite the leafy Cadogan Place Park.

In his novel *Nicholas Nickleby*, Charles Dickens wrote: 'Cadogan Place is the one slight bond that joins two great extremes; it is the connecting link between the aristocratic pavements of Belgrave Square and the barbarism of Chelsea.' These streets were also home to Fanny and Robert Assingham in Henry James' *The Golden Bowl*.

No.18 was the childhood home of writer and poet Lord Alfred Douglas, later the lover of Oscar Wilde. Former British prime minister Harold Macmillan's family home was at No.52. He was the grandson of Daniel Macmillan, co-founder of Macmillan publishers. Early authors on their roster included Charles Kingsley, who we'll meet later.

Lord Alfred Douglas (seated) and Oscar Wilde, May 1893

From the north end of Cadogan Place, walk west along Pont Street and turn left down Cadogan Square. ❷ Major General John Hay Beith, who wrote prolifically under his pen name Ian Hay, lived at No.21 in the 1930s. Poet and author Marguerite Radclyffe Hall lived at either No.39 or No.59 between 1911 and 1916. She is best known for her book *The Well of Loneliness*, a pioneering work of lesbian literature. She moved in 1916 to No.22 Cadogan Court on Draycott Avenue.

Dennis Wheatley, the author of thrillers and occult novels, lived at

No.60, ❸ and No.75 is the former home of Arnold Bennett, writer of the Clayhanger novels. He died from typhoid in the house in 1931.

Parallel to Cadogan Square to the west is Clabon Mews, ❹ used briefly as a location in the James Bond film *Skyfall*.

Continue west along Milner Street and Denyer Street to Draycott Avenue. Feel free to take a detour to Egerton Crescent ❺ to see the former homes of poet John Lehmann (No.31) and that of Lucas Malet, the pseudonym of novelist Mary St Leger Kingsley (No.27).

At Cadogan Court on Draycott Avenue you'll find where Marguerite Radclyffe Hall lived between 1916 and 1920.

Follow Draycott Avenue south and turn left on to Bray Place. At the end, turn right onto Blacklands Terrace, where you'll find John Sandoe Books, ❻ one of the city's best-loved bookshops. Irish novelist Edna O'Brien said: 'John Sandoe is an integral part of my life in London. It is quite simply the best bookshop anyone could wish for.'

Admittedly, a twenty-minute detour, but any fans of Jerome K. Jerome's ❼ hilarious novel *Three Men in a Boat* should walk to Nos.91–104 Chelsea Bridge Road, where he wrote the book.

Alternatively, walk west along the King's Road to Wellington Square, where William Boyd deduced that James Bond's fictional flat in *Moonraker* was at No.25. ❽ At the time of writing the book, the literary critic Desmond MacCarthy, a friend of Fleming's, lived there.

The next road along is Smith Street. No.50 is the house where writer Pamela Lyndon Travers, ❾ the creator of Mary Poppins, lived between 1946 and 1962. There is a blue plaque on the wall to commemorate her. The house was also the inspiration for the Banks' family home in the Disney adaption of the book.

Continue south along Durham Street and turn left onto St Leonard's Terrace to No.27. Here you'll see a blue plaque

in celebration of *Dracula* author Abraham 'Bram' Stoker, ❿ who lived at the house between 1847 and 1912. Joyce Grenfell, ⓫ known for her monologues, lived at No.21 and No.28 St Leonard's Terrace.

Continue back west along St Leonard's Terrace and right on to Radnor Walk. Poet laureate Sir John Betjeman ⓬ lived at No.29 between 1973 and 1984.

Now turn back on to the King's Road. On the right you'll find a large Waterstones bookshop. The itinerary continues west along the King's Road until you reach Manresa Road on the right. This is where, during the 1940s, Dylan Thomas ⓭ worked out of Wentworth Studios (Nos.1–8). Incidentally, 15 Manresa Road housed Chelsea's original public library.

Cross over the King's Road and on to Glebe Place. Cedar Studios is located at No.45, and was the home of John Galsworthy, ⓮ author of *The Forsyte Saga*. It was later the home of

John Osbourne, **15** whose play *Look Back in Anger* is considered a classic of the 'angry young man' group of writers.

Walk around Glebe Place and turn left onto Upper Cheyne Row to Oakley Street where you'll see the home of E.F. Benson **16** at No.10. Turn right onto Phene Street where you'll find the former home of novelist George Gissing. **17** You'll find a blue plaque here.

Return back west along Upper Cheyne Row and bear left on to Lawrence Street, one of the oldest roads in Chelsea. Poet and dramatist John Gay **18** lived at No.16 in 1712–14, as did Tobias Smollet, **19** author of *The Adventures of Roderick Random*, *The Adventures of Peregrine Pickle*, and *The Expedition of Humphrey Clinker*, apparently the favourite books of Charles Dickens as a child.

Henry James **20** had a room at No.10 Lawrence Street in which to write. The street was also once home to the cleric David Williams, who founded the Royal Literary Fund in 1790 to support authors. Beneficiaries included James Joyce, D.H. Lawrence, Dylan Thomas and Edith Nesbit.

Here we'd recommend a drink stop in The Cross Keys. **21** You'll be in good literary company. A blue plaque on the wall states that Dylan Thomas, J.M.W. Turner, Agatha Christie, John Singer Sargent, James Whistler and Bob Marley all enjoyed a drink in the pub (although not all together, sadly).

Now walk towards the Thames and right on to Cheyne Walk to see a remarkable concentration of literary greats. George Eliot (born Mary Ann Evans), **22** the author of *Middlemarch*, lived at No.4. The Scottish novelist and poet Naomi Mitchison **23** lived at No.1.

No.16 was the home of poet Dante Gabriel Rossetti, **24** who rented the house in 1862. He kept a large number of exotic animals in the house and garden, including a brown bear, a kangaroo and a wombat. The wombat was a particular favourite, and is said to have been the inspiration behind the dormouse in Lewis Carroll's **25** *Alice's Adventures in Wonderland*, Carroll being a regular visitor to the house.

No.21 Cheyne Walk was the home of Henry James, **26** Percy Wyndham Lewis and the artist James Whistler. It was also the site where Henry James died.

Bram Stoker **27** wrote the gothic classic *Dracula* at No.27 while working for

Reading List

The Chelsea Murders
Lionel Davidson

Offshore
Penelope Fitzgerald

Doctor Sleep
Madison Smartt Bell

Mrs Miniver
Jan Struther

Four and Twenty Blackbirds
Agatha Christie

Gorsky: A Novel
Vesna Goldsworthy

West End Girls
Jenny Colgan

actor Sir Henry Irving. (Whilst living here, Stoker rescued a drowning man from the Thames. Although the man died soon afterwards, Stoker was awarded a Royal Humane Society medal for his efforts.)

Moving along the road, we reach the Carlyle Mansions, **28** built in 1886. Many famous people have lived there, including the writers Erskine Childers, author of several detective books,

T.S. Eliot, Henry James, Ian Fleming, Somerset Maugham and historian Arnold J. Toynbee.

Farther along Cheyne Walk, past Battersea Bridge, are several houses built in 1777. Novelist Elizabeth Gaskell **29** was born at No.93.

Poet and essayist Hilaire Belloc **30** lived at

No.104, and a blue plaque here commemorates him, along with artist Walter Greaves.

Backtrack a little and walk up Danvers Street. *Gulliver's Travels* author Jonathon Swift **31** lived in a house on the west side of the street in the early 1700s. Continue to Paultons Square, another literary hotspot. Naturalist and writer Gavin Maxwell **32** lived at No.9. Jean Rhys, **33** author of *Wide Sargasso Sea*, lived in Flat 22 in Paultons House. And at No.48, you'll see a blue plaque dedicated to novelist and dramatist Samuel Beckett, **34** winner of the 1969 Nobel Prize for Literature. He lived here in 1934.

Head back west along the King's Road and take the next right on to Beaufort Street. Novelist Elizabeth Gaskell, **35** born at No.93 Cheyne Walk, lived at No.7 Beaufort Street from 1827 until 1829. The poet and playwright Thomas Sturge Moore **36** lived at No.31 in 1895, becoming friends with artist Charles de Sousy Ricketts, who lived at No.51.

Our final stop is the most satisfying.

Head back east along the King's Road and take the next left on to The Vale. From there, turn right on to Mallord Street. Here you'll see where A.A. Milne **37** and his family lived (No.11, later No.13) from the summer of 1919 until 1940. During his time in the 'prettiest little house in London', Milne wrote a collection of verses for children called *When We Were Very Young* (1924), which he dedicated to his son Christopher Robin. Later, he would write the famous *Winnie-the-Pooh* (1926), *Now We Are Six* (1927) and *House At Pooh Corner* (1928) books.

Of the house, he wrote: 'Any of you may find himself some day in our quiet street, and stop a moment to look at our house; at the blue door with its jolly knocker, at the little trees in their blue tubs ... at the bright-coloured curtains. We have the pleasure of feeling that we are contributing something to London.'

PONT STREET

CADOGAN SQUARE

SLOANE STREET

PAVILION ROAD

CADOGAN PLACE

2

1

4 **3**

EET

CADOGAN

ET

SLOANE SQUARE

LOWER SLOANE STREET

SPITAL ROAD

CHELSEA BRIDGE ROAD

CE

7

ITINERARY THREE

A

ARTISTIC CHELSEA

JAMES ABBOTT MCNEILL WHISTLER'S moonlit Chelsea, as seen in *Nocturne: Blue and Silver* (1871), is a still somewhat brooding place. A lone fisherman stands near a barge on the Battersea side of the Thames. Across the river, Chelsea Old Church can be made out. The original can be seen in Tate Britain, and its companion piece, *Variations in Violet and Green* (1871), at the Musée D'Orsay in Paris. In another piece, *Nocturne: Blue and Gold* (c. 1872–5), Whistler paints the old Battersea Bridge with the recognisable lights of the Albert Bridge in the distance. Whistler often employed the friendship of the brothers Henry and Walter Greaves as oarsmen to get the perspective he required, and the brothers, born in Cheyne Walk, became great friends with the artist. Walter, in particular, followed Whistler into his artistic calling, becoming a respected painter himself. His *Hammersmith Bridge on Boat-Race Day* (1862) shows the raucous excitement of the day, while his image of Old Battersea Bridge,

seen from Cheyne Walk, shows the boatyard his family owned. However, the seed of becoming a painter may have been planted before he met Whistler – his father was Joseph Mallord William (J.M.W.) Turner's boatman. In the Print and Drawings room of Tate Britain, you'll find Turner's depiction

Walter Greaves, *Hammersmith Bridge on Boat-Race Day*, 1862

of Chelsea from the late 1790s. Again, Chelsea is depicted from the Battersea side of the Thames and shows not only a rare image of London, but also one with uncharacteristic detail.

78   ITINERARY THREE

J.M.W. Turner, *Battersea Church and Bridge, with Chelsea Beyond, c.* 1797

This period of the later 1800s was a rich one for Chelsea's artistic scene. Over the centuries, the neighbourhood has been home to a great many artists. In Glebe Place, a series of studios were used by J.M.W. Turner, Scottish architect Charles Rennie Mackintosh, president of the Royal Academy Sir Alfred Munnings, Augustus John and Winifred Nicholson. And at various times in the Trafalgar Studios in Manresa Road you'd have found Henry James Brooks, Frank Brangwyn, Frank Dobson and Mervyn Peake working away. It was here where William Holman Hunt painted his famous *The Triumph of the Innocents* (1883–4).

William Holman Hunt, *The Triumph of the Innocents*, 1883–4

The artists aren't just remembered by a series of blue plaques (although there are plenty of those), but in some cases also left artwork. In Manresa Road, you'll find a sculpture by Andrew Sabin to celebrate sculptor Henry Moore, who taught at the Chelsea School of Art,

Andrew Sabin, *Painting and Sculpture,* 2013

and Moore's own *Two Piece Reclining Figure No. 1* (1959) is in the school's grounds. You'll also find David Wynne's *Boy with a Dolphin* on Oakley Street.

To walk the streets of Chelsea with this itinerary is to see the neighbourhood through the eyes of an artist. You'll see studios and homes of great painters, some of the artworks themselves, and also visit a pub painted by Walter Greaves and frequented by artists J.M.W Turner, John Singer Sargent and James Whistler.

Our artistic itinerary starts at the Cremorne Gardens, ➊ on the riverside at the eastern entrance from the Chelsea Embankment on Lot's Road. In the mid- to late-1800s, the area was dedicated to pleasure gardens and regularly packed with thousands of revellers. It was a colourful sight, and one that attracted local artists to paint it. Walter Greaves, who lived at No.104 Cheyne Walk, painted the dramatic scene of a balloon ascent at Cremorne Gardens. Incidentally, his father was a boatman in Chelsea and used to ferry J.M.W. Turner along the Thames as he painted some of his best-known pieces. Turner also lived on Cheyne Walk, and we'll visit them both later.

James Abbott McNeill Whistler, a friend of Walter Greaves, lived in The Vale, but also often painted Cremorne Gardens, notably in the works *Nocturne in Black and Gold – The Fire Wheel* and *Nocturne in Black and Gold – The Falling Rocket*. All of the art can be found online if you want to compare then and now. Be sure to search for *Dancing Platform at Cremorne Gardens, London* (1864) by Phoebus Levin for an insight into an afternoon in these pleasure gardens.

From Cremorne Gardens, walk up Edith Grove and left on to Edith Terrace. At No.13, you'll see a blue plaque that reads: 'Erected By The William Scott Foundation. William Scott CBE RA 1913–1989 Artist Lived and worked here 1962–1986.' Scott ➋ was known for his still-life and abstract paintings, and exhibited globally. His two sons founded the William Scott Foundation to raise awareness for the Alzheimer's Society, from which Scott died.

Return to the junction of the King's Road and turn left until you get to The Vale, where James Abbott McNeill Whistler ➌ lived at No.2 between 1886 and 1890. The painter, potter and tile-maker William de Morgan also briefly lived on The Vale with his artist wife Evelyn Pickering.

Whistler's house is on the corner with Mallord Street, named after Joseph Mallord William Turner. At No.28 is a house built as a studio for painter Augustus John, ➍ which is marked with a blue plaque. Actress and singer Gracie Fields later bought the house.

At the end of Mallord Road is Old Church Street, something of an artistic hotspot. The Hereford Buildings (Nos.49–51) is where sculptor and Royal Academician (and president) Sir Charles Wheeler ➎ lived. Artist Bernard Stern ➏ lived at No.18, and No.127 was the home of painter, potter and tile-maker William de Morgan and his artist wife Evelyn Pickering. ➐ They both died in this house.

William de Morgan, plate, c. 1890–1907

At No.143 is the Chelsea Arts Club, **8** founded in 1891 by a group of artists led by sculptor Thomas Lee. Members included Walter Sickert, George Clausen, Frank Brangwyn, John Singer Sargent, Henry Tonks, Philip Wilson Steer and James Abbott McNeill Whistler, who once entertained Claude Monet there. You can't miss its colourful exterior.

Also on Old Church Street, at No.155, you'll find a blue plaque that reads: 'London County Council John F. Sartorius 1775–c. 1830 Sporting Painter lived here from 1807 to 1812'. **9**

We're going to retrace our steps slightly and head back down the King's Road towards the Thames via Beaufort Street. Roger Fry, **10** a member of the Bloomsbury Group, lived at No.29 between 1892 and 1896. He wrote: 'As I understand it, art is one of the chief organs of what, for want of a better word, I must call the spiritual life.'

Continue down Beaufort Street to Battersea Bridge Gardens, where you'll find a bronze statue

James McNeill Whistler, *Arrangement in Grey and Black No. 1*, 1871

of the painter James Abbott McNeill Whistler by sculptor Nicholas Dimbleby. **11**

Back on the other side of the Battersea Bridge Gardens is J.M.W. Turner's **12** lodgings. While staying here, he assumed the name 'Admiral Booth' to maintain some anonymity. Later, he would die in the house, reportedly muttering the words 'the sun is God'. He became a familiar sight on the banks of the Thames, often holding a telescope and sketch-pad. There's a plaque to commemorate him at Nos.118–19, as is befitting one of the world's greatest-ever painters.

Heading back east, you'll see a blue plaque dedicated to painter Philip Wilson Steer, **13** who lived

at No.109 from 1898 until his death in 1942. He was a founder-member of the Chelsea Arts Club.

Walter Greaves **14** lived at No.104, which is situated behind his father's boat business. Greaves left some of the best documents of a bygone Chelsea, having lived in and painted the borough extensively. Writer Hilaire Belloc later owned the house, as did Chris Squire, the bass player of Yes.

James Whistler **15** lived at what is now No.96 Cheyne Walk between 1866 and 1878. It was in this house he produced his most famous works, including *Arrangement in Grey and Black No.1* (1871), better-known as 'Whistler's Mother'. He was a devoted disciple of the 'Matching' school, and is said once to have dyed a rice pudding green in order that it should blend with the walls of his dining room.

No.92 Cheyne Walk is Belle Vue House, built in 1771. The painter William Bell Scott **16** lived here between 1876 and 1890, becoming close friends with poet and painter Dante Gabriel Rossetti.

Charles Robert Ashbee, **17** architect, designer and one of the key proponents of the Arts and Crafts movement, lived at No.74. James Whistler died in this house on 17 July 1903. The house no longer exists, having been destroyed during an air raid in 1941.

The American-British sculptor Jacob Epstein **18** had a studio and residence at No.72 between 1909 and 1914.

Across Danvers Street is Ropers Gardens. Here you'll find a notable bronze statue called *The Awakening* by Gilbert Ledward, **19** a sculptor born in Chelsea. He was

a Royal Academician, president of the Royal Society of Sculptors and a member of the Chelsea Arts Club.

Continue east along Cheyne Walk. At No. 51 was once a pub called The Cricketers, which was regularly visited by artist George Morland. **20** It is said that instead of paying his bar bill, he painted a new sign for the pub.

No.31 was the birthplace of Walter Greaves. In front of the building, you'll also see *Boy with a Dolphin* by David Wynne. **21** It was unveiled in 1975.

No.22 was home to Dante Gabriel Rossetti **22** (although he's more

associated with No.16; see below), and it is here he painted *Beata Beatrix*, now housed in the Tate Gallery.

Next door at No.21 was once home to Whistler, and is also where author Henry James died.

The magnificent house at No.16 was home of poet Dante Gabriel Rossetti, who rented the house in 1862. From here, he entertained the artists and literati of the time. A painting by Henry Treffry Dunn depicts Rossetti reading proofs of *Sonnets and Ballads* to Theodore Watts-Dunton in the drawing room here. Rossetti also kept a menagerie of animals on the site, all of which

Henry Treffry Dunn, *Rossetti Reading Proofs of Ballads and Sonnets at 16 Cheyne Walk, London*, 1882

Glyn Warren Philpot, *Girl at her Toilet, c.* 1910

had the run of his back garden. His collection apparently included a kangaroo, peacocks, a black bear and a wombat (his personal favourite). The wombat was also loved by Rossetti's friend Lewis Carroll, who is thought to have based the dormouse in *Alice's Adventures in Wonderland* on the animal. Apparently, the landlords of No.22 continue to insert a clause in all new leases forbidding tenants 'to keep wombats' on the premises. There is a blue plaque here in his honour, and one to Algernon Charles Swinburne (1827–1909), who also lived here.

Return back to Lawrence Street and to The Cross

Key's pub. ㉓ The pub was painted by Walter Greaves around 1860, and a plaque on the wall features artists that regularly drank there. The list includes J.M.W Turner, John Singer Sargent and James Abbott McNeill Whistler. They could have added Rossetti to the list too, who met one of his muses here.

Walk east down Lordship Place to Cheyne Row. The artist Glyn Philpot ㉔ had his studio at No.14a between 1906 and 1909. The sculptor Charles James Pibworth ㉕ moved into the house in 1909 and lived here until 1943.

Farther north on Cheyne Row is No.30, the home of William de Morgan ㉖ and Evelyn Pickering. De Morgan is best known for his pottery and tile-making, and built a kiln in the back garden. He was also a painter and novelist, and claimed

that he made more money from writing than from pottery. The couple later moved to Upper Cheyne Row, The Vale and Old Church Street. No.30 was also the home and studio of Victorian artist Frederic, Lord Leighton.

Turn right on to Upper Cheyne Row. The satirical artist John Collett ㉗ lived at No.2 between 1766 and 1773. It was later inhabited by Charles James Lewis ㉘ between 1858 and 1883.

Return back to Glebe Place, a lovely and unassuming road that was home to Scottish architect Charles Rennie Mackintosh ㉙ and his artist wife Margaret Macdonald Mackintosh, who had adjoining studios at No.43 and No.45. Charles Rennie

Charles Rennie Mackintosh, stained glass design for House for An Art Lover, 1901

Mackintosh built No.49 Glebe Place for the landscape painter Harold Squire. **30** It was later used by Welsh painter Augustus John **31** between 1935 and 1940.

Nos.68–9 Glebe Place was the Joseph Turner Studio, **32** and there is a blue plaque in his honour that reads: 'The Studios of the Artist Joseph Turner 1811–1829'. There are also two other blue plaques here that state 'Sir Alfred Munning President Of The Royal Academy Lived Here 1920–1922' **33** and 'William McMillan Sculptor Lived Here 1921–1966'. **34**

John Singer Sargent,
Ellen Terry as Lady Macbeth 1889

Cross over the King's Road and on to Manresa Road, and witness another amazing concentration of artistic connections, including the world's most famous sculptor, Henry Moore.

No.2 Manresa Road is Henry Moore Court, which features a large black sculpture in the forecourt by Andrew Sabin. **35** The work, called *Painting and Sculpture*, is a representation of the artists of Chelsea College of Art, which used to be sited here. Henry Moore taught at the college between 1932 and 1939, and Andrew Sabin was a student and teacher there.

At No.16 you'll find the Trafalgar Studios, **36** a three-storey building purposely built for artists in 1878. Artists who have lived there include Henry James Brooks, best-known for his pictures of meetings and events, Welsh watercolourist and printer Frank Brangwyn, and artist and illustrator Mervyn Peake. Sculptor Frank Dobson, maritime painter Ernest Dade, and Arts and Crafts painter

and jeweller Nelson Dawson also rented studios here.

One of the first artists to rent a studio here was William Holman Hunt, **37** and it was here that he painted one of his most famous works, *The Triumph of the Innocents*.

Return to the King's Road, turn left, and walk a little along the road to No.181. In the 1890s, it was home to Charles Chenil's art materials shop **38** and briefly the home of the Chelsea Arts Club. By 1905, it was Chenil Galleries as well as a studio for Augustus John. Incidentally, Duke Ellington and his orchestra recorded here for Decca.

From here, it's a ten-minute walk to our penultimate stop: No.31 Tite Street. This was the studio of John Singer Sargent, **39** the leading portrait artist of his day. Many of his famous portraits were completed at this house, including his famous *Ellen Terry as Lady Macbeth* (1889), currently in Tate Britain.

Our final stop is No.7 Dilke Street, which is home to The London Sketch Club. **40** It was founded in 1898 as sketches became popular in newspapers and magazines. Its former members include Phil May, H.M. Bateman, Heath Robinson, Peter Blake, the journalist Reggie Bosanquet, Robert Baden-Powell and Arthur Conan Doyle.

William Heath Robinson,
How to Build a Bungalow 1935

Ⓜ

MUSIC & FASHION IN CHELSEA

THE KING'S ROAD. Three words that never fail to conjure a mental image. The name is shorthand for Mary Quant dresses and Mini Coopers, The Who and Mod tailors, or perhaps Vivienne Westwood and the first wave of punk. Maybe it's the Sloane Rangers, It girls and socialites. Even today, as chain stores and fast-food restaurants appear, the King's Road (always with the definitive article) remains a byword for a lively fashion scene. It was the concentration of artists and musicians in Chelsea that came first. The fashion boutiques followed the antique markets that dressed the 1960s. Then came the pubs, the restaurants and the hangouts.

The Rolling Stones are, of course, Chelsea's most famous musical residents, with all of the Stones, including your author, residing and rehearsing in the borough. Led Zeppelin had their office on the King's Road, and Eric Clapton was a regular in its restaurants. When John Lennon and Yoko Ono as The Plastic Ono Band launched 'Give Peace A Chance' on 3 July 1969, they chose Chelsea Old Town Hall for the venue.

The tailors on the west end of the King's Road dressed some of the most stylish people of the 1960s and 1970s. The Beatles, The Rolling Stones, Jimi Hendrix and David Bowie all got their clothes from their shops; a decade later, it was The Clash, Sex Pistols, Chrissie Hynde, Patti Smith, Deborah Harry and Bob Marley. Stores such as Vivienne Westwood's Sex are firmly embedded in the annals of musical folklore. It was in this shop where Malcolm McLaren (Westwood's boyfriend at the time) saw the potential in a spunky young regular called John Lydon, asking him to front the Sex Pistols.

The pubs, restaurants and coffee shops of the King's Road naturally attracted the stars of the day. Patrons of the popular La Famiglia Italian restaurant included Brigitte Bardot, David Bailey, Michael Caine, Jean Shrimpton, Princess Margaret, Peter Sellers, Ian La Frenais, Kylie Minogue

The Chelsea Drugstore, July 1968

and Ronnie Wood. (Now *there's* a dream dinner party list!) Even simple sandwich shops would be graced by greatness: Mick Jagger, John Lennon, Yoko Ono, John Wayne, Lauren Bacall, Humphrey Bogart, Judy Garland and Christine Keeler all ate at S. Boris on the south side of the road.

One establishment even made it into song. In 'You Can't Always Get What You Want' by The Rolling Stones, Jagger sings:

I went down to the Chelsea Drugstore
To get your prescription filled.
I was standing in line with Mr. Jimmy
And, man, did he look pretty ill.
We decided that we would have a soda,
My favourite flavour, cherry red.

We have photos to imagine what the King's Road would have looked like in the 'Swinging Sixties', but many of the establishments are long gone, replaced by new boutiques, modern developments or, in the case of the Chelsea Drugstore, a McDonald's, where you can at least still get a soda, although not one you'd be likely to find in the lyrics of a hit single.

Our music and fashion itinerary runs the length of the King's Road and shoots off in various directions for worthwhile stops. Take it as a 'then and now' excursion, enjoying the independent shops, pubs and coffee shops along the King's Road as it is now whilst learning about how it was in the past. The spark of young creatives still hang out here, and perhaps you'll see the icons of the future.

There's only one place this itinerary could start, and that is Sloane Square. ❶ It sits on the boundary between Belgravia and Chelsea. There are few places in London so synonymous with a scene. It's the hangout of the Sloane Ranger, the upper-middle-class socialite who makes their home in Chelsea. The term was first used in 1975 in *Harpers & Queen* magazine by Peter York and Ann Barr to describe a tribe of people who were living in the area. York and Barr would go on to release *The Official Sloane Ranger Handbook* in 1982; in the centre of the book's cover was Lady Diana Spencer.

Sloane Square is named after Sir Hans Sloane (1660–1753), heir to the land at that time. The first square appeared in the late 1700s, and was simply a grass lawn surrounded by railings. At that time, fields extended all the way to where London Victoria station is now. Worth a look is the relief on the 1953 Venus Fountain in the middle of the square, which shows King Charles II and Nell Gwynn.

There are two significant buildings on the square. The first is the Royal Court

King's Road 1965

Theatre, ❷ which opened in 1888 with a run of plays by George Bernard Shaw. It became a cinema in 1932, but bomb damage during the Blitz forced it to close in 1940. Its heyday was still to come, however, when the English Stage Company moved into the renovated theatre in 1954. John Osbourne, part of the 'angry young man' movement, showed his play *Look Back in Anger* (1956) there, and this was followed by *The Entertainer*, starring Laurence Olivier. Over the years, the avant-garde approach led to it premiering plays by writers including Hanif Kureishi, Jean-Paul Sartre, Bertolt Brecht and Samuel Beckett, as well as being

the site of the premiere of *The Rocky Horror Picture Show* in 1974.

The other notable building on the square is the Peter Jones department store, ❸ which played an integral role in Chelsea's fashion scene. It has been on this site since 1877. Following Peter Jones' death in 1905, it was bought by John Lewis, and continues to be owned by the John Lewis Partnership today. The building you see here today was completed in 1936 and is Grade II* listed.

Begin your time-skipping journey west along the King's Road. Our first musical stop is at No.31, which was the home of composer Percy Grainger

(1882–1961) ④ between 1908 and 1914. You'll see a blue plaque on the wall that reads: 'Percy Grainger 1882–1961 Australian Composer Folklorist and Pianist lived here'. He was born in Australia but rose quickly in Chelsea society, earning money by playing in the homes of patrons and then touring the country. He was particularly interested in British folk music.

Across the road at No.50 was The Chelsea Cobbler, ⑤ which made bespoke shoes, and was particularly admired by members of The Rolling Stones. Another popular stop for the band was No.98, which was the Chelsea Kitchen, ⑥ where they might run into Northern Irish footballer and Chelsea resident George Best.

Continue to Duke of York Square, which leads to the Saatchi Gallery. ⑦ When the gallery hosted *Exhibitionism*, the first international exhibition by The Rolling Stones, three giant tongues dominated the square outside the gallery.

The Stones' folklore continues at No.49, on the corner of the King's Road and Royal Avenue.

Although today it's a McDonald's, it used to be the Chelsea Drugstore, ⑧ as immortalised in the song 'You Can't Always Get What You Want' (see the introduction for the lyrics). Over its three floors were bars, food stalls, a record store, boutiques and, yes, a pharmacy.

A little farther along, at No.138a on the corner of the King's Road and Markham Square, was Bazaar, ⑨ opened by Mary Quant and Alexander Plunkett-Greene in 1955. Quant's trademark black-and-white dresses were perhaps the defining look of the King's Road fashion scene, if not the entire 1960s.

Fashion designer Mary Quant, 1966

If you stay on the same side of the road and cross Markham Street, you'll find The Pheasantry ⑩ in the middle of the block. This Georgian building, built in 1769, is so-called because pheasants were once raised on the site for the royal household. A blue plaque on the wall reads: 'Princess Seraphine Astafieva 1876–1934 Ballet Dancer lived and taught here 1916–1934'. During her time, Astafieva taught prima ballerinas Alicia Markova and Margot Fonteyn. During the 1960s and 1970s, it was variously a private members club and a nightclub, and is where Andrew Lloyd Webber and Tim Rice discovered Yvonne Elliman. The upper floors of the building were flats, with residents including Eric Clapton, journalist Martin Sharp (editor of *Oz*), Germaine Greer, Clive James, and photographer Robert Whitaker, who was responsible for the controversial 'butcher' photo used on the original cover of The Beatles' album *Yesterday* & *Today*.

On the next block, at No.162, was I Was Lord Kitchener's Valet. ⑪ During the late 1960s, the shop was frequented by the pop musicians of the time, including various members of The Rolling Stones. Lord Kitchener's Thing was another outlet on the King's Road, one of several in London.

Almost next door, at No.168, was the All Kinds boutique, **12** which counted Tony Curtis, the Four Tops, The Temptations, and several footballers of the time as customers.

John Michael Ingram's boutique, **13** one of the earliest on the King's Road, having opened in 1957, was at No.170. It was one of the original retailers of the Mod style.

Between 1967 and 1970, the Club dell'Aretusa **14** was at No.107, which counted among its celebrity guests Princess

I Was Lord Kitchener's Thing

Margaret, Sammy Davis Jr, David Bailey and Twiggy, as well as Brian Jones and Keith Richards of The Rolling Stones.

Another well-known spot was Picasso coffee bar on the corner of the King's Road and Shawfield Street at No.127. **15** It was popular with Eric Clapton, The Rolling Stones and other musical stars of the

day, and its clientele made it the place to see and be seen. Opened in 1958, it eventually closed in 2009.

The next road on the left is Flood Street. In the Chelsea Manor Studio at Nos.1–11 was the Michael Coopers Photographic Studio. **16** This is where the sleeve of *Sgt. Pepper's Lonely Hearts Club Band* was put together.

The remarkable building on the corner of Flood Street was the Margaret Morris Club. **17** Margaret Morris was a British dancer, choreographer and teacher, who founded the club in 1915. Members included Augustus John, Jacob Epstein, Katherine Mansfield, Ezra Pound, Siegfried Sassoon, Wyndham Lewis and Charles Rennie Mackintosh.

Dandie Fashions

Picasso coffee bar

This 1956 psychedelic Bentley was owned by fashion maverick and co-owner of Dandie Fashions, John Crittle. Painted in a similar colourful style to the exterior of the shop, it was used to chauffeur their clients to parties and clubs around town. The car was later passed to The Beatles when they invested in Dandie Fashions in 1968.

Also on this strip of buildings was the Top Gear boutique, **18** which opened in 1965 at No.135. The shop had the famous Mod bull's-eye on its front canopy. It became Acme Attractions in 1974, and was frequented by artists including The Clash, Sex Pistols, Chrissie Hynde, Patti Smith, Deborah Harry and Bob Marley. It closed in 1977.

The Countdown **19** boutique was at No.137 between 1965 and 1971. Regular customers included various members of The Beatles, The Rolling Stones and Marianne Faithful.

Continue along the King's Road to No.161, where Dandie Fashions **20** opened in 1967. The co-owner, Tara Browne, died in the high-profile car accident, which is referred to in The Beatles' 'A Day In The Life'. The Beatles were customers of the boutique, along with The Rolling Stones and Jimi Hendrix. Most notably, David Bowie bought his Ziggy Stardust outfit from the shop.

Across Chelsea Manor Street, at Nos.165–79, is Chelsea Old Town Hall. **21** This was where John Lennon and Yoko Ono as The Plastic Ono Band launched 'Give Peace A Chance' on 3 July 1969.

Next door, at Nos.181–3, was Charles Chenil's art materials shop. **22** In later life, it would become a recording studio, and was where Duke Ellington and his orchestra recorded for Decca.

One of most remarkable buildings in Chelsea is Argyll House, **23** the oldest house on the King's Road, dating back to 1723. It was built for John Perrin by the Venetian architect Giacomo Leoni, whose monogram appears on the gate. It was owned by Lady Sibyl Colefax between 1922 and 1937. Her parties were notorious at the time, and once included Fred and Adele Astaire, who

Queen of Punk Rockers, Pamela Rooke aka Jordan at Sex shop on the Kings Road, December 1976

entertained fellow guests one evening. Another occasion saw George Gershwin play piano with Arthur Rubinstein and Cole Porter standing on either side of him.

Thomas Arne (1710–78), ㉔ the composer of 'Rule Britannia', lived his final years at No.215. Arne also composed music to be played at Ranelagh Gardens in Chelsea. Peter Ustinov lived here in more recent times.

Move along to No.239 and to the former location of The Gateways Club, ㉕ on the corner of Bramerton Street. First opened in 1931, it became the longest-surviving lesbian nightclub in the world. It was popular in the 1960s with celebrities such as Diana Dors and Dusty Springfield.

On the next strip, on the other side of Bramerton Street, was the original site of the Chelsea Antiques Market. ㉖ It helped define the look of the 1960s, with members of The Rolling Stones, in particular Brian Jones, buying Moroccan clothing here.

No.251 was another unlikely epicentre of 1960s culture. The Sandwich Shop ㉗ served the likes of Mick Jagger, John Lennon and Yoko Ono. Next door, at No.253, was the Emmerton & Lambert boutique, ㉘ again popular with members of The Rolling Stones.

The cinema on the corner of Old Church Street used to be an artificial ice rink called the Glaciarium. ㉙ For part of its life it was the King's Road Theatre, which held the first live performance of *The Rocky Horror Picture Show*.

Across the road at No.304 was The Alkasura boutique, ㉚ particularly popular among the glam rockers of the 1970s, with the likes of Marc Bolan among the customers.

At No.328 was a 1960s hangout called The Casserole. ㉛ Regular visitors included The Rolling Stones and The Beatles.

On the corner of Beaufort Street was The Roebuck public house. ㉜ It was built in the 1890s, and became a popular pub during the 1960s and 1970s. It was a regular haunt for Malcolm McLaren and the Sex Pistols.

Another pub, the Man in the Moon (No.392), ㉝ stood at the corner of the King's Road and Park Walk, and was where Adam and the Ants played some early gigs. It is now a restaurant.

Although there's still a tailors at No.406, it is no longer the Modern Outfitters, ㉞ which counted Bob Dylan, Keith Richards and David Bowie among its customers. The owner, Lloyd Johnson, designed the clothes for the classic Mod film *Quadrophenia*.

One of the few remaining boutiques is at No.430. **35** Hung On You was launched here in 1966. In 1969, it became the Mr Freedom, clothing members of The Rolling Stones and The Beatles. However, it was the next iteration that established its place in music folklore. In 1971, Vivienne Westwood and Malcolm McLaren opened Sex, a boutique that became the centre of the punk movement despite only being open between 1974 and 1976. Malcolm McLaren was managing The Swankers from the shop, members of which would go on to form the Sex Pistols. It was in this boutique that McLaren met John Lydon and persuaded him to join the band. Pistols bass player Glenn Matlock worked in the shop, and other notable proponents of the punk movement shopped here, including Chrissie Hynde, Adam Ant and Siouxsie Sioux. The shop is now the World's End, and was still part of Vivienne Westwood's fashion empire when she died. The World's End 'backwards clock' (with 13 hours) is still there.

As you wander down into the World's End area of Chelsea, you'll pass the former offices of Led Zeppelin and the headquarters of their Swan Song Records (No.484). **36**

At No.488 was Granny Takes a Trip, **37** the first 'psychedelic' boutique. The façade constantly changed, and at one point there was a 1948 Dodge car that looked as though it had crashed through the front. Rod Stewart, Ronnie Wood, Bill Wyman and Keith Richards were all customers.

One of the key sites in the history of The Rolling Stones took place at the corner of the King's Road and Slaidburn Street. The Wetherby Arms pub, **38** opened in 1881, was a regular rehearsal space for the band, and was where this author first auditioned, becoming a founder member in 1962. It closed in 1971.

Here is where our excursion along the King's Road comes to an end, but there are many more places in Chelsea with an unusual musical and fashion history. Before continuing towards the Thames, perhaps take a table at the La Famiglia **39** restaurant just around the corner, at No.7 Langton Street. It has long been a place for the Chelsea scenesters to eat. Celebrities who have been spotted there include Brigitte Bardot, David Bailey, Michael Caine, Princess Margaret, Peter Sellers, Kylie Minogue, Bill Wyman and Ronnie Wood of The Rolling Stones.

Actor Michael J. Pollard outside Granny Takes A Trip c. 1965

The Who filming a live set for German TV at the Duke of York's HQ, November 1966

The 606 Club **40** on Lot's Road is another great place to visit (be sure to check their listings first). Eric Clapton and Ronnie Wood have played there, and there's a particular focus on jazz. To get there, continue west along the King's Road to Tadema Street and then Tadema Road to Lot's Road. The club is on the right.

It's worth the walk back along the Thames – which is always a lovely stroll – to hit our final few stops on this musical and fashion itinerary.

Walk east along Lot's Road, onto Cremorne Road and past Cremorne

Gardens and Battersea Bridge to Cheyne Walk. No.48 was the home of Mick Jagger in 1968. **41** The most infamous incident of his time here happened in May 1969, when he was arrested for marijuana possession. Just the other side of Lawrence Street is the Carlyle Mansions, **42** home to Rolling Stones' drummer Charlie Watts, as well as the composer Richard Addinsell, who is best known for his *Warsaw Concerto*,

written for the 1941 film *Dangerous Moonlight*.

Farther along Cheyne Walk is the Chelsea Embankment Gardens, where you'll find a statue dedicated to composer and Chelsea resident Ralph Vaughan Williams (1872–1958). **43** He lived at No.13 Cheyne Walk between 1905 and 1929.

Perhaps most fittingly though, we should finish in a pub. The Cross Keys **44** in Lawrence Street (which makes an appearance in two of our other itineraries) has a plaque on the wall that states: 'The Cross Keys Heritage Dylan Thomas, J.M.W Turner (painter), Agatha Christie, John Singer Sargent, James McNeill Whistler (painter), Bob Marley 1708–2012 celebrated figures drank here'. A blue plaque in honour of Bob Marley can be found at No.42 Oakley Street.

Chelsea is a borough that continues to evolve at a rapid rate. It's been the centre of the 'Swinging Sixties', the glam rock 1970s and the punk movement. Sloane Square is the playground for the rich young things of London, and the boutiques along the King's Road still attract the wealthy and famous of today. What scene will emerge next from Chelsea, we can't possibly say. But we do know something will. We watch with interest.

CHELSEA STREETS

A TO Z

CHELSEA STREETS *A TO C*

In which you will meet Karl Marx, novelist Elizabeth Gaskell, Laurence Olivier and the fictional intelligence officer George Smiley, featured in eight of author John Le Carré's novels. You'll also discover where Hollywood legend Judy Garland died and hear about the remarkable life of actress Dorothea Jordan, who took Drury Lane by storm in the 1790s, and then mothered fifteen children, including ten by the Duke of Clarence, the future William IV.

Politicians who made their homes on these streets include William Wilberforce, who was fundamental in abolishing the slave trade, Prime Minister Harold Macmillan, and Aneurin 'Nye' Bevan, the architect of the National Health Service. It was an earlier politician, Sir Thomas More (1478–1535), who put Chelsea on the map. Several of the streets in this section lie on his estate.

Alpha Place

Here you will find the location of The Hut, a Scout Hut rebuilt in 2015 to create a community space behind the Hall of Remembrance in Flood Street. There is also a Peabody Estates development of the same name.

Anderson Street

Anderson Street is named after John Anderson, a trustee of James Colvill, whose nursery ground was on this site. This street is situated in the heart of Chelsea, close to the King's Road and Sloane Square, and benefitting from the shops and restaurants the area offers. It has an early 'Chelsea' road sign.

No.4: This was the home of Karl Marx (1818–83) and his family in 1849. After six months living there, bailiffs evicted them for non-payment of rent, and they left Chelsea.

No.7: This house was built in 1845 and is a fine example of Regency and early Victorian influences.

Ann Lane – *see Cremorne Estate in the Miscellany.*

Apollo Place

Apollo Place is located on the site of an original mews, but has been redeveloped to a degree that no original mews properties survive. It is a cul-de-sac off Riley Street and now contains just five properties used for residential and commercial purposes. In the Second World War, a high-explosive bomb fell directly onto the mews, damaging some of the properties. It is part of the Cremorne Estate. It has a very early black-and-white road sign with just the street name.

Ashburnham Road

Named after the location of Ashburnham House, home to John Ashburnham, 2nd Earl of Ashburnham (1724–1812). The road runs the length of what was once the great lawn.

Astell Street

Named after Mary Astell, a pioneering feminist and a forerunner of the suffragettes. In 1709, she set up a Anglican charity school at the Royal Hospital for daughters of Chelsea Pensioners. During the Second World War, there was a food office sited here.

Basil Street

Basil Street runs west off Sloane Street and north off Hans Crescent. The Basil Mansions are here.

No.8: The Basil Street Hotel, built in 1910, is an Edwardian-style hotel with the charm of an English country house.

Battersea Bridge Gardens

Located on the south side of Chelsea Embankment and west of Battersea Bridge, there is a bronze statue here of the painter James Abbott McNeill Whistler (1834–1903) looking over the Thames. It was erected in September 2005 and is the work of sculptor Nicholas Dimbleby. There are also two seats here with dedications to earlier Chelsea residents.

Beauchamp Place

Beauchamp Place (pronounced 'Beecham') was named Grove Place until 1885. It was once known for its brothels and lodging houses, but since the Edwardian era, antique shops and high-end fashion boutiques have dominated the street. Womenswear designer Lalage Beaumont is based here. The San Lorenzo restaurant has been here since 1963, and has been popular among actors, musicians, artists and celebrities ever since. It has an old blue street sign that is probably Victorian. It reads 'Beauchamp Place S.W.'

Beauchamp Place looking towards Brompton Road, 1977

No.10: The Knightsbridge Hotel.

Nos.13–14: Claverley Court Apartments.

No.33: The Beaufort Hotel.

No.45: Beaufort House Apartments.

Beaufort Street

Beaufort Street runs north from Battersea Bridge to the King's Road. From 1766, it was laid out across the site of Beaufort House and its grounds. There are five large, redbrick residential buildings named Burleigh House, Cadogan House, Dacre House, Kingsley House and Winchester House. Collectively known as the Sir Thomas More Buildings, they were erected in 1903–4 and display a variety of decorative plaques on their front walls.

No.7: Novelist Elizabeth Gaskell (1810–65), who was born at 93 Cheyne Walk, lived here from 1827–9.

No.17: Mulberry Close, a large apartment building.

Half-way up Beaufort Street from the river, on the eastern side, is a church fronted by a statue of Jesus on the Cross. On the adjoining building to the north, on the southern wall of No.28, there is a coloured mosaic honouring Sir Thomas More and dedicated as follows: 'Saint Thomas More Chancellor of England, Martyred for his faith on Tower Hill 1535, lived here. It was from this house that he went for his trial and his imprisonment in the Tower of London.'

Beauchamp Place was also a sixteenth-century mansion of the Seymour family, whose titles included Viscount Beauchamp. It belonged to Edward Seymour, Viscount Beauchamp, who became the Earl of Hertford and was the son of a Lord Protector of England.

Beaufort Gardens

Beaufort Gardens is unique in that the gardens are gone and the square is lacking buildings at the eastern end. After Richard Lloyd's death in 1859, his executor and trustee, William and Charles Quentery, teamed up with Thomas Stimpson, a builder, to redevelop the estate, while the remaining lots were sold to Jeremiah Little, another local builder. Architect George Adam Burn, who was responsible for the rebuilding of the Red Lion pub on Brompton Road, designed the five houses at Nos.43–7, and most likely the rest of the houses here, which each have four main storeys with an attic above. The square was named Beaufort Gardens by the Quenterys in 1863, and both sides were finished by 1870.

No.28: Allen Hall, a former nineteenth-century convent, which since 1975 has been the Seminary of the Roman Catholic Archdiocese of Westminster. The Seminary Garden is one of the largest private gardens in Chelsea, dating back to 1524, when Sir Thomas More purchased land in Chelsea and Kensington for his Great House. Although the house is long gone, a central courtyard garden contains a fountain and shrubs, while the main garden has a lawn surrounded by roses, flowering shrubs and trees. A path leads to a secluded walled garden, beyond which we find More's mulberry tree, and finally an area planted in *c.* 2004 as the St Thomas More Mulberry Walk.

No.29: The artist Roger Fry (1866–1934) lived here from 1892 to 1896.

No.31: The poet Thomas Sturge Moore (1870–1944) lived here in 1895, and befriended Charles de Sousy Ricketts at No.51.

Nos.38–40: Beaufort House, on the junction with the King's Road.

Sir Thomas More

Saint Thomas More, Chancellor of England, martyred for his Faith on Tower Hill 1535, lived here. It was from his house here that he went for his trial and his imprisonment in the Tower of London.

In around 1525, Thomas More, lawyer, statesman and Chancellor of the Duchy of Lancaster for Henry VIII, bought twenty-three acres of land in Chelsea. He built himself a large home by the river, later to be called Beaufort House. Henry VIII frequently travelled down the Thames to his residence for visits. More became Lord Chancellor in 1529, but opposed Henry's divorce and resigned in 1532, retiring to Chelsea. He also strongly fought against the dissolution of the monasteries, an act that eventually led him to be tried for treason and beheaded in 1535. His house was demolished in 1740. Chelsea Park Gardens and Beaufort Street now sit on the site. A mosaic (left) honouring Sir Thomas More is at No.28.

HISTORICAL CHELSEA

No.51: Artist Charles de Sousy Ricketts (1866–1931) lived here until 1902.

Major-General Charles George Gordon (1833–85) lived in this street before his expedition to Khartoum, from which he never returned. The street has an early 'Chelsea' road sign.

Blacklands Terrace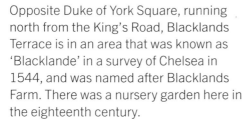

Opposite Duke of York Square, running north from the King's Road, Blacklands Terrace is in an area that was known as 'Blacklande' in a survey of Chelsea in 1544, and was named after Blacklands Farm. There was a nursery garden here in the eighteenth century.

No.7: This is the site of a former public house called Alma.

Nos.8–9: The Five Fields restaurant.

Nos.10–12: The John Sandoe bookshop, the oldest established bookshop in Chelsea. John Sandoe founded this shop in 1957. Prior to this, the premises

were used by three separate concerns at the same time: a dress shop (before that it had been a poodle parlour), a second-hand bookshop and a secretarial business. Today, the bookshop has a bias towards the humanities as well as an excellent children's department.

Blantyre Street

Runs south from the King's Road, and west of Glebe Place. The Blantyre Arms public house is on this street. The Chelsea Reach Tower, St John's Church and Mission Hall are at the intersection of Blantyre Street and what was Dartrey Road. St John's Church was originally situated on Tadema Road. At first, open-air services were held in the area from 1873, before a permanent church was opened in 1876 to serve the development of the World's End estate. The church sponsored a wide range of charitable and social activities, and worked with the Salvation Army. It was bombed in 1940 and services were moved to a mission at St John's Community Church in Blantyre Street. In 1973, the parish was united with St Andrew's on Park Walk.

Bourne Street

Bourne Street is a long, mainly residential street lying east of Sloane Square. Samuel Archbutt, a Victorian developer, built some of the houses in c. 1824, such as Nos.37–45, which were designed originally as workers' cottages.

No.35: The Francis Holland School.

St Mary's Church (Church of England) is on this street. It was built 'quickly and cheaply' in 1874 to provide ministry to the poor living in the nearby slums of Pimlico. The Carmel Church Hall is also here, built in 1937–8, and is home to the Grosvenor Club, a members-only club.

Bramerton Street

Located on the southern extension of Glebe Place, Bramerton Street was built on the former rectory gardens. Part of this street, previously known as Caledonian Terrace, was built between 1830 and 1860. The name was changed in 1878, when the northern part was under construction, and very little has changed in nearly 100 years. The former Chelsea footballer Joe Cole had a house here in recent times.

No.4: Sculptor Charles James Pibworth lived here from 1899 to 1901.

No.37: William Joyce, otherwise known as 'Lord Haw-Haw', lived here for a while.

Bray Place

One of the streets north of the King's Road, opposite Duke of York Square. It acquired its name from a grant of

manorial property and land made to Sir Reginald Bray (1440–1503) by Henry VII, in recognition of Bray's help in the king's bid to gain the crown. It has two very early road signs (pre-1917).

Britten Street

Britten Street, between Dovehouse Street and Sydney Street, is named after J. Britten, who was a trustee of St Luke's Church, which was built about the same time as the street. A foundation stone lies there inscribed 'This stone was laid in the presence of The Guardians by Thomas Symons Esqre their chairman on the 19th day of February A.D.1973'.

No.13: The Builders Arms public house.

No.28: Britten House.

Brompton Arcade

Brompton Arcade is at 13–31 Brompton Road and was built in 1903–04. The arcade could be entered through a stone archway and had rows of shops on either side. In 2018, the building was demolished, except for the stone front elevations, which will be incorporated into the new building.

Brompton Place

Brompton Place is off the Brompton Road and home to a small row of nineteenth-century terraced houses originally known as Lloyd's Place after the landowner.

Brompton Road

Brompton Road starts at the Knightsbridge underground station, runs south-west through a residential area, and ends at Brompton Cross, which becomes Fulham Road. The street is replete with five-star hotels and wide pavements, and there are many top restaurants and shops along it. The Church of the Immaculate Heart of Mary, commonly known as the Brompton Oratory, is also here. Just east of this was the Brompton Road underground station, which, due to a lack of traffic, closed on 30 July 1934.

Nos.87–135: The world-famous Harrods department store.

No.150: The Embassy of Uruguay.

Burnaby Street

Burnaby Street is one of the streets north of Lots Road, and was named after a brother of Admiral Sir William Burnaby, who lived for some time in the neighbourhood. The street has an early 'Chelsea' road sign.

No.4: At ground level, this house front features a charming wall plaque depicting five children, with one blowing a pipe and one riding a hound.

No.32: On the junction with Uverdale Road is the Chelsea Ram public house. The pub sign depicts a Chelsea pensioner in red with a ram on a lead. It was refurbished and reopened in 1995. Knick-knacks adorn the interior walls and much of the furniture is antique.

Burnsall Street

Burnsall Street is north of the King's Road, east of Britten Street, and was originally called Brewer Street until 1928. It was renamed in memory of Martha Burnsall, who had established a charity in 1805 for 'poor decayed housekeepers'. The Flying Colours art gallery is here.

Bury Walk

Bury Walk was possibly named because it led to a burial ground, the site of which was later taken over by St Luke's Church in Sydney Street. The street shows the varying styles of development from the 1830s to the present day. It is a mews-style through road between Fulham Road and Cale Street, parallel to Stewarts Grove, and contains properties used for a mixture of residential and commercial purposes. During the Second World War, several high-explosive bombs fell onto Sydney Street, as well as next to and directly onto the Walk itself.

No.22: This is a strange house, with a castellated top. There is a plaque on the wall here that states 'Sophie Fedorovitch 1893–1953 Ballet & Opera Designer Lived Here'.

No.41: A cute little house of some character.

Bywater Street

A cul-de-sac that runs north of the King's Road, opposite Wellington Square, and is named after Thomas Bywater, who was a landowner in the area. The Georgian townhouses here are very attractive. Built in the 1850s on the site of a nursery garden, Bywater Street was originally called Addison Place.

No.9: The home of the fictional intelligence officer George Smiley, featured in eight of author John Le Carré's spy novels. The 1997 BBC series *Tinker Tailor Soldier Spy*, starring Sir Alec Guinness, was partly filmed here.

Cadogan Gardens

Located north of the Peter Jones department store and running parallel to the King's Road, this location has attracted personalities including radicals, artists and poets. More recently, it became home to a private members club.

No.11: The Cadogan Gardens Hotel, built by Lord Chelsea in the late nineteenth

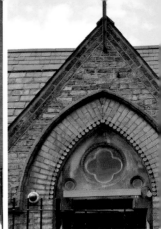

century, replaced four separate Victorian townhouses.

No.19: There is a school here with a highly decorated front.

Nos.21–2: These houses have highly decorated entrances.

Cadogan Gate

Cadogan Gate runs west off Sloane Street and is residential.

Cadogan Lane

Cadogan Lane is a partly cobbled through road between Cadogan Place and Pont Street, with an additional cul-de-sac section on the opposite side of Pont Street. It was originally the stable and coach houses for the main houses on Cadogan Place. At some time between October 1940 and June 1941, a high-explosive bomb fell directly on to the mews. It contains residential and commercial properties.

No.4: The property was home to Mr and Mrs Mickey Deans, and it was there on 22 June 1969 that Hollywood legend Judy Garland died, suffering heart failure. Her husband Mickey awoke to find her dead on the toilet.

Cadogan Place

Cadogan Place is named after Earl Cadogan and runs parallel to Lower Sloane Street on the west side. It gives its name to the extensive Cadogan Place Gardens.

No.30: Mrs Dorothea Jordan (1762–1816) lived here from 1812. She adopted the name when she arrived from Ireland with her mother in 1782. She had already been on stage in Ireland, and soon appeared at the Drury Lane Theatre, where Lord Byron thought she was superb. She caught the eye of the unmarried Duke of Clarence (the future William IV) in 1790 and had ten children by him. She had a previous daughter by her theatre manager in Dublin, and in London a further three by Sir Richard Ford. Her relationship with Clarence was good, until George III, concerned that none of his sons had produced a legitimate heir, ordered them to marry, and Clarence abandoned her.

No.44: William Wilberforce (1759–1833) lived here briefly in 1833. As a young man, he left university, was elected MP for Hull, and soon became a member of the young political 'fast set' in London.

In 1787, he founded the Proclamation Society Against Vice and Immorality, and began his forty-six-year battle for the abolition of slavery. His first great step was the Slave Trade Act of 1807, which effectively abolished the legal slave trade. When he was seventy-three, he was stricken with an attack of influenza, and in early July 1833 he arrived at this house, which his cousin Mrs Lucy Smith had lent him. However, his illness proved too much for him and he died on 29 July 1833. Ironically, the culmination of his life's work, the Emancipation Act, abolishing slavery in British possessions, was passed in August 1833, a month after his death.

No.52: The London birthplace and family home of Harold Macmillan (1894–1986), who was prime minister of the United Kingdom from 1957 to 1963.

No.79: The former home of Lord and Lady Colin Campbell, who provided Victorian London with a sensational divorce trial in 1886.

The original Chelsea House was here, and the London residence of the Cadogan family. In its earlier days, it was situated on the site of the Duke of York Square redevelopment in the King's Road. Its most recent manifestation was at the eastern end of the northern terrace of Cadogan Place. Chelsea House was demolished in 1935 and replaced by a residential block (also called Chelsea House), which now occupies the site.

Charles Dickens wrote about this street in his novel *Nicholas Nickleby* (1838–9). It is also the home of Fanny and Robert Assingham in Henry James' novel *The Golden Bowl* (1904).

Cadogan Square

Located south of Pont Street, east of Lennox Gardens and west of Sloane Street, Cadogan Square was also named after Earl Cadogan. Whilst it is mainly a residential area, some of the properties are used for diplomatic and educational purposes. It is known for being one of the most expensive residential streets in the United Kingdom.

The Square is on the site of Henry Holland's grand house and grounds (*see Sloane Square*), and was built in 1877–8 by the Cadogan and Hans Place Estate Ltd. It was one of the first significant developments in London to use red brick, rather than the usual yellow brick and stucco.

In November 2014, a house balcony collapsed here, killing two men and

injuring six others. The square has a pre-1917 road sign, possibly Victorian.

No.21: Major General John Hay Beith, CBE (1876–1952) lived here in the 1930s. He was a British schoolmaster and soldier, but is best remembered as a novelist, playwright, essayist and historian writing under the pen name Ian Hay.

No.26: The building has a hanging metal sign featuring a dog.

No.31: South African actress Moira Lister (1923–2007) lived here in 1972.

No.39 or No.59: The writer Marguerite Radclyffe Hall (1880–1943) lived here from 1911 to 1916.

Nos.54–8: The buildings were designed by William Young in 1877 for Lord Cadogan. The architect J.J. Stevenson was largely responsible for the south side, which was built in 1879–85. The east side was built in 1879 by George Thomas Robinson.

No.60: The writer Dennis Wheatley (1897–1977) lived here from 1960 to 1970. Opposite this house is a view into the square, where one can see the

sculpture titled *Dancer With Bird* (1975) by David Wynne (1926–2014).

No.68: Sussex House School for Boys (founded 1952), which was built by Norman Shaw.

No.75: The novelist and filmmaker Arnold Bennett (1867–1931) lived here from 1922 to 1930. Bennett was the author of the Clayhanger novels, amongst others. He died in his house in Baker Street after contracting typhoid from drinking tap water in France.

No.81: Home to the American socialite Barbara Daly Baekeland, who was murdered by her son Antony in November 1972.

Other celebrities who have lived in Cadogan Square include stop-motion animator Ray Harryhausen, and film stars Christopher Lee and Boris Karloff.

Cadogan Street

This street runs horizontal to the King's Road behind Peter Jones department store. St Mary's Roman Catholic Church is here, built in the 1870s by the same architect of Westminster Cathedral. It followed the establishment of Roman Catholicism in Chelsea with St Thomas More's School in 1845.

Cale Street

Cale Street crosses Sydney Street beside the Royal Brompton Hospital and was named after Judith Cale (d.1717), who established an annual fund of 23 shillings each for six poor widows.

William Sutton left his fortune to build the historic Sutton Dwellings here, which were used to house families on low income suffering from poor living standards.

The Sutton Estate was built in 1913, and more than 2,000 people have found a place to live there. The estate comprises several buildings with the house names Elbourn, Flamstead, Gadebridge, Hammerfield, Icknield, Jenningsbury, Kingsmill, Leverstock, Maylands, Nettleden, and Oatwell.

No.27: The former site of The Blenheim public house. The name 'Blenheim' is still featured in white lettering at the top of the building.

Callow Street

Callow Street runs parallel to Beaufort Street on the western side. It is named after John Callow, a member of a family of publicans who established a building business in the area c. 1840 and was employed by the Cadogans to lay out a number of streets in Chelsea.

Camera Place

Camera Place is between Limerston Street and Park Walk, south of Fulham Road. At No.6 is The Sporting Page pub, originally built in 1856 as the Odell Arms. This site was first listed as three Chelsea villas. It was rebuilt in 1974 as the Red Anchor but still retains a Victorian lamp over the entrance.

Carlyle Square

Carlyle Square was originally laid out around 1821, but it changed in the mid-1920s when Chelsea Park Gardens took its place. Even now, it retains the atmosphere of a rural village.

No.2: Osbert Sitwell (1892–1969) occupied this house for forty years, and it was here where the young composer William Walton (1902–83) and the poet Edith Sitwell (1887–1964) produced the first private performance of *Fagade*. The blue plaque here states: 'Park Lane Group Sir Osbert Sitwell Bt CH Author and Essayist lived here 1919–63'.

No.6: The grand theatrical couple Dame Sybil Thorndike (1882–1976) and Lewis Casson (1875–1969) lived here. Dame Sybil began her theatrical career during 1904–7 with a tour of America. She met Casson in 1907, married him a year later, and became a close associate of George Bernard Shaw, who wrote the play *Saint Joan* for her to play the title role. The couple celebrated their sixtieth wedding anniversary in 1968, but Casson died a year later. There is a blue plaque here that reads: 'Dame Sybil Thorndike 1882–1976 Actress Lived Here 1921–1932'.

No.18: One of the most notorious inhabitants, the Soviet spy Kim Philby (1912–88), lived here from 1945 until his defection to the USSR following his betrayal of British secrets.

No.22: Sir David Frost lived here for several years until he died in 2013. He held his annual garden fete in Carlyle Square Garden, which was attended by royalty, parliamentary members, celebrities from the worlds of film and theatre, writers, artists, musicians and sports personalities.

Caversham Street

Caversham Street is situated north-west of the Royal Hospital Road and opposite the Chelsea Physic Garden. It is residential and was heavily bombed in the Second World War.

Christ Church was built to the designs of Edward Blore (1787–1879) and was consecrated on 26 June 1839. A new west front, designed by W.D. Caroe, was added before the First World War, and a new entrance porch by G.G. Woodward was built in 1933.

No.22: The London School of Tennis Ltd.

Nos.27–33: Hayden Piper House, built in 1992.

The mews off Caversham Street is small and residential.

Charles II Place

Situated directly off No.77 King's Road, close to Markham Square, these large modern-style mews houses were built *c.* 1989. It is a gated and secure site that is closed to the public.

Chelsea Cross

Chelsea Cross is a small section of road at the junction of Fulham Road and Old Church Street. It is home to a close-knit community of twenty-four specialist showrooms, with everything from bespoke furniture and upholstery, hand-painted wallpaper, fabrics, carpets and eighteenth-century and vintage antiques to silver, art and rare books, as well as a flower stall and two delicious Italian restaurants. Its road sign is underneath the road sign for Queen's Elm Parade. There is another 'Chelsea Cross' road sign across Fulham Road opposite.

Chelsea Manor Gardens

Chelsea Manor Gardens runs parallel with the King's Road, and is immediately behind Chelsea Old Town Hall. It was the site of the municipal swimming baths, which today is the Chelsea Sports Centre, comprising a sports hall, fitness room, dance studio and a swimming pool. A former garage was demolished to make way for Chelsea Towers, which were erected on the site.

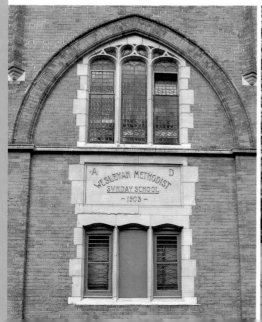

Chelsea Manor Street

Chelsea Manor Street runs from the King's Road, east of the Chelsea Old Town Hall. On the north-west side is a stone entrance with a blue notice board headed 'Kensington and Chelsea Register Office Chelsea Old Town Hall'. The building opposite has a stone plaque inset low down on the wall that reads: 'This Stone Was Laid By The Rt Hon George Thomas MP Speaker Of The House Of Commons 23 October 1982'. Previously simply Manor Street, it passed through the former great garden of New Manor House, the home of Katherine Parr.

The Wesleyan Methodist Church is here, on which there is a wall plaque headed 'Wesleyan Methodist Sunday School 1903'. The church tower was destroyed during wartime bombing and the church was declared unfit for worship. In the 1970s, it was rebuilt and included a drop-in centre and counselling service. Twenty-one homes for the elderly were added and leased to a charitable trust.

There is a blue plaque here dedicated to designers Edward McKnight Kauffer (1890–1954) and Marion Dorn (1896–1964), who lived in Flats 139 and 141, respectively. The actors Sybil Thorndike (1882–1976) and Lewis Casson (1875–1969) lived together in Flat 98 at one time.

Other buildings here include Daver Court, Friese Greene House, Meriden Court and Grove Cottages. Chesil Court is here at the junction with St Loo Avenue. The residential Grove Buildings and Grove House are also here.

Further down is Swan Court, built in 1931. During the Blitz, in September 1940, a bomb fell on the north-east corner of the block, causing much damage but fortunately no injuries.

Agatha Christie lived on and off for 28 years in a one-bedroom flat in Swan Court. Here she wrote *The Mousetrap* and the Poirot story *Third Girl*. She also wrote the Poirot story *How Does Your Garden Grow* featuring the Chelsea Flower Show.

No.43: This building has n old entrance headed 'Mothercraft Training Home', built in the 1930s to support mothers, nurses and midwives. (*See Flood Walk*).

Chelsea Park Gardens

Situated to the north of the King's Road and south of Fulham Road, and therefore conveniently close to the local shops, restaurants and transport facilities. This is on part of the land previously owned by Sir Thomas More in the time of Henry VIII. Built sometime between 1914 and 1923, it was previously a silk farm and is part of the Carlyle Conservation Area. It is made up of attractive Arts and Crafts houses on quiet, leafy streets.

Kim Philby

The scandal surrounding Kim Philby (1912–88), who lived in the basement flat at No.18 Carlyle Square, resonated around the world. Philby, a Cambridge graduate, started working for the Secret Intelligence Service in 1940, rising quickly through the ranks during the Second World War. He

was appointed first secretary to the British Embassy in Washington in 1949. From this time, he passed intelligence to the Soviet Union. He helped fellow double agents Donald Maclean and Guy Burgess escape to Moscow. Despite being publicly accused of espionage (for which he was exonerated in 1955), Philby continued working for the Secret Intelligence Service before finally being discovered in 1963. He fled to Moscow and lived there until his death in 1988.

Chelsea Square

Chelsea Square lies just off of Old Church Street and north of the King's Road. In June 1893, the old Brompton Fire Station opened on the north side of what was then known as Trafalgar Square, but is now known as the South Parade. It closed when the new Chelsea Fire Station was opened on the King's Road in 1965.

Cheltenham Terrace

Cheltenham Terrace borders Duke of York Square on the south-west side, and was built by John Tombs in the 1840s, who came from Upton St Leonard's, near Cheltenham (hence the name).

In 1841, the National Society for the Promotion of Education leased Whitelands House, a three-storey Georgian house, as a women's teacher training college. Opened in 1842, the house was never considered adequate for the increasing student numbers, and further college buildings were added in 1850, 1890 and 1899. The original Whitelands House was demolished in 1891. The college chapel, dedicated to St Ursula and begun in 1881, was decorated with twelve windows of female saints, designed by Burn Jones and manufactured by William Morris. The chapel contents were successfully moved when the college was relocated to Wandsworth in 1931, where Queen Mary officiated at the opening ceremony. The ten-storey apartment block that now stands there was named Whitelands House in memory of the previous building.

Chesham Street

Runs between Belgrave Square and Pont Street, and is on the eastern boundary of Chelsea. It was first laid out in 1831. It includes a number of listed buildings and expensive apartments.

Chester Cottages

A paved, mews-style cul-de-sac that is approached through an entrance under a building in Bourne Street, east of Sloane Square. The cottages are part of the Sloane Square Conservation Area.

Cheyne Gardens

Cheyne Gardens are on the west side at the southern end of Chelsea Manor Street.

No.1: The building has a blue circular plaque to Henry VIII that states: 'King Henry VIII 1491–1547'.

No.23: On this roof is a metal cockerel motif. It is not a weather vane.

Cheyne Mews

Cheyne Mews is a partly cobbled cul-de-sac approached through an entrance between 23 and 24 Cheyne Walk. It contains five properties used for residential purposes. The large blue plaque here is mentioned in the Cheyne Walk section below.

Cheyne Place

Cheyne Place has a parade of buildings on the north side of Royal Hospital Road in a sought-after area, with great views over the historic Chelsea Physic Garden and Battersea Park beyond.

Cheyne Row

Cheyne Row was named after the Cheyne family, who were Lords of Chelsea Manor, and is one of the oldest streets in Chelsea. Some houses were built soon after William Cheyne inherited the manor of Chelsea in 1698, and a row of houses on the west side, built in 1703, still survive. The street has an early road sign.

KING HENRY VIII 1491–1547
Close to this site stood the King's Manor House. Part of its boundary wall adjoins Cheyne Studio

No.2: The property features an old iron boot scraper, which has recently been painted with a small face similar to the faces that have been painted on the Chelsea Embankment seats.

No.7: The front door here is actually in Lordship Place. It has a religious semi-circular plaque above the entrance door featuring the Virgin Mary and Christ Child surrounded by four infant angels.

No.10: This house dates from the late eighteenth century, and in the early 1900s was the residence of Margaret Damer Dawson (1873–1920), musician, anti-vivisection campaigner and, together with Nina Boyle, founder of the Women's Police Service. She also helped to found a home for abandoned babies and was awarded the OBE for services to

her country during the First World War. She died of a heart attack in 1920, aged forty-seven. On the front wall of the house is a simple grey plaque to her honour titled 'Margaret Damer Dawson Lived Here'. There is a monument to Dawson in the form of a decorated bird bath on the Chelsea Embankment Gardens (*see the Miscellany*).

No.14: A pretty little house named Cheyne Cottage.

No.14a: The artist Glyn Philpot (1884–1937) had his studio here in 1906–09, and sculptor Charles James Pibworth (1878–1958) lived here *c.* 1909–43. The house is now named Gt. Cheyne Studio.

Nos.15–17: Across the road is Vere House. It is named after the De Vere family, who were Lords of the Manor of Kensington for 500 years. The house is surrounded by decorative metal railings.

No.16: High up on the south side of the house is an old stone plaque set into the wall. It reads: 'This Is Cheyne Row 1708', with the 'w' of the 'Row' being a cross between an 'n' and a 'w', and the 'n' ending with an upward curl.

I discovered that this is how the letter 'w' was written in the 1700s (and earlier) having seen examples of the same lettering in some of the Chelsea Old Church memorials.

No.18: High on the front wall is a small plaque (possibly pewter) of a crown above two hands shaking, with the number '80585' below. It is a solid lead fire insurance plaque from the Hand in Hand Fire & Life Insurance Society, one of the oldest British insurance companies, founded in 1696 at Tom's Coffee House in St Martin's Lane. It was one of the fire insurance companies founded after the Great Fire of London.

No.24: Formerly No.5, it was once the home of the great essayist and historian Thomas Carlyle (1795–1881). Artist Leigh Hunt found him and his wife Jane this house, which stands on part of the grounds of Henry VIII's Manor House. There is a white plaque inset in the front wall of the house in Carlyle's honour.

No.30: The potter and tile-maker William de Morgan (1839–1917) moved here in 1872 and built a kiln in the garden. Later, in need of larger premises, he moved to Orchard House on the junction with Upper Cheyne Row. During his ten years there, he created much of his best work, including the tiles installed in

Leighton House on the edge of Holland Park. The house is the former home and studio of Victorian artist Frederic, Lord Leighton (1830–96) and is now open to the public. He also made tiles for luxury liners. De Morgan was also a competent painter and novelist, and claimed that he made more money from writing than from pottery. He was married to the painter Evelyn Pickering, and in 1882 they moved to The Vale, situated off the King's Road. When his rambling house there was wanted for redevelopment, he moved to 127 Old Church Street.

Another famous resident who lived in Cheyne Row was the philanthropist Luke Thomas Flood (*see Flood Street*).

On the junction of Cheyne Row and Upper Cheyne Row was the site of Orchard House (mentioned above). It became available in 1892 for the Roman Catholic Church to build a church there. Designed by Edward Goldie, the foundation stone was laid on

7 June 1894. The Catholic Church of Our Most Holy Redeemer & St Thomas More was opened the following year, on 23 October 1895.

On 14 September 1940, the church was struck by a high-explosive bomb. Among the eighty people who were sheltering in the crypt and basement below it, nineteen were killed and many more injured. After the war, the church was repaired. On the altar is a relic from Sir Thomas More's vertebrae, which came from the convent in Bruges, where his adopted daughter Margaret Clements was a nun.

Cheyne Walk

Cheyne Walk takes its name from William Lord Cheyne (1657–1728). The first of these houses was built on the site of the gardens of Henry VIII's palace, and became the home of the Cheyne family until 1712, when Sir Hans Sloane bought the estate. He sold some of the land as building plots, and Cheyne Walk became one of the most desirable residential areas in London. The street has a modern 1965 road sign reading 'Kensington &

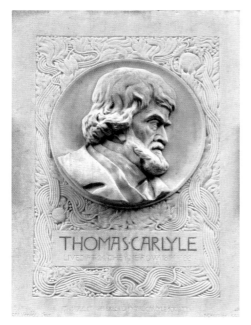

Chelsea', an earlier 'Chelsea' road sign, as well as a very early, plain black-and-white road sign headed 'Cheyne Walk S.W.', possibly Victorian. Heading west towards Battersea Bridge, the attractive Georgian houses that face the river are as follows:

No.1: This building was rebuilt in 1887–8 on the site of an earlier eighteenth-century house. The prominent actor-manager Seymour Hicks (1871–1949) lived here in 1937. The highly decorated doorway is actually in Flood Street on the west junction with Cheyne Walk. Beside it is a very old black-and-white sign on the house wall, crudely headed '1 Cheyne Walk'.

No.2: This property was built c. 1717 and re-fronted in 1879. The actor John Barrymore (1882–1942) lived here in 1924–5.

No.3: The house next door was also built c. 1717. Sir John Goss (1800–80) lived here while he was organist at the Old Church and St Paul's Cathedral. Resident in 1840–51 was Admiral William Henry Smith (1788–1865), Vice President of the Royal Society and a founder of the Royal Geographical Society. The house was acquired in 1942 by the National Trust to house the Benton Fletcher Collection of musical instruments. These are now at Fenton House in Hampstead.

Rolling Stones founder member Keith Richards bought this house in 1968 for £55,000 and moved here in May 1969. He was arrested for drugs here in June 1973 and sold the house in late 1992.

No.4: Built in 1718 and with an attractive doorway, residents have included the artists William Dyce (1846–7) and Daniel Maclise (1861–70). It was also the residence of George Eliot (born Mary Ann Evans) (1819–80), one of the leading novelists of her day, best-known for *Middlemarch* (1871–72).

After her husband's death in 1878, she married Johnny Cross, and moved here on 3 December 1880. A few days later, she attended a concert at St James' Hall, Piccadilly, where she contracted a chill, which developed into laryngitis. She died on 22 December, aged fifty.

No.5: This property was also built in 1718. John Camden Neild (1780–1852) lived here from 1814. Despite inheriting a fortune of £250,000, Neild lived a miser's life. He attempted suicide in 1828, and although his housekeeper faithfully looked after him for another twenty-five years, and more than once saved his life, she received nothing in his will. Upon his death in 1852, he left his entire fortune of £500,000 to Queen Victoria. In recent times, this house became the residence of the High Commissioner of Cyprus.

No.6: This home was built in 1718 for Joseph Danvers (*see Danvers Street*). From 1765 to 1782, the house was occupied by Dr Dominicetti's Fumigatory Steam Baths, for the treatment of anything from asthma to leprosy. His patients included the Duke of York and Sir John Fielding, but the business eventually collapsed, and in 1782 Dr Dominicetti left England hopelessly in debt. The house later became a boarding school for choristers of the Chapel Royal, including the future composer Sir Arthur Sullivan (1842–1900). Half a century later, Noel Coward failed the audition to join the company.

No.8: Replete with an arched inset wall statue of a young boy holding a large fish.

No.10: Occupied by former prime minister David Lloyd George from 1924 to 1925.

No.13: The philosopher Bertrand Russell (1872–1970) lived here briefly in 1903. The composer Ralph Vaughan Williams (1872–1958) lived here from 1905 until 1929, and there is a statue in his honour in the Embankment Gardens.

No.14: Bertrand Russell lived here in rented rooms in the autumn of 1902, when he was engaged in completing *The Principles of Mathematics*, one of his major works with his close associate

Alfred Whitehead. He moved next door to No.13, but returned here briefly in 1904.

No.16: Formally Tudor House, the property was built in 1717 and renamed Queen's House in 1882, having once been occupied by Catherine of Braganza (1638–1705). It is one of the most magnificent houses on Cheyne Walk. The ghost of a bear was regularly seen in the gardens here in the nineteenth and early twentieth centuries. The creature was thought to be one of the bears that were baited to death on the site in the sixteenth century, but it could have also been one of the animals owned by poet Dante Gabriel Rossetti (1828–82), who rented the house in 1862. He entertained and worked with all

52

of the artists and literati of the time, and kept a menagerie of animals, all of which had the run of his back garden.

They included a kangaroo, a black bear and a wombat. The wombat, which was much admired by Lewis Carroll, is thought to have been the model for the dormouse in Carroll's *Alice's Adventures in Wonderland* (1865). The wombat is still remembered in Cheyne Walk, and the landlords of No.22 continue to insert a clause in all new leases forbidding tenants to keep them on the premises. There is a blue plaque here in honour of Rossetti and novelist Algernon Charles Swinburne (1827–1909), who also lived here.

No.17: Thomas Attwood (1783–56), a pupil of Mozart and later organist at St Paul's Cathedral, lived and died at this house. Writer Naomi Mitchison (1897–1999) was married in 1916 and spent most of the next five years here.

No.18: Rebuilt in 1867, this house became the well-known coffee house Don Saltero. John Salter, who was once a servant to Sir Hans Sloane and was also addicted to collecting curiosities, owned three coffee houses in Chelsea before settling for Cheyne Walk. His first venture, probably on the corner with Lawrence Street, was in 1675, when coffee houses were all the rage in London. This famous establishment in Cheyne Walk opened about 1718. He died in 1728, but his daughter carried on the museum and coffee house until 1758. It was finally turned into a tavern in 1799, and the house became a private residence in 1867.

Nos.19–26: Built on the site of Henry VIII's Manor House in the early 1750s. No.19 has an old carved stone pillar set into the front wall.

No.21: The painter James Abbott McNeill Whistler lived here in 1890. The novelist Henry James died here in 1916, after having been awarded the Order of Merit. The writer Wyndham Lewis (1882–1957) lived here between 1935 and 1936.

No.22: This is a wonderful house, and was home at various times to Algernon Charles Swinburne, Meredith and Hall Caine, and Dante Gabriel Rossetti during his widowhood. It was the house where he painted *Beata Beatrix*, which now hangs in Tate Britain. He moved to No.22 in 1862 and remained here until his death, twenty years later.

Nos.23–24: Between No.23 and No.24 is Cheyne Mews, a part-cobbled cul-de-sac that contains five properties used for residential purposes. A large blue plaque here states as follows: 'King Henry VIII's Manor House stood here until 1753, when it was demolished after the death of its last occupant, Sir Hans Sloane'. Nos.19–26 Cheyne Walk were built on its site in 1759–65. The old manor house garden still lies beyond the end wall of Cheyne Mews and contains some mulberry trees said to have been planted by Queen Elizabeth I.

No.27: Abraham 'Bram' Stoker (1847–1912), the Dublin-born author of *Dracula*, lived here while he was working as business manager for the legendary actor Sir Henry Irving and writing the novel that would make him famous. While here, he rescued a drowning man from the Thames, but the man died soon after, and Stoker was awarded a Royal Humane Society medal for his efforts. He would later move to No.18 St Leonard's Terrace.

No.31: The site is on the corner of where Oakley Street joined the Chelsea

Dorothea Jordan

Dorothea Jordan (1762–1816), who lived at No.30 Cadogan Place, must have made quite the impression on everyone she met. She moved to London from Ireland with her mother in 1782, and followed her passion for the stage to perform at Drury Lane Theatre. Lord Byron was known to be an admirer, but it was the Duke of Clarence, the future William IV, who courted her, and together they had ten children. She also had one daughter with her theatre manager in Dublin and three more children with Sir Richard Ford. She was later abandoned by her lovers and children, and died alone in Saint Cloud, France, where she is buried.

Embankment. This scenic and historical approach to Chelsea from Albert Bridge was replaced in 1968 by a block of flats named Pier House. The lost buildings included the Pier Hotel (1844) and adjoining premises, including Henry Job's former coffee rooms, the artist-haunted Blue Cockatoo Café. Chelsea artist Walter Greaves (1846–1930) was born here. On the pavement is a statue of a boy and a dolphin.

No.37: This house is on the site of the old public house called the Magpie and Stump. It was there in Tudor times when Henry VIII, then Lord of Chelsea Manor, granted it a strip of land. In 1803, conspirators led by Colonel Despard met here to plot the murder of George III and steal the Crown Jewels. The Pye, as it was called, managed to survive the creation of the Embankment but fell victim to a fire in 1886. The building was replaced by a house of the same name eight years later, and built by the Arts and Crafts architect Charles Robert Ashbee (1863–1942). This too was lost in the

redevelopment of a dreary block of flats in 1968, but his other houses at No.38 and No. 39 still survive.

Nos.43–5: These houses were built in the early eighteenth century on the site of Shrewsbury House, which had been built in 1519 and was situated by the river between today's Cheyne Row and Oakley Street. The occupier, the 4th Earl of Shrewsbury, was Privy Councillor to Henry VIII, and his son Richard was born at Chelsea. The 6th Earl, who was the fourth (and most unhappy) husband of the famous Bess of Hardwick (1527–1608), left the house to her.

Along with four homes in London and Hardwick Hall in Derbyshire, Bess of Hardwick was the second-wealthiest woman in England after Queen Elizabeth I. Shrewsbury House was demolished in 1813, although parts remained among houses in Cheyne Walk in 1928. There are wall signs here to Shrewsbury House.

No.46: In June 1875, the Cheyne Centre began here as the Cheyne Hospital for Children, founded by a Mr and Mrs Wickham Flower. Its aim was to take children suffering from chronic disease who would otherwise be excluded from general hospitals. It soon expanded into five houses in Cheyne Walk that were rebuilt as the Chelsea Hospital for Spastic Children in 1889. Recently, the building was converted into apartments. The hospital moved some of its operations to the Chelsea and Westminster Hospital in Fulham Road, and others to West Wickham in Kent.

Nos. 46–8: These were originally three separate dwellings (built *c.* 1711) on the site of the Three Tuns public house. The original bowling green that was there is now part of Cheyne Row.

No. 48: Rolling Stones founder member Mick Jagger bought this house for £50,000 in May 1968. In May the following year, he was arrested for possession of marijuana there and fined £200. He was still living there in early 1971, before self-imposed exile to the south of France. He sold the house in the 1980s.

No. 49: The Feathers, one of the oldest inns in Chelsea, was on this site. It is referred to as early as 1664, and stood at the eastern corner of the junction of Cheyne Row and Cheyne Walk. It had extensive gardens to the rear extending almost to Glebe Place. During a coin shortage in 1666, the landlord Thomas Munday issued his own halfpenny tokens, which was the norm with traders at the time.

No. 50: The King's Head and Eight Bells public house was situated at the western corner of Cheyne Row and Cheyne Walk, and was one of the many public houses lining the riverside before the Embankment was constructed. In 1871,

it boasted that it had been in existence for over 100 years. The present building dates from 1886, and there are cellars here thought to be Tudor. During the first half of the twentieth century it was a venue for many Chelsea artists. In the postwar years, it became 'the ultimate Chelsea pub' with artists and writers such as Dylan Thomas, and the Chelsea pensioners.

In the 1960s came disaster, when the owners, Whitbread, changed it into an American-styled bar. The restyling was a failure, and in 2002 it was put up for sale, later becoming a restaurant.

No. 51: On the corner of Lawrence Street and Cheyne Walk was an inn called The Cricketers, which was one of the many drinking places patronised by the artist George Morland (1763–1804). The Thames Coffee Shop was located here in 1865, when the row contained five small shops and the pub, all facing the river. These buildings were swept away with the construction of the Embankment in 1886, and the Carlyle Mansions has occupied the site ever since. The block has panels of birds and flowers on the

façades facing the river and on the Lawrence Street side to the west. These apartments have had many famous residents living there, as follows:

No.1: Composer Richard Addinsell (1904–77).

No.10: Writer Erskine Childers (1870–1922).

No.11: Actor Gordon Harker (1885–1967).

No.12: Rolling Stones founder member Charlie Watts (1941–2021).

No.12 or 14: Historian Reginald Blunt (1908–69).

No.19: Poet T.S. Eliot (1888–1965) c. 1915.

No.21: Writer Henry James (1843–1916) from 1913.

No.24: Writer Ian Fleming (1908–64).

No.27: Writer Somerset Maugham (1874–1965) in 1904.

No.59: The artist William Holman Hunt (1827–1910) lived here between 1850 and 1853. The house was eventually demolished when the Cheyne Hospital for Children was rebuilt in 1875. The hospital was later moved, and the building was renamed Courtyard House and converted into luxury flats.

Nos.62–3: These houses were east of the Old Church, and formerly part of a terrace of five properties called Church Row or Prospect Place. They were built c. 1686 when Thomas Lawrence owned them. Dr Francis Atterbury lived at No.63, as did Nicholas Sprimont (1716–71) in 1755–6, who was the proprietor of the Chelsea Porcelain Works in Lawrence Street.

No.72: Sculptor Jacob Epstein (1880–1959) worked and lived here from 1909 to 1914.

No.74: Charles Robert Ashbee designed this house and lived there from 1898–1902. James Abbott McNeill Whistler moved here in 1902, where his late wife's sister and her mother took care of him. He continued to paint, but died there on 17 July 1903. He was buried alongside his wife in Chiswick Old Cemetery. This row of houses was destroyed in an air raid in April 1941.

Crosby Hall: This fifteenth-century hall once formed part of Crosby Place, erected c. 1466 at Bishopsgate for Sir John Crosby, grocer and wool-man, who was prominent in the affairs of the City. Fire destroyed most of the building in the seventeenth century, but the great hall survived. In 1910–11, the hall was moved from the City stone by stone, to its present site almost opposite Battersea Bridge, on the corner of the Chelsea Embankment and Danvers Street. It was partially enclosed by a new Tudor-style building, erected in 1926–7 after funding became available. This became the headquarters and hostel of the British Federation of University Women.

In 1949, writer Sydney R. Jones said: 'Crosby Hall withstood the onslaught [of the Second World War], kept its roof over its head, and so remained triumphant'. It is a Grade II listed building. Over the front entrance are the words 'Meritum Pertinacia Fortitude Et Fidelitas' ('Merit, Pertinacity, Strength and Loyalty').

No.90: On the eastern junction with Beaufort Street is More's House, with a very decorative doorway and a coloured tiled entrance.

Crosby Hall

years. He then sold the house to John Studzinski, an American investment banker, who reportedly saw ghosts in the house.

Nos.93–4: These houses were built in 1777. The novelist Elizabeth Gaskell was born at No.93. Her mother died within a week of her birth.

No.96: James Abbott McNeill Whistler moved to No.2 Lindsey Row (now 96 Cheyne Walk) in 1866 and lived here until 1878. The works he produced here included portraits of his mother and Thomas Carlyle. He was a devoted disciple of the 'Matching' school, and is said to have once dyed a rice pudding green in order that it should blend with the walls of his dining room.

No.98: The great engineers Marc Isambard Brunel and his son Isambard Kingdom lived here from 1808 until about 1825. It was in the latter year that the senior Brunel began what was to be an extended and hazardous venture – the building of the Thames Tunnel – which, after his death, his son Isambard eventually completed. Today it is part of the London underground system. There is a blue plaque here to their honour that states: 'Sir Marc Isambard Brunel 1769–1849 and Isambard Kingdom Brunel 1806–1859 Civil Engineers Lived Here'.

Rolling Stones founder member Mick Jagger bought this house in 2015 (other references state that he bought the house in 2009).

No.91: This is Belle Vue Lodge. It was built in 1771 on the western junction of the Embankment and Beaufort Street, on land that had formerly been part of the grounds of Beaufort House. The land had earlier been an orchard, which accounts for the fig trees seen in that part of Chelsea. Luke Thomas Flood (1775–1860), a benefactor of Chelsea parish, was here in 1829, and the artist Charles Conder (1868–1909) lived here in 1904. It has a beautifully decorated entrance.

No.92: This is Belle Vue House. Also built in 1771, it has largely the same history as Belle Vue Lodge (*see above*). The large garden here has a mulberry tree that was supposedly planted by Sir Thomas More. The first owner was James Hackett, the royal coach-maker, whose business in Long Acre made him the Rolls-Royce of his day. The painter William Bell Scott lived here from 1876 to 1890. The house was bought by author Ken Follett in 1984, who lived here with his family for the next seventeen

Nos.98–100: This is Lindsey House, built in 1674 on the site of an earlier house from 1630. Its most notable owner was Count Zinzendorf, who in 1751 established the Moravian Brethren here, a displaced Protestant sect that had suffered persecution in Central Europe. From here they led a simple life until the Count's death in 1770, when they were forced to leave. Their chapel and burial ground still survive. In 1775, the house was divided into separate dwellings, at which time it lost many of its exterior features. There is a large plaque here that reads as follows:

'Lindsey House built 1674 by Robert Bertie 3rd Earl of Lindsey incorporates a house which Sir Theodore Mayerne Court Physician built on the site of Sir Thomas More's Farm reconstructed in 1752 by Count Zinzendorf as the London headquarters of the Moravian Brethren sub-divided 1774 as 1–7 Lindsey Row altered in the nineteenth century and again in 1952'.

No.101: James Abbott McNeill Whistler moved to rooms in Lindsey House in Lindsey Row (now 101 Cheyne Walk) from 1863–6. The mansion was originally built by Sir Théodore de Mayerne (1573–1655), court physician to King James I and King Charles I.

No.104: This was the home of the Chelsea artist Walter Greaves. His father owned a boat business on the riverfront here. There is a blue plaque that states: 'Walter Greaves 1846–1930 Artist Lived Here 1855–1897', and another stating 'Hilaire

Belloc 1870–1953 Poet, Essayist and Historian Lived Here 1900–1905'. In 1980–81, Chris Squire, the bass player of the group Yes, lived here.

No.108: There is a blue plaque on the front wall here that reads as follows: 'John Tweed 1863–1933 Sculptor Lived Here'.

No.109: The painter Philip Wilson Steer lived here from 1898 until his death in 1942. He was a founder member of the Chelsea Arts Club. There is a blue

Thomas Hosmer Shepherd, *Lindsey House*, 1850

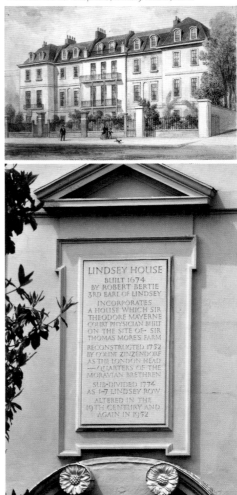

plaque here honouring him that reads: 'Philip Wilson Steer 1860–1942 Painter Lived and Died Here'. A later resident was Cecil King, who owned the *Daily Mirror*.

No.112: This was once the Santa Cruz Italian restaurant. It was replaced by the Busabong Tree restaurant in 1993, which closed in 2002. The Painted Heron took its place, but has since closed.

No.113: Here on the pavement at the junction with Munroe Terrace is where The Rolling Stones had some photos taken at their very first photo session by Philip Townsend, in May 1963.

Nos.118–19: The artist Joseph Mallord William Turner (1775–1851) had lodgings here, and was obsessive in retaining his anonymity among his neighbours, assuming the name 'Admiral Booth'. With his telescope and his sketch-pad, Turner became a familiar figure along the shore of the Thames, and much of his best work was done here. He died

here, six days before Christmas in 1851, muttering 'the sun is God'. He left much of his unsold work to the National Gallery. There is a square grey plaque here that says: 'Joseph Mallord William Turner Landscape Painter. B.1775-D.1851 Lived & Worked in this House'.

No.120: There is a blue plaque here in honour of Sylvia Pankhurst (1882–1960), the great campaigner for women's rights, who lived here.

Christchurch Street

Christchurch Street runs parallel to the south of Redburn Street and north of the Chelsea Physic Garden. It contains Christ Church, which was built in 1839 as a church for the working-class people in the area. The street has an old 'Chelsea' road sign.

No.1: Cheyne Place, which has an unusual stairway entrance.

No.4: Durham Cottage, which was purchased by Laurence Olivier in June 1937 for himself and Vivien Leigh, and was their London base until 1956.

Christchurch Terrace is beside Christchurch Street. At No.6 is The Surprise public house, built in 1903, with a hanging sign of a ship in full sail.

Clabon Mews

Clabon Mews consists of two part-cobbled through roads with a cul-de-sac section off Cadogan Square. The mews was originally stable and coach houses for the main houses in the square, and is fairly large, containing seventy-five properties used for residential and commercial purposes. In 2012, the mews was used as a filming location for the James Bond film *Skyfall*.

Cliveden Place

This is a wide residential street north-east of Sloane Square. Nos.19–25 are four-storey terraces built in the early nineteenth century and are Grade II listed. Labour MPs Aneurin 'Nye' Bevan (1897–1960) and Jennie Lee (1904–88) lived at No.23 between 1944 and 1954. A blue plaque has been hung on the wall of the house. Aneurin 'Nye' Bevan was one of the key architects of the National Health Service, while Jennie Lee played a leading role in the development of the Open University.

Clover Mews

Clover Mews is a cobbled lane off Dilke Street and Swan Walk, just east of the Chelsea Physic Garden. It is a largely untouched mews, previously used as stabling with accommodation above for staff and now a beautiful residential area. The mews is part of the Royal Hospital Conservation Area.

Coulson Street

Coulson Street was named after Thomas Coulson, a butcher from Clerkenwell,

who was heir to James Colvill, the nursery ground owner, in the first half of the nineteenth century. The terraced houses here were built in the mid-nineteenth century. The street has an old 'Chelsea' road sign.

Cremorne Road

Located just north of Lots Road, it was named after the Cremorne Gardens.

Nos.23/25: The properties here (and others on each side) have unusually decorated entrances.

No.37a & 39a: Cremorne Mansions has white decorated doorways, above which are highly decorated coloured stained-glass windows with the house names.

No.42: The very cute Toll House with a clock above.

The Cornwall Mansions are also here.

Culford Gardens

Culford Gardens lies just behind the Peter Jones department store to the north, and were named after Culford Hall, near Bury St Edmunds, which was a Cadogan family property. The Culford Mansions are at Nos.11–20.

Battersea Bridge

CHELSEA STREETS *D TO F*

In which you will meet Alexander Fleming, who discovered penicillin, poet John Donne, Sir Clive Sinclair, and two remarkable civilian Second World War heroes. You'll see the flat where The Rolling Stones was founded and visit the studio where the sleeve for Sgt. Pepper's Lonely Hearts Club Band *was designed. You'll also meet the notorious Nazi propagandist William James Joyce, who was given the moniker 'Lord Haw-Haw'.*

Danube Street

Danube Street is south of Cale Street and was formerly called Little Blenheim Street. It was named after Marlborough's victory at the Battle of Blenheim in August 1704, a significant battle of the War of the Spanish Succession. The village of Blenheim is on the Danube, hence the street name. There are a few residential properties here, but the street is mainly a go-between.

Danvers Street

🄷 🄻

Danvers Street runs between Paultons Square and the Chelsea Embankment. It was developed on the site of Danvers House and its grounds. Buildings were built in the early years of the eighteenth century. The eastern side of Crosby Hall is here, at the western junction with Cheyne Walk. Jonathan Swift (1667–1745) lived in a house on the west side in 1711.

No.18a: Atterbury House.

No.18b: Stallwood House.

No.20: Fleming House, named after the most famous resident of this street, Alexander Fleming (1881–1955), the discoverer of penicillin, who lived here from 1929 until his death. A blue plaque to his honour is as follows:

'Greater London Council Sir Alexander Fleming, 1881–1955 Discoverer of Penicillin, Lived Here'.

Rolling Stone Bill Wyman bought the penthouse flat at Fleming House and lived there with his family from February 1991 to July 1995.

Beside 20 Danvers Street is Lavender Close, a private cul-de-sac for the Fleming House residents' parking.

Denyer Street

Denyer Street is north-east of Draycott Avenue, close to Fulham Road, and was named after Elizabeth Denyer. In her will in 1821, she left an annual fund to be distributed among eight poor spinsters in Chelsea.

No.47: The Shuckburgh Arms public house, a Grade II listed building, was here. Built in the mid-nineteenth century, it was briefly called Finnigans Wake. It closed in 2006.

Dilke Street

Dilke Street is close to the Chelsea Embankment and east of the Chelsea Physic Garden. It was named in 1875 after Sir Charles Dilke, the MP for Chelsea (1868–86), who was born and lived for many years in Sloane Street. His political career terminated when he was cited as a co-respondent in a sensational divorce case (*see Sloane Street*).

No.7: In 1838, a sketching society was formed, an activity which grew in importance with the increase of illustrated magazines, newspapers and books. The group became the Langham Sketching Club (meeting at Langham Place in the West End), and in 1898 it was officially formed as The London Sketch Club. In 1957, the club moved here. The doorway also features a plaque titled 'The London Sketch Club' and a smaller plaque below titled 'The English Gardening School'.

Donne Place

Donne Place was named after poet John Donne (1573–1631), who stayed for a period at Danvers House. It is residential, and the street displays a variety of pleasant houses.

No.32: A blue plaque is on the wall in honour of Sir Clive Sinclair, entrepreneur and inventor. He is best known for launching mass-market computers.

Dovehouse Green

Dovehouse Green is the small square opposite the Chelsea Old Town Hall on the north side of the King's Road, which leads to Chelsea Farmers Market. Early maps show that in 1827 it was referred to as a 'Burial Ground' with a workhouse at the rear. Poverty existed in Chelsea, and this Victorian workhouse, erected in 1843, played its part in the lives of these poor people during those times. In 1860, it was dubbed a 'Graveyard', but by 1878 its name had been changed to 'Chelsea Workhouse'. It changed again in 1894 to 'Recreation Ground' and had a mortuary at the rear. This was still the case when the Second World War commenced.

Several tombs and gravestones surround the green, as well as a central obelisk that features a faded heraldic shield, above which is very faded and undecipherable lettering due to weather wear.

There are plaques on the east wall here.

There is a small brass plaque to two civilian war heroes that states: 'In memory of Anthony Smith, G.C. (George Cross) who on February 23rd, 1944 carried out an heroic act of rescue following a bombing raid near to this place [Sydney Street] and was awarded the George Cross and the Freedom of the Borough of Chelsea, and Albert Littlejohn, B.E.M. (British Empire Medal) who was honoured for his role in the same rescue.'

Another small plaque states: 'In remembrance of 457 civilians killed in Chelsea by enemy action 1939–1945'.

There are two large blue plaques beside these. The top plaque states: 'To celebrate the silver jubilee of Elizabeth II 1952–1977 and the Golden Jubilee of the Chelsea Society 1927–1977 the old burial ground given by Sir Hans Sloane in 1733 was laid out anew by the Chelsea Society in collaboration with the Royal Borough of Kensington and Chelsea and named Dovehouse Green'.

The plaque below that is from later, and states: 'Dovehouse Green was refurbished by The Royal Borough of Kensington and Chelsea to celebrate the Golden Jubilee of HM Queen Elizabeth II 1952–2002 and was re-opened in June 2003 by The Worshipful The Mayor Councillor Christopher Buckmaster.'

The circular pale-blue wall plaque states:

'The Royal Borough Of Kensington & Chelsea Environment Award 1979'.

Dovehouse Street

Dovehouse Street runs from the King's Road north to the Royal Marsden Hospital, and was previously named Arthur Street. In Dovehouse Close, a dovecote is shown on Hamilton's 1664 map of Chelsea.

Here is the Chelsea Hospital for Women, which was originally at 78 King's Road in 1831. It was moved here in 1914, and the foundation stone reads: 'This stone was laid on June 9th AD. MCMXIV [1914] by the right honourable George Henry 5th Earl Cadogan K.G. PC who presented this site to the Hospital'.

Over the entrance door, the inscription is as follows: 'This Hospital Was Opened By H.M. Queen Mary July 11th 1916'. The hospital was eventually incorporated into Queen Charlotte's Hospital at Stamford Brook.

Nos.53–5: This house has an egg-and-dart decorated doorway.

No.111: The Jonathan Yeo art studio.

No.127: Dove House.

No.145: The Le Colombier restaurant, established in 1998.

No.153: The Crown public house.

The British actor Anthony Hopkins lived in this street before his move to America.

Draycott Avenue 🅛

Draycott Avenue runs parallel with Sloane Avenue, between the King's Road and Fulham Road. It was initially named Marlborough Road, and the Marlborough Primary School, built in 1878, is here. The street was renamed Draycott Avenue in 1906 after Anna Maria Draycott, who married Sir Francis Shuckburgh. The street has an early 'Chelsea' road sign.

Here is Avenue Court, with a blue plaque that states: 'English Heritage Sir Archibald McIndoe 1900–1960 Reconstructive Surgeon lived here in flat 14'.

There is an old timbered house between Bray Place and Coulson Street, with leaded light windows.

The Guinness Trust Buildings, built in 1892, are on this street. Aimed at supporting the 'labouring poor', they also provided boiling water and club rooms with newspapers, books and games.

Peter Jones (1843–1905) first set up in business here, but disaster struck during works to develop two shops into one. Whilst knocking through, the walls collapsed and an apprentice was killed. Jones' wife was temporarily buried, although she survived. The Peter Jones department store is still on the King's Road and is now owned by John Lewis.

Another Draycott Avenue tradesman of this period was Thomas Crapper (1836–1910), the sanitary engineer whose

name has become synonymous with his business. Several of the early water closets he manufactured were named after streets in this vicinity.

The writer Marguerite Radclyffe Hall (1880–1943), who always called herself 'John', was able to carve out a life of her own with the aid of a substantial inheritance. She lived at 22 Cadogan Court on the street from 1916 to 1920. She was best known for the classic lesbian book *The Well of Loneliness*.

No.96: The Queen's Arms public house was here in 1851. It was rebuilt in 1904

Draycott Place

Draycott Place is north of the King's Road off Sloane Avenue, and is a street of beautiful buildings in red brickwork with highly decorated entrances, with most being built between 1889–91. There are many terraced buildings in the 'Pont Street Dutch' style here, with façades reminiscent of the distinctive gables and varied fenestration of Dutch seventeenth-century buildings. Draycott House is here. The street has an early road sign and a pre-1917, plain black-and-white road sign headed 'Draycott Place SW.'

No.10: Featuring decoration above the door of plants and a baby's face.

No.12: Featuring decoration above the door of plants and a smiling face.

No.20: This property has decoration above the door of a devil with what looks like mermaids on each side. To the side is a bricked plaque of a horse with wings.

No.22: Above the door is decoration of winged horses on either side.

No.27: This house has a white entrance in an almost Chinese style.

Nos.29–31: These properties have a stunning decorated entrance and a curved balcony.

Nos.37–9: A stunningly decorated double-entrance and squared balcony.

Nos.41–3: The buildings have a redbrick entrance in an almost Chinese style.

No.42: The Draycott apartments.

No.52: It has a decorated entrance in stone that dates from 1907.

No.59: The building has a heraldic plaque in red brickwork.

Draycott Terrace

Draycott Terrace is a residential street between Draycott Place and Cadogan Street. It is home to St Mary's Rectory, a late-nineteenth century building originally home to the priest for St Mary's on Cadogan Street.

Dudmaston Mews

Dudmaston Mews is behind the Royal Marsden Hospital and was originally the stable and coach houses for the salubrious houses on the surrounding streets. In the Second World War, a high-explosive bomb fell onto Chelsea Square, south of the Mews, next to Bury Walk and directly on to the mews itself.

Duke of York Square 🅼

Duke of York Square is off the King's Road, west of Sloane Square, and is dominated by a statue of Sir Hans Sloane (1660–1753). The building of the square, located opposite Peter Jones, was started in the reign of King George III (1760–1820). Between 1801 and 1803, the government bought the site, along with the manor house sited there, which had previously been the seat of the Cadogan family. They housed the Royal Military Asylum for the Children of Soldiers of the Regular Army on it. It was designed to accommodate 1,000 orphans – 300 girls in the south wing and 700 boys in the north wing. The girls' accommodation was moved to Southampton in 1823, and the boys took over the whole building until they left in 1909. After this date, the Territorial Army turned it into their barracks.

The Saatchi Gallery, Duke of York Square

In 1985, a refurbishment and stone-cleaning programme was carried out, with splendid results bringing out the original colour of the brick and stonework. On the top of the stone archway are carvings of war relics.

The building was fully vacated in 2003 and is now the home of the famous Saatchi Gallery, which shows international contemporary art.

In April 2016, *Exhibitionism*, the first international exhibition on The Rolling Stones, opened, taking over the entire two floors of the gallery. Three giant Stones tongues dominated the square.

No.30: Frederick Court. There are modern statues by Allister Bowtell of a man leap-frogging a road post and a seated lady watching him.

Durham Place

Durham Place is off Smith Street on the western side, and it is said to have been where Queen Elizabeth I supped with the Earl of Leicester in May 1566. A mansion

stood there named Ship House in 1694; it was later named Durham House and demolished around 1920. The street was built in 1790 by Mr Richardson.

No.2: There is a stone carving of a man's face over the entrance here.

No.3: Ormonde House.

No.4: The modern Durham House is here.

Nos.5–6: Conway House.

No.10: The Chelsea High School was here between 1891 and 1894.

Edith Grove

Edith Grove is named after Edith Gunter, who was the daughter of the developer of what had previously been the market gardens. Her father, James Gunter (1731–1819), a successful Mayfair confectioner, had started purchasing land in 1801 (*see Gunter Grove*). The street's southern end was built in the 1870s on the site of Ashburnham Hall and its market gardens. The east side of Edith Grove and the streets opposite were poorer-quality housing that was ultimately replaced between 1969 and 1977.

The street has an old 'Chelsea' road sign and another very old one, undoubtedly Victorian, with painted white lettering on a black background, which is very damaged and faded.

Chelsea Community Baptist Church here has a varied past. In 1854, it was the West Brompton Congregational Church and was a thriving centre for worship, but in 1944, during the Second World War, the original building was destroyed. The parishioners met for the next sixteen years along with the Salvation Army in the Old Chelsea Police Station. From 1960 to 1991, the church underwent numerous changes and reorganised itself with the Chelsea Baptist Church as the Edith Grove Christian Centre. After several years, the church again reorganised itself as the Chelsea Community Church.

Nos.6–8: At the centre of the upper wall is a carving of a lion holding a shield featuring a lion inset below a crown. It is precisely like the statuette at No.452 King's Road.

No.10: High up on this house, between the windows, is a statue of a reclining greyhound.

No.11: It is an interesting house, with leaded light windows.

No.12: Mulberry Lodge.

No.14: Mulberry Place.

No.15: Here are the Editha Mansions, dated 1897. There is a highly decorated doorway and a decorated coloured-tile entrance. On either side of the entrance are a series of wall plaques with the face of a wolf, a sleeping face, and a plaque with acorns.

Nos.17–21: Destroyed in an air raid in the Second World War.

Nos.17–19: This is now Little Chelsea House, a modern apartment block.

No.19: This was the home of the American writer and socialite Muriel Draper (1886–1952) and her husband, the tenor Paul Draper (1886–1925). They were at the centre of London's musical, literary and artistic life, and they hosted a series of musical gatherings in the studio behind their house.

No.25a: This is a very narrow, peculiar-shaped house.

No.36: The modern Chelsea Community Baptist Church.

No.102: The first-floor flat was rented by Rolling Stones founder Brian Jones, who was joined there by Mick Jagger and Keith Richards from August 1962 to September 1963.

Edith Terrace

Edith Terrace is a pleasant tree-lined residential road that joins Edith Grove and Gunter Grove, north of the King's Road.

No.11: Esher House, a residential building.

No.13: On the front is a blue plaque that reads: 'Erected By The Williams Scott Foundation. William Scott CBE RA 1913–1989 Artist Lived and worked here 1962–1986.'

Egerton Crescent

Egerton Crescent runs off Egerton Gardens and was developed in the mid-1800s along with Egerton Terrace by James Bonnin, prior to the latter being built by Alexander Thorn.

No.27: Lucas Malet, the pseudonym of the novelist Mary St Leger Kingsley (1852–1931), lived here in 1902.

No.31: John Lehmann (1907–87), the English poet and man of letters, lived here from 1945.

No.40: Major-General William Frederick Cavaye (1845–1926), British military officer and politician, lived here.

Other celebrities who have lived in this street include British journalist and broadcaster David Frost (1939–2013), the English theatre and film director Tony Richardson (1928–1991), and the British theatrical impresario and film producer Michael White (1936–2016), who bought the house from Richardson. Australian theatre and film director Jim Sharman (born 1945) also lived on this street.

Egerton Gardens

Egerton Gardens runs roughly south-west to the north-east of Brompton Road. Much of it was built by Alexander Thorn, who also built Cremone Wharf. This new road was linked to what was then Brompton Crescent. The area was

gerton Crescent

renamed after Lord Francis Egerton, 3rd Duke of Bridgewater and son of the first Earl of Ellesmere.

No.17: Major-General Charles Edmund Webber (1838–1904) lived here and was the street's first occupant in 1887.

Nos.22–8: The Franklin Hotel was created by combining four houses.

No.31: This building was designed by Thomas Henry Smith and later changed to flats. Judge Sir Ronald Waterhouse (1926–2011) lived in one of the flats between 1957–8.

No.38: William Romilly, 2nd Baron Romilly (1835–91), died in a fire here in 1891 along with two of his servants.

No.53: Florence Tyzack Parbury (1881–1960), the socialite, author, musician, painter and traveller, lived here.

Another notable building on this road is Mortimer House.

Egerton Place

Egerton Place is an expensive residential street in a prestigious location.

Egerton Terrace

Egerton Terrace is a quiet, tree-lined residential street in the heart of fashionable Knightsbridge.

Nos.17–19: The Egerton House Hotel, originally built in 1843.

Ellis Street

Ellis Street is just off Sloane Street and full of trendy little boutiques.

Elm Park Gardens

Elm Park Gardens is on the junction of The Vale and Fulham Road, and was once the massive Chelsea Park, with a grand mansion surrounded by cedars, mulberry trees and elms (hence the name Elm Park Gardens). The existing development was laid out between 1878 and 1885.

The street has a very early, plain black-and-white road sign headed 'Elm Park Gardens, SW.'

No.32: There is a blue plaque to 'Sir Stafford Cripps 1889–1952 Statesman born here'.

No.34: Featuring a blue plaque that reads: 'Joyce Grenfell (1910–1979) Entertainer and Writer lived here in Flat No.8 from 1957 to her death in 1979'.

Elm Park Lane

This is a cute mews cul-de-sac entered through an arched brick entrance and is residential.

Elm Park Road

Elm Park Road is north of the King's Road and crosses The Vale. The street is residential and has an old 'Chelsea' road sign and an even earlier, pre-1917, plain black-and-white road sign headed 'Elm Park Road SW.'

Elystan Place

Elystan Place is situated between Cale Street and Sloane Avenue, and is a sought-after place to live.

Nos.3–5: Ranelagh House.

No.87: The Elystan Mansions, with a decorated entrance.

Thackeray Court is here and is a residential building.

Elystan Street

Elystan Street runs between Fulham Road and Cale Street at the junction with Whitehead's Grove. It was formally called College Street, and Mr Whitehead developed much of the area. Formerly part of Chelsea Common, the land was let out for building purposes as early as 1790. The houses in this street, dating from the 1830s and 1840s, were ruthlessly demolished after 1929, when fourteen acres of housing were sold off to developers. The Cadogan family can trace their ancestry back to a Welshman named Cadwgan ap Elystan, hence Elystan Street. The street was renamed in 1913 and has two early road signs from around this date.

Byron Court is here, and the street has many popular restaurants.

No.12: Crown Lodge.

No.43: The site of the Marlborough Arms public house, built in 1901. There are two redbrick wall plaques, one decorated with leaves stating 'The Marlborough Arms', while the second features a vase with a flower dated '1901'. The pub closed in 2003.

No.53: This house has a highly decorated and attractive entrance.

Embankment Gardens

Embankment Gardens is a roughly crescent-shaped road off the Chelsea Embankment and just east of Tite Street.

Nos.11–12: Chelwood House.

Nos.22–3: Riverpark Court. The central arched entrance on this residential building is highly decorated with four child angels and an additional small angel face on either side. West of the entrance was a smaller entrance which has been subsequently replaced with a window.

Chelsea Court is here, with an imposing entrance on the Chelsea Embankment.

Fernshaw Road

Fernshaw Road is a situated between Gunter Grove and Edith Grove. It is

The London Sketch Club, formerly the Langham Sketching Club, was formed in 1838 out of the Artists' Society. Sketching had grown in importance with the increase of illustrated magazines, newspapers and books. In 1957, the club moved to No.7 Dilke Street. This gentleman's club became a centre for artists, illustrators and writers. Members would meet every Friday night for dinner, and spend two hours drawing on a subject and discussing the work (before embarking on an evening of cheese and beer). Members have included Phil May, H.M. Bateman, John Hassall, Christopher Nevinson, Heath Robinson,

Peter Blake, the journalist Reggie Bosanquet, Robert Baden-Powell and Arthur Conan Doyle.

residential, and the Fernshaw Mansions are here. It was once home to the literary agent of Joseph Anton, the alias that Salman Rushdie chose whilst in hiding after being 'sentenced to death' after the publication of *The Satanic Verses* (the names is a combination of Conrad and Chkhov). In April 2013, several homes were evacuated after the roofs of three terraced houses collapsed.

First Street

First Street is residential and runs south from Walton Street to Mossop Street.

Flood Street Ⓜ

Flood Street was once Robinsons Lane, perhaps named after Sir Ernest Robinson, the developer of Ranelagh Gardens. It has also been known as Queen Street and initially as Pound Lane. It may have been down this road that Samuel Pepys rode to the Swan Inn on the river, famed for its association with the Doggett's Coat and Badge race rowed by the Thames watermen.

It was later named after Luke Thomas Flood, who had lived in Cheyne Row.

He had been treasurer of the Chelsea charity schools and a public benefactor, and left £3,000 to the parish in 1860 for charitable uses. He helped many poorer children, providing bread, clothing and apprenticeship payments, which helped increase academic achievement. A service is still held at St Luke's & Christ Church dedicated to his memory. The street has two pre-1917 plain black-and-white road signs, both of which are headed 'Flood Street. SW'.

The Trafalgar pub was here and was originally called Lord Nelson, but was demolished in 2019.

Here are the Chelsea Manor Studios and Swan Court, stretching between here and Chelsea Manor Street.

No.30: The Violet Melchett Clinic is concerned with child health. The dedication over the entrance says: 'The Violet Melchett Infant Welfare Centre Chelsea Health Society'.

The Hall of Remembrance here is used for community activities, including a night shelter in cold weather and a nursery.

On the afternoon of 18 April 1964, The Beatles rehearsed for a show here, together with Long John Baldry, Millie Small, P.J. Proby and Cilla Black

No.72: The Rossetti Studios are here and are reached through an archway. Inside is a wall plaque that states: 'Rossetti Studios Erected By Edward Holland 1894'.

No.74: Rossetti House, a residential building.

No.76: St Loo Cottage is here, set back and reached through an entrance.

The last building on Flood Street's western junction with Cheyne Walk is the highly decorated doorway named No.1 Cheyne Walk.

Moving up the east side of the street from Cheyne Walk to Robinson Street are the Cheyne Court residential buildings.

No.87: The Coopers Arms public house. The original Coopers Arms, licensed in 1831 as a beer house, was demolished in 1874 and rebuilt forty feet south of its original position to allow for the extension of Redesdale Street into Queen Street (then called Flood Street). There is a hanging sign of a working cooper (a person who makes beer barrels), with an oval plaque of a sheep attached above headed 'The Ram Brewery Wandsworth' and an iron support lettered 'Est. 1831'.

No.77: William James Joyce, the Nazi propagandist known as 'Lord Haw-Haw', lived here from 1928 to 1930 with his first wife Hazel and their daughter.

No.33: Writer Quentin Crewe lived here in 1960.

No.19: Former prime minister Margaret Thatcher and her husband lived here in 1991.

No.15a: Here is an old building with a gabled roof.

On 30 March 1967, at Michael Coopers Photographic Studio, 4 Chelsea Manor Studios, 1–11 Flood Street, the sleeve of *Sgt. Pepper's Lonely Hearts Club Band* was assembled.

There are two old buildings at the King's Road end on the east side: one with beautiful stained-glass windows and a pointed roof, while the other has three gables and a flat roof.

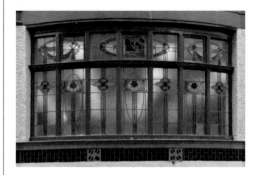

Flood Walk

Flood Walk is west of Flood Street, crosses Chelsea Manor Street, and has an early road sign. No. 30 is the entrance to the former Violet Melchett Infant Welfare Centre. Built 1930–31 it was a new development in the field of child welfare at the time of its construction, being the first to incorporate a Mothercraft Training Home affiliated with the Mothercraft Training Society and a day nursery (original entrance on Flood Street). The Chelsea Sports Centre is also here, and on the corner of this street and the King's Road is the Kensington and Chelsea Registration Office.

Franklin's Row

Franklin's Row is residential and runs south-west from Duke of York Square to Royal Hospital Road. It was named after Thomas Franklin, a farmer turned builder who built the first four properties and a public house here in 1699. He also created the roadway around three sides of Burton's Court. The residents of this late-Victorian apartment block have the pleasure of overlooking a pleasant,

fenced green, purchased in 1687 to provide an extension to Royal Avenue but which is now used for sporting activities.

The Royal Hospital Tavern was here in 1900.

A white standing post here reads 'Kensington Trust 1823'.

Fulham Road (south side)

Fulham Road (south side) is a major street that runs the length of Chelsea's northern boundary, but only the south side of Fulham Road belongs to Chelsea. It contains rows of commercial establishments throughout and also has residential properties. From east to west is as follows:

No.81: The Michelin House was constructed as the first permanent UK headquarters and tyre depot for the Michelin Tyre Company Ltd. The building opened for business on 20 January 1911. The building has three large stained-glass windows based on Michelin advertisements of the time, all featuring 'Bibendum' (otherwise known as the Michelin Man). Around the front are several decorative tiles showing famous racing cars of the time that used Michelin tyres. More tiles can be found inside the front of the building. People walking into the reception area of the building are still greeted by a mosaic on the floor showing Bibendum holding aloft a glass of nuts, bolts and other hazards, proclaiming 'Nunc Est Bibendum' (Latin for 'Now is the time to drink'). The reception area also features more decorative tiles around its walls.

Michelin moved out of the building in 1985 when it was purchased by the publisher Paul Hamlyn and Sir Terence Conran. Together, they embarked on

William James Joyce

William James Joyce, the Nazi propagandist, lived at No.77 Flood Street from 1928 to 1930 with his first wife Hazel and their daughter (he also lived at No.44 Jubilee Place). He joined the conservative group the Junior Imperial League, but moved further right, later joining Oswald Moseley's British Union of Fascists. He gave his last pro-fascist speech in Sloane Square in August 1939. The next night, he fled to Germany and began his infamous radio propaganda broadcasts throughout the Second World War. Jonah Barrington of the *Daily Express* coined his nickname, 'Lord Haw-Haw'. At the end of the war, he was captured in Germany and sentenced to high treason. He was hanged in Wandsworth Prison on 3 January 1946, becoming the last person in Britain to be sentenced to death for treason.

a major redevelopment that included restoring some original features. The development featured Hamlyn's Octopus Publishing offices, Conran's Bibendum Oyster Bar restaurant, and a Conran shop. All three businesses opened in August 1987.

No.131: This is the Thurloe Court apartment building, with two entrances on Fulham Road.

No.169: This is the very popular Theo Fennell jewellery shop.

No.203: The Royal Marsden Hospital, which stands at the junction of Fulham Road and Dovehouse Street, was instituted in 1851 by William Marsden (1796–1867). His wife's death from cancer may have caused Marsden's interest in treating the disease. He believed that a specialist hospital for cancer treatment was needed, but met opposition from the *British Medical Journal* and Queen Victoria, who saw no need for hospitals devoted to a single illness.

Marsden's hospital was the first in the world dedicated solely to treating cancer, and was built here in 1862. That building is now the centre block of the present enlarged hospital. Heiress Angela Burdett-Coutts, a strong supporter of the enterprise, laid the foundation stone in 1859. The two turreted wings were added in 1883. There is a plaque inset high on the Fulham Road wall which says: 'In Memoriam Cordeliae Read Obiit 1872' ('Obiit' meaning 'she died'). However, I haven't managed to discover who this lady was.

The hospital's name is relatively recent, having been used only since 1954. It was called the Cancer Hospital for much of its life and became the Royal Cancer Hospital in 1936 when Edward VIII was patron. The building is now called the Royal Cancer Hospital (Free) Institute of Cancer Research.

Nos.243–5: This was the site of the Queen's Elm pub.

Nos.251–3: Green & Stone of Chelsea, a famous supplier of art materials that traded in the King's Road for ninety years before being relocated here on 29 September 2018.

No.333: Here is The Goat, an Italian restaurant and cocktail bar. It was originally a pub called The Goat, which in 1725 became The Goat in Boots. It reverted to its original name in 2013.

No.369: The Chelsea & Westminster Hospital. The first hospital on this site was conceived in 1876 and officially opened as the St George's Union Infirmary in February 1878. It was renamed St Stephen's Hospital in 1925. It joined the National Health Service in 1948 and continued until 1989, when it was closed. The new hospital was rebuilt on the site and officially opened by Her Majesty The Queen in 1993.

Fulham Road, looking west, June 1955

Duke of York Square

CHELSEA STREETS *G* TO *M*

In which you will meet A.A. Milne (and his son Christopher Robin, who was born in Chelsea), Dylan Thomas (who called living in London 'capital punishment'), Gracie Fields, Mark Knopfler of Dire Straits, Gianluca Vialli and Laurence Olivier. You'll also learn about a house built on a medieval plague pit, visit the scene of a grisly murder, and see where Dylan Thomas, J.M.W. Turner, Agatha Christie, John Singer Sargent, James Abbott McNeill Whistler and Bob Marley used to drink (although sadly not all together).

Gertrude Street

Gertrude Street is a broad, attractive residential street north of the King's Road between Edith Grove and Limerston Street.

No.15: Central London Community Healthcare NHS Trust. St Mary Abbots Rehabilitation and Training (SMART) was registered as a charity here in 1985.

Glebe Place

Glebe Place was built on the former

kitchen gardens on glebe lands (i.e. owned by the parish) of the Chelsea Rectory, hence the name. Much of the street was laid out around 1870. It comprises two parts: a spacious road of Victorian houses and artists' studios, while its shorter bottom section contains a few picturesque houses that are reminders of a rural past. The street has an early 'Chelsea' road sign.

No.4: One of many of the houses that have decorated doorways.

No.35: The fine redbrick West House, with an old boot scraper. It was built in 1868–9 by the architect Philip Webb for the artist George Price Boyce.

Nos.43a–45: The Scottish architect and artist Charles Rennie Mackintosh (1868–1928) and his wife had these adjoining studios from August 1915 to 1923.

No.44: The front of this building features a white circular plaque of a lady.

No.45: John Galsworthy (1867–1933), novelist and playwright best remembered for *The Forsyte Saga*, lived at Cedar Studios here. It was later the home of the author John Osborne, who was given the sobriquet 'angry young man' for his play *Look Back in Anger* (1956). Today, the building houses the Cedar Studios, which are populated by artists. The No.5 studio is the Glebe Garden Gallery.

No.47: A metal seat, highly decorated with fern leaves, is outside the property.

No.49: Scottish architect Charles Rennie Mackintosh built this studio for the painter Harold Squire. It was home to Augustus John (1878–1961) from 1935 to 1940.

No.50: This sizeable art deco-style house has beautiful decoration, including four statues of ladies on the topmost roof. It was built between 1985 and 1987 for the advertiser Frank Lowe. Ed Glinert described it as a folly in *The London Compendium*. Following a two-year reconstruction project, this unique residence was redesigned to serve as the perfect canvas for displaying art. The double-height living space features professional gallery lighting and specially commissioned pieces by Georgian artist Tamara Kvesitadze. A newly constructed basement includes a 40-foot-long corridor that leads into a spacious dining room with a large aquarium inset into one of the walls.

Doubling as a family home and an artistic residence, it has expansive outdoor spaces, including a spectacular timber-decked terrace that spans the entire roof. The entrance column has the house number, and a stone statue of a young girl is on top.

No.51: This is the Chelsea Open Air Nursery School, built in 1928, which has a cute, coloured plaque.

No.60: Glebe Studios, owned until recently by art collector Ivor Braka.

No.66: Another redbrick building, with two wall decorations: one of a circular flowered plaque with a capital 'W', and below it, an upright plaque with a semi-circular vase of flowers.

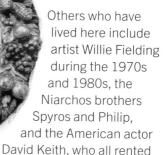

Nos.68–9: This was the Joseph Turner Studio, and there is a blue plaque in his honour that says: 'The Studios of the Artist Joseph Turner 1811–1829'. Two other blue plaques state: 'Sir Alfred Munning President Of The Royal Academy Lived Here 1920–1922' and 'William McMillan Sculptor Lived Here 1921–1966'.

No.70: The door to this property is beautifully decorated and studded. The wall decorations include a leaf and white floral plaques, and a circular religious plaque of Mary and Jesus surrounded by six angels.

No.73: Formerly The Studio. Several artists who have had studios in the street include Augustus John and Winifred Nicholson.

Others who have lived here include artist Willie Fielding during the 1970s and 1980s, the Niarchos brothers Spyros and Philip, and the American actor David Keith, who all rented houses here.

Glynde Mews

Glynde Mews is off Walton Street in the Royal Borough of Kensington and Chelsea, and is an excellent example of a redeveloped mews. It consists of several modern properties lining a cul-de-sac.

Godfrey Street

Godfrey Street is a residential street immediately north of the King's Road, opposite Radnor Walk. It was possibly named after Walter Godfrey, a Chelsea landowner, or corn chandler John Godfrey, who held land by the King's Road in the 1830s. Cottages were built on this street to house labourers and their families in cramped accommodation.

Nos.20 & 22: Both houses have charming white circular wall plaques of women dancers.

No.40: The plaque here is titled '1931'.

No.53: The Chelsea Toys Store.

Grove Cottages

Grove Cottages is a small residential street off Eaton Terrace, just west of Chelsea Manor

Street. It was developed in the 1900s originally as working-class dwellings and known as Grove Buildings. The land was given freely by Lord Cadogan on condition that the tenants had incomes of less than 25s a week (around £1.20 today). A number of flats were associated, meaning they had shared toilets and were without bathrooms, with the municipal baths only 200 yards away.

Gunter Grove

Gunter Grove is a large, tree-lined residential street west of Chelsea between the King's Road and Fulham Road. It is named after the Gunter family, who developed the former nursery fields between Brompton Cemetery and Stamford Bridge, the home of Chelsea Football Club, during the early nineteenth century. This one-way thoroughfare has a heavy traffic load from the Thames Embankment heading for Heathrow Airport, Oxford and the West Country.

No.1: Here is a blue English Heritage plaque that reads: 'Arthur Ransome (1884–1967) Author of *Swallows and Amazons* lived here 1904–1905'. He rented the ground-floor flat of the building, and during his time there, he published a collection of essays called *The Souls of the Streets*. He also briefly shared the lodgings with poet Edward Thomas.

Guthrie Street

Guthrie Street is a cul-de-sac that runs north of Cale Street and is named after George James Guthrie (1785–1856), an army surgeon who popularised new treatments for amputations and gunshot wounds during the Napoleonic Wars. Dame Unity House, a small patient accommodation for the Royal Marsden Hospital, is here at No.2a.

Halsey Street

Halsey Street is north of Cadogan Street and is residential. The two terraces were developed on open land in the 1840s.

No.14: This house has Chelsea's oldest and largest fig tree in its rear garden. It is more than 9m high, with a 7.6m diameter canopy of fruit-bearing branches that intricately twist across the back walls. It dates back to 1847, when the house was built.

Hans Crescent

Hans Crescent runs south of Brompton Road and sits opposite Harrods department store. The area was

redeveloped between 1892 and 1908, and New Street (from 1904 part of Hans Crescent) took its character chiefly from Harrods. The Hans Crescent Hotel was built in 1896, and for decades was one of the most exclusive hotels in London. It is now part of Harrods Estates, and exists as luxury apartments with a tunnel connecting to the store.

Hans Place

This late-eighteenth-century private square, situated south of Harrods, was designed by Henry Holland as part of his Hans Town development. Little remains of the original development for which the garden of Hans Place was laid out. Most of the houses in the area were established in 1875. Three house survive from Holland's development: 15, 33, and 34.

Hasker Street

Hasker Street is south of Walton Street, between First Street and Ovington Street, and is one-way. It is residential and is within walking distance of Sloane Square, Knightsbridge and South Kensington. It has no redeeming features.

No.43: Bertrand Russell had a pied-à-terre here, but spent much of his later years in north Wales with his fourth wife.

Hemus Place

Hemus Place is north of the King's Road and east of Chelsea Manor Street. It is a small roadway between buildings and has no houses. In 1937, it was named after William Hemus Rayner, a Cadogan family builder.

Henniker Mews

Henniker Mews is a pretty, cobbled mews south of Fulham Road and west of Beaufort Street. It was named after John Wright Henniker Wilson (1800–72), who married Mary Wilson, the heiress of Chelsea Park.

No.16: A plaque here states: 'On 15th January 1913 Bamford & Martin Ltd Manufacturers of the first Aston Martin cars commenced business here'.

Hobury Street

Hobury Street is a one-way tree-lined street in World's End, north of the King's Road and east of Edith Grove. Houses here include Georgian townhouses. George Meredith, poet and novelist lived at No.7.

Holbein Mews

Holbein Mews is a partly cobbled through road off Holbein Place, leading to Lower Sloane Street. It was initially developed at the end of the nineteenth century as stable and coach houses for the leading homes on Sloane Gardens and Holbein House. It is now residential with some commercial activity. During the Second World War, a high-explosive bomb fell on to Sloane Gardens, just above Holbein Mews, causing some damage to the properties there.

Holbein Place

Holbein Place is on the west side of Sloane Square and has interior designer Nicholas 'Nicky' Haslam's showroom and trade office at Nos.10–14.

No.18: This was once the Como Lario Italian restaurant, which opened in 1986 and was frequented by celebrities including Pierce Brosnan, Nigella Lawson and Gary Lineker. It is now closed.

Hortensia Road

Hortensia Road is principally residential, and runs west of Gunter Street and north of the King's Road. The site was formerly occupied by the Royal Exotic Nurseries, which gave its name to Hortensia Road, a new road created in 1903. London County Council acquired it in 1905, and the Carlyle School was opened here in November 1908 for the secondary education of more than 500 girls. The school was used as a hospital in the First World War and then became a grammar school. Boys were later admitted, but the school moved to Pimlico in 1969 and became a nursery in 1971. The Carlyle Building now hosts the English National Ballet School. Hudson House is also here.

Ives Street

Ives Street is west of First Street, north of Mossop Street and, at the time of the 1891 census, the properties at Nos.27–9 were the London Provincial Dairy.

No.1a: The Vita Boutique Fitness health club is here.

No.15a: The Bluebell Cottage School for children aged two to five was here, but closed in 2020.

Ixworth Place

Ixworth Place is south of Fulham Road and west of Sloane Avenue. It was named after the Suffolk village of Ixworth, which the Cadogan family owned. The street has two very early, plain black-and-white road signs headed 'Ixworth Place, S.W.', one of which is probably Victorian.

The Oratory School Hall is here and has a religious plaque above the entrance door featuring Mary with baby Jesus and four child angels.

Ixworth Hall is here and is used for a variety of events.

No.35: The four-star Myhotel Chelsea.

No.37: Katharine Pooley Design Studio.

The Samuel Lewis Trust Dwellings are on the corner of Ixworth Place and Elystan Street, with highly decorated walls on each side.

Jubilee Place

Jubilee Place is a pleasant residential street opposite Radnor Walk and north of the King's Road. It was so-named in 1810 to celebrate the fiftieth anniversary of King George III's reign. The main buildings here include Jubilee House, Radnor Mansion and Arundel Court.

No.3: The Michael Hoppen Gallery is here. It opened in 1992 and showcases up-and-coming fine art photographers.

No.4: The Pheasantry House is here and is a residential building.

No.44: William Joyce (aka 'Lord Haw-Haw') lived here at one time.

Justice Walk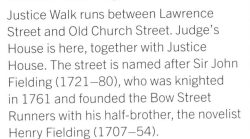

Justice Walk runs between Lawrence Street and Old Church Street. Judge's House is here, together with Justice House. The street is named after Sir John Fielding (1721–80), who was knighted in 1761 and founded the Bow Street Runners with his half-brother, the novelist Henry Fielding (1707–54).

The Court House was built in the early eighteenth century and witnessed hundreds of trials, most of which dealt with highway robberies committed by footpads along the dark lanes between Chelsea and the capital. Convicted criminals were taken on the short walk to prison ships moored on the River Thames before being shipped to British penal colonies. After the last prisoner was sentenced, the Court House – one of the few buildings surviving from Chelsea's early days – became a wine warehouse before becoming home to a warren of tiny artists' and architects' studios. This historic building is the only surviving local courthouse jail in the capital.

I took photos in 2002 (*above, left*) of the hanging sign of a judge at Justice Walk, and I retook photos in 2012 (*above, right*) when the sign was badly worn. Now it is no more, having been taken down.

No.1: Justice House. When I saw it in 2002 it was named Justice Cottage.

No.2: This house has a decorated doorway.

The Judge's House has a decorated doorway but no number.

The large house at the end of the north-west side was once a Wesleyan Chapel with a schoolroom beneath, and Queen Victoria once attended a service there. Peter Jones, founder of the famous Sloane Square department store, and Thomas Carlyle were more frequent attendees.

Kimbolton Row

Kimbolton Row is a small, gated, mews-style cul-de-sac off Elystan Street containing just six properties. At some time between 1940 and 1941, some high-explosive bombs fell on to Fulham Road, not far from the row, causing some damage. It has a pre-1965 road sign headed 'Kimbolton Row. S.W.3'.

A BRIEF HISTORY OF THE KING'S ROAD

IT IS HARD TO BELIEVE that today's busy street was once a quiet country footpath, little more than a cart track. During the reign of King Charles II (from 1660 to 1685), he had the road constructed as a private carriage route between his palaces at Whitehall and Hampton Court. It was patrolled at night by royal troops, and the only people allowed to pass down it were the king and holders of special passes. Conveniently for the king, the road passed Sandford Manor too, in present-day Fulham, which at the time was the home of his mistress Nell Gwynn ('pretty, witty Nell' as Samuel Pepys once described her).

In 1719, Sir Hans Sloane led the local property owners to successfully petition for access to the King's Road. In the late eighteenth century, King George III (1760–1820) would journey on it to visit his palace at Kew, crossing the river Westbourne via the Bloody Bridge, and passing Chelsea Old Church (also known as All Saints) on the way. It was he who finally granted permission for local roads to join it.

By the early nineteenth century there were still fields, farms and thatch cottages on both sides, while the Chelsea village was still centred around Chelsea Old Church beside the river. By 1830, shops had begun to appear beside the villas along the highway, and the road was widened to accommodate the increased traffic. By 1869, it had become the centre of development in the parish, changing the focus of the village away from the river. This would later cause the more modest Georgian terraced houses to be replaced by Victorian and Edwardian buildings, and then apartment blocks in the twentieth century.

Modern clothes retailing in the King's Road really began with Mary Quant, who set up her first shop here in the late 1950s at Markham House. It was just a few steps from the Markham pub, which enjoyed an unexpected rejuvenation as the shop became fashionable. The road, stretching from Sloane Square past Chelsea Town Hall to the World's End, became the centre of 'Swinging London'. It was filled with countless pubs, restaurants and boutiques. The small, useful neighbourhood shops closed as the boutique owners moved in and the 'beautiful people' of the Sixties arrived.

THE KING'S ROAD

A M

*In which you shall meet The Beatles, Jimi Hendrix and David Bowie,
who bought his Ziggy Stardust outfit from a King's Road boutique. We'll
also see the house that on one memorable occasion entertained Edward VIII
and his bride-to-be Wallis Simpson, Arnold Bennett, Virginia Woolf, Hilaire
Belloc, Max Beerbohm and Winston Churchill.*

*And imagine the sandwich shop that served celebrity clients including
John Lennon, Christine Keeler, John Wayne, Lauren Bacall and Humphrey
Bogart, or the coffee shop that was frequented by Michael Caine and Terence
Stamp. But the King's Road is probably best known for its fashion boutiques.
In the 1960s, they dressed the likes of Tony Curtis, the Four Tops,
The Temptations, Rod Stewart, Marc Bolan and Bob Dylan. In the 1970s, it
was The Clash, the Sex Pistols, Chrissie Hynde, Patti Smith, Debbie Harry
and Bob Marley, who all headed to the King's Road for clothing and drinks.*

*You'll also see where The Rolling Stones held their first rehearsals
(and auditioned the author of this book).*

The King's Road North Side (even numbers)

Nos. 36–42: This is the highly decorated Sydney Smith building, built in redbrick in 1887. It is residential, with a row of shops and boutiques.

No. 50: The Chelsea Cobbler shoe shop opened here in 1967, and was popular with musicians of the day, including members of The Rolling Stones.

No. 72: The Colville Tavern public house, which was built in 1856. It closed down in 1969 when the Lord John clothing chain took over the site.

No. 98: The Chelsea Kitchen opened here in 1962, and was very popular with members of The Rolling Stones and Northern Irish footballer George Best.

No. 114: Actress Joyce Grenfell was living here in 1946.

No. 120: This was the premises of Thomas

Crapper, who walked to London as an 11-year-old boy, became an apprentice to a plumber in nearby Sydney Street, and later started his own business, which was synonymous with his name. Crapper became a plumber to royalty and was responsible for improvements at Sandringham and Windsor. He sold out to his partners in 1904, and it was they who relocated the showroom to the King's Road. It closed in 1966.

No.138: Here was the Markham Arms public house, open from 1856 to 1991. It is now a bank.

No.148: This was previously occupied by Box Farm between 1680 and 1900. The Electric Theatre (one of London's first purpose-built cinemas) was built here in 1913. It later became known as the Classic Cinema until it closed in 1973. It briefly reopened as a live venue, but was demolished in 1978.

Nos.152–4: The Pheasantry is a historic Georgian building built in 1769. In 1865, it was occupied by Samuel Baker, who raised pheasants for the royal household. By the 1920s and 1930s, its rooms contained the studio of dance teacher Serafina Astafieva, who taught prima ballerinas Alicia Markova and Margot Fonteyn. There is a blue plaque dedicated to her that reads: 'Princess Seraphine Astafieva 1876–1934 Ballet Dancer lived and taught here 1916–1934'.

The ground floor and basement was a members-only club until 1966. It then became a nightclub that survived into the 1970s, and was where singer Yvonne Elliman was discovered by Andrew Lloyd Webber and Tim Rice. The upper building was apartments. Famous residents included Eric Clapton, journalist Martin Sharp (editor of *Oz*), Germaine Greer, Clive James and photographer Robert Whitaker, who was responsible for the controversial 'butcher' photo used on the original cover of The Beatles' album *Yesterday & Today*. The Pheasantry was redeveloped in 1971 and currently houses shops, apartments and a pizza restaurant.

No.162: The clothing boutique I Was Lord Kitchener's Valet was here from 1967. It was frequented by the pop musicians of the time, including various members of The Rolling Stones.

No.168: This was the All Kinds boutique, where many famous customers shopped, including actor Tony Curtis, the Four Tops, The Temptations, and many footballers of the time.

No.170: John Michael Ingram's boutique was one of the earliest on the King's Road, having opened in 1957. Being one of the original retailers of the Mod style, it designed clothes for TV personalities, including Patrick McGoohan for the cult TV series *The Prisoner*.

Nos.180–2: The Eleusis Club, which evolved from a branch of the Reform League, was here until its lease expired in 1902. The Chelsea Electric Palace was operating here prior to 1910, and changed in 1912 to the Cadogan Electric Palace, advertising pictures and variety shows until 1914. However, with new purpose-built cinemas becoming popular, this soon faded away and a new shopping terrace followed its demolition.

No.188: Cygnet House, an apartment block with a traditional entrance.

CHELSEA TOWN HALL

Chelsea Vestry Hall was built on the King's Road in 1858, together with public baths and a scientific institution. A new hall was built in 1887 at the rear of the old one, fronting Manor Gardens. Later, incorporating this building, the Chelsea Old Town Hall was built between 1906 and 1908. There is a plaque inset in the wall attesting to this: 'Metropolitan Borough Chelsea Erected 1906–8'. It also mentions two mayors during that time, namely W.J. Mulvey J.P. Mayor (1905–6) and the Hon. W. Sidney J.P. Mayor (1906–8). Inside were murals emphasising Chelsea's artistic, literary and scientific heritage.

The building's use as an administrative town hall was abandoned after the creation of the Royal Borough of Kensington and Chelsea in 1965 and the opening of the new town hall complex in Kensington. Its principal use was for recreation, a registry office and the Chelsea Library. There is an early bell on the roof and a modern clock.

Set into the outer wall is an early public drinking fountain, no longer in use, headed 'Metropolitan Drinking Fountain & Cattle Trough Association', and a small black plaque nearby that states: 'These trees [on the pavement in front] are in memory of Basil Marsden Smedley O.B.E. 1902–1964 who loved and served Chelsea'.

During the First World War, the street was lit by gas lamps, but these were partly masked in 1917 when night-time air raids by zeppelins became a threat.

Nos.200–4: The Lord Nelson public house was here in 1806 and was rebuilt in 1933. In 1970, the pub's name was changed to The Trafalgar and it operated as a 'discotheque with a fairground'. The opening ceremony saw film stars Julie Ege and George Lazenby pulling the first pint.

Nos.206–8: The Gaumont Palace cinema opened on this site in 1934. It was modernised in 1960 and renamed the Odeon in 1963 before closing in 1972. A new Odeon cinema was opened a year later, but closed in 1981. Film distributors Artificial Eye took it over and renamed it the Chelsea Cinema in 1983. The cinema was taken over once again by the Curzon group in 2006 and is now named Curzon Chelsea.

No.232: Here was the old Chelsea Post and Sorting Office, which was converted and extended in 2007 to provide affordable housing with a shop below. The original 'Post Office' title is still visible above the present shop.

Nos.232–42: The Chelsea Palace of Varieties replaced the Wilkinson Sword factory in 1902, and attracted all the leading stars of the day. It featured music hall entertainment, staging the likes of George Robey, Vesta Tilley, 'Wee' Georgie Wood and Gracie Fields, and relied heavily on income from the annual pantomime. It declined rapidly after the Second World War despite featuring a mixture of circus and nudity. It was used as a TV studio from 1956 and hosted a Radio Luxembourg talent contest that was won four weeks in a row by the Chas McDevitt Skiffle Group. The band went on to record the song 'Freight Train' with Nancy Whiskey, which became a hit in both the UK and the US. In 1957, the building was leased to Granada Television, who remodelled it for use as their 'Studio 10'. TV shows produced in this studio over the next eight years included 154 episodes of *The Army Game* and three series of a variety show called *Chelsea at Nine*, which featured many top acts who were appearing live in London. Billie Holiday gave her last recorded performance here in February 1959. Granada abandoned the building in 1966 and it was demolished in 1969, to be replaced by apartments and a furniture store.

No.250: This building was used as the old Chelsea Register Office. It was here where Bessie Wallis

Warfield married her second husband, Ernest Simpson, in 1928, becoming Mrs Wallis Simpson. Her third husband would be Prince Edward, the Duke of Windsor, formerly King Edward VIII, who abdicated his throne to marry her. It was also the venue for Judy Garland's 1969 marriage to Mickey Deans, with singer Johnnie Ray as their best man. Judy died a few months later.

Nos.250–250a: The foundation stone of these two buildings was laid here by William Lawrence, the Chairman of the Board of Guardians, on 21 May 1883. The Board of Guardians' offices were held here from that time. In 1903, the building was enlarged, with a second foundation stone laid on 8 April 1903 by James Jeffery, LCC Chairman of Guardians. A decorated roof plaque above 250a says 'CG 1903'.

No.264: The present Chelsea Fire Station was built in 1964 for London County Council on the site of a regency terrace dating from 1810. It is a typically modernist building, built as part of the scheme that included Chelsea School of Arts.

No.298: This was the Rose & Crown pub, which was built around 1719. It was rebuilt in 1838 and the name changed to The Cadogan Arms. It closed in early 2016.

No.304: The Alkasura boutique opened here in 1969 and was a favourite of Rod Stewart and Marc Bolan. It closed in 1975.

On the wall above this shop there is a strange, pre-1917 road sign titled 'Vale Terrace' in black and white, with 'S.W' in red. This can only mean that at one time this was the name of this part of the King's Road, The Vale itself being a street a little further west.

No.328: The Casserole, which opened in 1960, was a trendy 'camp' restaurant frequented by various members of The Beatles and The Rolling Stones, as well as many others in the Sixties.

No.344: The two-floor apartment above the Brora shop was bought in 1982 by Rolling Stones founder member Bill Wyman, and is used as living accommodation and an office for his Ripple companies to this day.

No.350: In 1923, the Blue Bird Company was here, a very upmarket garage of a kind new to London at the time. It sold petrol and contained repair shops and car showrooms, together with lounges and club rooms for customers. Malcolm Campbell and his son Donald's land speed record vehicles were apparently named after this establishment. It became an

ambulance station during the 1950s, and in 1997 it was converted to the Bluebird restaurant, café and shops.

No.352: There is a carving of a cow's head on the front wall here, denoting that this building was previously a Wright's dairy shop (*see No.46 Old Church Street and No.69 King's Road*).

No.354: The Roebuck public house was built here in the 1890s, and was an integral part of life here in the Sixties and Seventies. Later it was redeveloped into the Beaufort House restaurant and cocktail bar.

No.380: Here is the entrance to buildings set back from the road, with a plaque above headed 'The Porticos'.

No.382: This was the William Ashford dairy in 1939.

No.392: The Man in The Moon public house, built around 1813, stood at the corner of the King's Road and Park Walk, and contained a fringe theatre for about twenty years. Adam and The Ants played some of their early gigs here before it closed in 2003, when it became the Eight Over Eight restaurant.

No.406: Johnson's The Modern Outfitters was here in 1978, supplying designs to Bob Dylan, Keith Richards, David Bowie and many others. The owner, Lloyd Johnson, later designed the Mod clothes for the film *Quadrophenia* (1979).

It is also the site of the Brickbarn Close residential apartment buildings.

No.430: The Hung On You boutique was here from 1966, to be replaced in 1969 by the Mr Freedom boutique. Members of The Rolling Stones and The Beatles were customers at both establishments. In 1971, Vivienne Westwood and Malcolm McLaren opened Sex here.

No.452: Standing beside the front door of this private house is a stone carving of a rampant lion that looks very regal. It is holding a shield containing the figure of a smaller rampant lion with a crown above its head.

No.484: This was the headquarters of Swan Song Records, started by Led Zeppelin in 1974 following the end of their contract with Atlantic Records. They left following the closure of the company in 1983, and the building was turned into apartments.

No.488: Granny Takes a Trip was opened here in February 1966 by artist Nigel

Waymouth, his girlfriend Sheila Cohen and John Pearse. It was probably the very first 'psychedelic' boutique, and was famous for the mural of a Native American chief and its 1967 'Jean Harlow' mural.

The shop was sold in late 1969 to Freddie Hornik, who had previously worked at Chelsea's Dandie Fashions. Hornik had introduced velvet suits and stack-heeled boots to the leading rock stars of the era, such as Rod Stewart, Ronnie Wood, Bill Wyman and Keith Richards. The business closed in 1974.

No.500: The building is at the junction of the King's Road and Slaidburn Street. The Wetherby Arms public house opened here in 1881, and would later become part of Rolling Stones history. Brian Jones, Mick Jagger, Keith Richards and Ian Stewart rehearsed regularly in the back room there (*see the small door on the far left*). This is also where Bill Wyman auditioned and became a founder member of The Rolling Stones in

December 1962. The pub closed in May 1971, and the site became a variety of establishments.

No.550: Stanley House was not the first building on this site. Sir Arthur Gorges (*see Gorges House*), who was a friend of the poet Edmund Spenser, had built an earlier house here in the early seventeenth century. Gorges was a cousin of Sir Walter Raleigh and, like him, was a naval man. He died in 1625, and two years later the property passed into the possession of his daughter, the wife of Sir Robert Stanley. It was rebuilt in *c.* 1691 as Stanley House.

The National Society bought Stanley House in 1841 to create a college for their own schoolmasters. The first principal was the Rev. Derwent Coleridge, son of the poet Samuel Taylor. Four-time prime minister William Gladstone (1809–98) was a supporter. The Society later added a children's school to the original building. During the First World War, the college was converted to the

Second London General Hospital to help cope with the thousands of wounded troops evacuated from the battlefields of France and Belgium. The current building, St Mark's College, was renovated in 2002 and has a copy of the Elgin Marbles in a frieze around the dining room walls.

No.552: This is a small building opposite Lots Road on the north side, at the entrance to the Coleridge Gardens, which are set far back from the road.

The King's Road South Side (odd numbers)

No.31a: The composer Percy Grainger lived here from 1908 to 1914. There is a blue plaque here in his honour: 'Greater London Council Percy Grainger 1882– 1961 Australian Composer Folklorist and Pianist lived here'.

No.33: The Whitelands Girls Boarding School was here from 1772 to 1841. In the early 1930s, it was briefly occupied by Oswald Moseley and his British Union of Fascists, and became known as the 'Black House'. The building was demolished in 1935.

No.39: This was the laboratory of William Friese-Green (1855–1921), the inventor of the modern celluloid movie film, who patented his movie camera in 1888.

No.49: The White Hart public house originally stood at No.49. It was replaced by the Chelsea Drugstore in July 1968, and it was revolutionary for its long opening hours – sixteen hours a day, seven days a week. Over three floors, it

included bars, food outlets, a chemist, a newsstand, record store and boutiques, but pressure from the local residents forced its closure in May 1971. It is mentioned in the 1969 Rolling Stones song 'You Can't Always Get What You Want' ('I went down to the Chelsea Drugstore, to get your prescription filled'). It is now sadly a McDonald's restaurant.

No.69: This was once Wright's Dairy, and the name can be seen in three white panels above the terracotta 'cow's head' insignia. The Wrights were cow keepers and dairy farmers and it was acknowledged to be the finest dairy in the district .

No.77: This small alleyway is shown as No.77 King's Road and is headed 'Leading to Charles II Place SW3'.

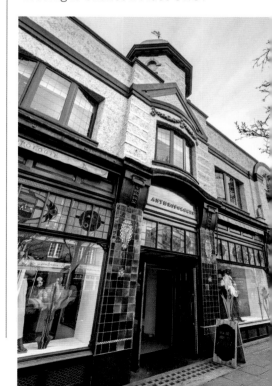

No.107: The Club dell'Aretusa was here from 1967–70, and among its celebrity customers over the years were Princess Margaret, Sammy Davis Jr, David Bailey, Twiggy, Brian Jones and Keith Richards of The Rolling Stones.

No.119: The Commercial Tavern public house was built on this site in 1842. In 1958, it was renamed The Chelsea Potter in commemoration of ceramics artist William de Morgan (1839–1917), who founded a pottery in Chelsea in 1872. This is a very popular establishment at the present time.

No.121: In 1875, the firm Taylor, Son and Gosnells, perfume distillers, was offering distilled and toilet waters, fancy soaps, pomades and 'preparations for the teeth'. When the business outgrew its buildings, it was relocated to larger premises at the Bloomsbury Distillery, 45 New Oxford Street. Later, it became the ironworks factory of Green & London, makers of decorated metal coal hole (or manhole) covers (*see pages 36–7*).

No.127: The Picasso coffee bar opened here in 1958 and was frequented by, amongst others, actors Michael Caine and Terence Stamp. David Hemmings was also a regular during the filming of Michelangelo Antonioni's 1966 film *Blow-Up*. The Picasso finally closed in 2014.

Nos.131–41: This building on the junction with the King's Road and Flood Street is beautifully decorated with plain green and flowered tiles, and a variety of stained-glass windows. In 1915, Margaret

Morris (1891–1980), a British dancer, choreographer and teacher, founded the Margaret Morris Club, whose members included Augustus John, Jacob Epstein, Katherine Mansfield, Ezra Pound, Siegfried Sassoon, Wyndham Lewis and Charles Rennie Mackintosh, among others. The club was still functioning here in the 1920s. She was the first proponent of the Isadora Duncan technique in Great Britain. In 1972, at the age of eighty-one, she trained the dancers for the hit musical *Hair* in Glasgow.

No.135: The Top Gear boutique opened in 1965 and sold Mod clothing to the rich and famous, with eye-catching bull's-eyes on its front canopy and carrier bags, a logo later popularised by The Who. It was taken over by Acme Attractions in 1974 and was frequented by artists such as The Clash, the Sex Pistols, Chrissie Hynde, Patti Smith, Deborah Harry and Bob Marley. It closed in 1977.

No.137: The Countdown boutique was here from 1965 to 1971, and regular customers included various members of The Beatles, The Rolling Stones and Marianne Faithful.

No. 149: Actress Joyce Grenfell lived here from 1939–46, and from 1952–6.

No. 155a: This is the front entrance of the Chelsea Methodist Church.

No. 161: Dandie Fashions opened here at the beginning of 1967, by which time co-owner Tara Browne had died in a high-profile car accident. The incident was immortalised in The Beatles song 'A Day In The Life'. Members of The Beatles, The Rolling Stones, Jimi Hendrix and David Bowie were all customers, and it was Dandie that supplied Bowie's famous Ziggy Stardust outfit. These premises were later occupied by Proud Galleries, with an excellent display of rock 'n' roll, fashion and pop culture photography.

No. 163: The Jean Machine, founded here in 1971, was part of a chain of stores selling jeans.

Nos. 165–79: Chelsea Old Town Hall was here from 1886 to 1965, and was the venue for John and Yoko's media launch of the Plastic Ono Band on 3 July 1969. It is now a venue for concerts, fashion shows and antique fairs.

There are a series of plaques across its walls. The large grey stone plaque reads: 'Metropolitan Borough of Chelsea Erected 1906–08 by Mayor W.J. Mulvey, etc'. The small black plaque inserted there reads: 'These trees are in memory of Basil Marsden Smedley O.B.E 1901–1964 who loved and served Chelsea'.

To the right is the grey edifice titled: 'Metropolitan Drinking Fountain & Cattle Trough Association'.

Nos. 181–3: Charles Chenil's art materials shop opened here in the 1890s and was the home of the Chelsea Arts Club for a while in 1903. It developed into the Chenil Galleries in 1905, devoted to collections and exhibitions. From 1910, Augustus John had his studio here. In 1925, the galleries were relaunched and had their heyday.

In 1933, when the space was being let out, Duke Ellington and his orchestra recorded here for Decca. At the outbreak of the Second World War, it was used for civil defence. Afterwards, the building was sold to the council, and local art exhibitions were held here, as well as X-ray sessions. In 1977, the galleries became privately owned again and

were usually used to sell antiques. Planning consent was granted in June 2010 for a new residential and retail scheme providing new apartments and townhouses.

Nos.191–3: The Chelsea Conservative and Unionist Association was here in 1885. The foundation stone was laid on 18 May 1887 and the club finally opened in 1888. The lease of the building expired in 1935, following which the Club withdrew to join with the South Stanley Conservative Club further along the King's Road.

Nos.195–7: A public house called The Six Bells was on this site in 1722, and it was still surrounded by fields until 1799. In 1895, there was a popular bowling club here with a green at the rear. By the late 1930s, the bowling green and the outbuildings had been demolished, and the public house was seriously bomb-damaged during the Second World War. The site was rebuilt around 1949 and was still named the Six Bells. Ten years later, it was reopened as The Bird's Nest at the Six Bells.

In 1984, it became the Henry J. Beans public house, which was replaced in March 2015 by the Ivy Chelsea Garden Restaurant. It is a Grade II listed building.

A photograph from 1903 shows the Six Bells public house with a façade unchanged from today. It includes the four devils on the plinths — two of which are illustrated here.

No.203: The circular plaque here states: 'The Royal Borough of Kensington & Chelsea Environment Award 2007'.

No.211: This is the site of Argyll House, the oldest house still existing on the King's Road. It was built in 1723 for John Perrin by the Venetian architect Giacomo Leoni, whose monogram appears on the gate. The house got its name from the residence of the 4th Duke of Argyll in 1769. Between 1922 and 1937 it was occupied by society hostess Lady Sibyl Colefax. It is alleged that the future Edward VIII was introduced to Wallis Simpson at one of her soirees here. Other notable guests included Arnold Bennett, Virginia Woolf, Hilaire Belloc, Max Beerbohm, Winston Churchill and Yehudi Menuhin. Fred and Adele Astaire entertained the guests one evening, and George Gershwin played piano on another occasion, with Arthur Rubinstein and Cole Porter standing on either side of him. The evening was rounded off by a rendition of folk songs by Jan Masaryk, son of the future Czech president.

No.213: This house was built in the 1720s, and was once home to *The Third Man* and *Oliver!* film director Sir Carol Reed. His life is commemorated by a blue plaque reading: 'Sir Carol Reed (1906–1976) film director lived here from 1948–1978'. Judy Garland and her family rented the house from Reed for a period in 1960.

No.215: Composer Thomas Arne (1710–78) lived his last years at this residence. He was famous for his composition of the patriotic song 'Rule Britannia'. In 1745, he was engaged as composer to the pleasure ground of Vauxhall Gardens and also composed music to be played at Ranelagh Gardens in Chelsea. From 1904 to 1920, the actress Ellen Terry (1847–1928), who was one of the beauties of her time, lived here. In 1864, she married the celebrated painter George Frederick Watts, but they separated a year later, and she then went to live with architect Edward William Godwin and had two children by him. In 1876, she was at the Royal Court in Chelsea for a long run. She had a long and storied career, and was consistently popular and admired as an actress. In more recent times, actor Peter Ustinov occupied the house.

No.239: The Gateways club, on the corner of Bramerton Street, was the longest-surviving lesbian club in the world. First opened in 1931, it became popular with artists and celebrities such as Diana Dors and Dusty Springfield in the 1960s, and was used for scenes in the 1968 film *The Killing of Sister George*, starring

Beryl Reid and Susannah York. It closed in September 1985.

Nos.245–53: These shops and stalls are on the site of the Chelsea Antiques Market, which was frequented by members of The Rolling Stones, particularly Brian Jones, who bought Moroccan clothes and jewellery here.

No.251: S. Boris, a sandwich shop, opened here in 1969, and was frequented by many notable customers, including Mick Jagger, John Lennon, Yoko Ono, John Wayne, Lauren Bacall, Humphrey Bogart, Judy Garland and Christine Keeler.

No.253: This was the home of the popular Emmerton & Lambert boutique, which was frequented by members of The Rolling Stones. It was replaced in 2005 by the Northcote Gallery.

No.259: This was the ironworks factory of Charles Leonard Hacking, a maker of decorated metal coal hole covers (*see pages 36–7*).

In 1934, it became Green & Stone, the traditional and long-established art and craft supplies shop and picture-framers, and was frequented by artists including Gerald Scarfe, David Hockney and Damien Hirst. It closed on 28 September 2018 owing to structural problems with the building, and relocated to 251–3 Fulham Road.

No.273: The Stockpot restaurant, one of the oldest restaurants on the King's Road, was here and was frequented by the likes of Eric Clapton in recent years.

Nos.279–81: The Glaciarium, an artificial ice rink created using the technology invented to freeze meat, was here in 1876. In 1910, the site was occupied by The Palaseum roller-skating rink. It was renamed King's Picture Playhouse a year later, and in 1943 it became the Ritz. Remodelled again in 1949, it became the Essoldo Chelsea until 1972, when it was renamed the Curzon, before closing a year later. It reopened as the King's Road Theatre for live performances, notably the first live version of *The Rocky Picture Horror Show*. Having closed in 1979, it reopened a year later as the Classic and is now a Cineworld.

No.283: This building has an unusual door with a clock above.

Nos.293–301: Stanley Terrace, marked above with the name and dated 1840.

No.295: Sculptor Charles James Pibworth lived here from 1948 until his death ten years later.

Nos.303–23: These are the Argyll Mansions, a large apartment building. The site was formerly a late eighteenth-century house in use by Dr Lee for his surgery. It was demolished in 1903 when the Argyll Mansions were built.

No.357: The popular Worlds End Bookshop.

No.381: The Moravian Church is here. It was founded in 1742 by its members, who had come to London from Europe. The chapel was destroyed in an air raid in 1941 and the congregation began worshipping in chapels of various denominations. In the 1960s, it was decided to re-establish the Fetter Lane Congregation at the Chelsea site, and this is where the congregation has

worshipped ever since. The blue sign with white and yellow lettering outside reads: 'The Moravian Church in Great Britain and Ireland The Fetter Lane Congregation etc'. In January 2016, a plaque honouring Ernest and Mary Gillick was unveiled at their former home here. Mary was best known for her effigy of Queen Elizabeth II, which had been used on coins from 1953–70.

No.383a: This was the site of The Globe public house in 1881. It was later renamed The Water Rat, but closed in 2004.

No.385: The Chelsea Police Station was here in 1852. It was rebuilt east of that structure and opened in 1897. A newer station opened in Lucan Place in 1939 and was still in use in 2002. The station

at 385 King's Road became a community centre, but was replaced by offices and shops in 1985. Nearby is a very old, pre-1917 road sign, possibly Victorian.

No.397: This is now the Frantoio Italian restaurant, which replaced the very popular Leonardo's restaurant on this site. It is frequented by a host of celebrities that include Bill Wyman, Michael and Shakira Caine, Johnny Gold, Bob Geldof, Jimmy Nail, Ian La Frenais, and the former England and Crystal Palace football manager Roy Hodgson, as well as many Chelsea footballers.

No.433: This was formerly Rileys public house.

Nos.441–57: This is the World's End Nurseries, Chelsea's longest-established garden centre.

No.459: This was the World's End Distillery tavern, which existed during the reign of Charles II. It is mentioned in William Congreve's play *Love for Love* (1695) as being 'in the middle of nowhere'. A narrow alley (called Hobs Lane and World's End Passage) ran down to the river and was commercially important, as many of the customers came by boat from the City. The pub was rebuilt in 1897, and there is a popular restaurant here. The decorated plaque on the front of the building has ugly faces and two lions' heads inset.

To the immediate west of The World's End Distillery is the World's End estate, which is a small square lying back from the King's Road, which had a highly decorated shelter of multicoloured tiles. The Chelsea Theatre is located here at No.7. It was established as the Chelsea Theatre Centre in 1992 under the artistic

direction of Francis Alexander. The building has recently been refurbished, and reopened in September 2003 with a programme of new works.

Standing on the western junction with Edith Grove are the Guinness Trust residential buildings, which include Capel House, O'Gorman House and Winch House.

No.529: World's End Health Centre.

No.533: The Furniture Cave is here, and is where Rolling Stone Bill Wyman bought many items of antique furniture throughout the 1980s and 1990s.

No.535: This was the headquarters of the independent record label Cube Records, which was launched in 1972 by music publisher David Platz. It was also the UK office for Essex Music. It folded in the 1970s, becoming part of Elektra Records. The building has since been demolished, although the new Plaza 535 building here still houses the Essex Music group.

Lamont Road Passage

Lamont Road Passage is in World's End, a little north of the King's Road and west of Beaufort Street, and is residential. No. 1 was once home to Chamberlin Powell & Bon, one of the leading architectural practices in post-war Britain and responsible for the Barbican Estate.

Langton Street

Langton Street is just north of the King's Road and east of Edith Grove. It was named after Thomas Langton, a Lambeth timber merchant who built in this area in the 1850s. It is residential and has several restaurants.

No.7: Established in 1966, the building is home to the popular La Famiglia Italian restaurant, created by the godfather of Italian chefs, Alvaro Maccioni. Celebrities who regularly ate there included Brigitte Bardot, David Bailey, Michael Caine, Jean Shrimpton, Princess Margaret, Peter Sellers, Ian La Frenais, Kylie Minogue, and Bill Wyman and Ronnie Wood of The Rolling Stones.

Lavender Close

Lavender Close is a small private cul-de-sac for residents' parking only, and runs down the north side of Alexander Fleming House on Danvers Street. It has an early road sign titled 'Lavender Close SW3', with the 'SW3' in red and no mention of Chelsea.

Lawrence Street
🅷 🅻 🅰 🅼

Lawrence Street is one of the oldest roads in Chelsea. Its name comes from Sir Thomas Lawrence, a goldsmith who lived in the earliest known Chelsea Manor House. He bought the manor and the house, located at the northern end of today's Lawrence Street, in 1583. He died ten years later and was buried in a chapel in Chelsea Old Church, which became known as the Lawrence Chapel. Several other family monuments can also be seen there. The house was demolished early in the eighteenth century. The street was previously adjacent to the Thames, but after the Embankment was constructed, the road and river were physically divided, as they are today.

There is a simple black-and-white road sign titled 'Lawrence Street' here, and another very old and battered road sign with white lettering on a blue background that is probably Victorian.

Monmouth House was here, owned by the Duchess of Monmouth, and consisted of four houses originally situated at the top of Lawrence Street.

The King's Mansions and the Lawrence Mansions residential buildings are here, the latter having a neat entrance.

No.1. An old public house, The Cross Keys, is here. First opened in 1708, it was painted by Walter Greaves around 1860 and shows just how open the street was to the Thames in those days. It sadly closed in 2012 and was boarded up. Following a petition signed by 2,200 local people, the new owners reopened it as a public house and restaurant.

There is a blue plaque there that reads:

'The Cross Keys Heritage
Dylan Thomas

The Cross Keys in 2002 (above) and after reopening in 2015

J.M.W Turner (painter)
Agatha Christie
John Singer Sargent
James Abbott McNeill Whistler (painter)
Bob Marley
1708–2012
Celebrated figures drank here'.

No.10: This is Lawrence House. Henry James (1843–1916) used rooms here to write while he lived at his club.

No.16: John Gay (1685–1732), the creator of *The Beggar's Opera*, lived here in 1712–14. Tobias Smollett (1721–71) was also a resident here. Smollett's three novels, *The Adventures of Roderick* *Random*, *The Adventures of Peregrine Pickle*, and *The Expedition of Humphrey Clinker*, were among Charles Dickens' favourite children's books. On the front wall, a large square blue plaque reads: 'London County Council Chelsea China was manufactured in a house at the north end of Lawrence Street 1745–1784 Tobias Smollett novelist also lived in part of the house 1750 to 1762'.

On the north-west side of Lawrence Street, where the above plaque is displayed, is where the superb Chelsea porcelain was made under the ownership of Sir Everard Fawkener. The business was passed on to the French silversmith Nicholas Sprimont, who built the Chelsea Porcelain Works on the corner of today's Justice Walk. Sprimont sold the business to James Cox in 1769, when he became too ill to continue. Cox then sold it on to William

Duesbury in Derby. Several maker's marks were incised on this Chelsea porcelain, but most often it was a Red Anchor, which today is the symbol of the Chelsea Society.

No.19: On the wall is a coloured plaque commemorating a lady named, I believe, Angya (or Ingya) Di Remini. However, the plaque is very worn and hard to read, and I've been unable to find any further references to her.

Others who lived on this street in early times included Sir John Fielding (the Bow Street magistrate) and cleric David Williams (1738–1816), founder of the Royal Literary Fund, who set up a home and a school here in 1773.

Lennox Gardens

Lennox Gardens are west of Clabon Mews and south-east of Walton Street. It was formerly the site of the Prince's Cricket Club, established here in c. 1870 by George and James Prince, who had founded the club in 1858. The cricket ground had been laid out on the former Cattleugh's nursery gardens, which were famous for their pines. There were a skating rink and racket courts here, as well as the cricket field, and in 1870 there were 700 members of the 'nobility and gentry' with exclusive membership. *Wisden Cricketers' Almanack* of 1872 described it as 'grand and quick and one of the finest playing grounds in England'. It also became the original home of lawn tennis.

The field's lease expired in 1885, and the Lennox Gardens and Lennox Garden Mews were built here, becoming one of the most exclusive garden squares in Chelsea. The houses are a mixture of Gothic and Baroque detail constructed between 1882 and 1886. In 1928, the central garden was described as

being surrounded by a thick privet hedge with an ornamental garden and a well-kept lawn.

On the corner of Lennox Gardens and Pont Street is the St Columba Church of Scotland (1883), built in grey stone to an unusual shape. It has the royal insignia over the side door.

No.8: Dates from 1880 and has a blue plaque erected in 2004 by English Heritage, inscribed 'Count Edward Raczynski 1891-1993 Polish Statesman Lived here 1967–1993'.

No.11: Mitford House. Mrs Percy Mitford was living here in 1918. It became Knightsbridge School in 1968.

Nos.39 & 43: These houses have highly decorated doors.

John Dunbar and his wife Marianne Faithfull lived in a flat here in the late 1960s, and James Gilbey of the Gilbey gin family owned one of these apartments. It was here that he would meet Diana, Princess of Wales, during their romance in the summer of 1989.

Lennox Garden Mews

Lennox Garden Mews is a private cobbled through road off Milner Street, leading to Walton Street. It was initially

laid out as the stable and coach houses for the main houses in Lennox Gardens. The houses here were built between 1882 and 1886, and are used for residential and commercial purposes. The mews is part of the Hans Town Conservation Area.

Limerston Street

Limerston Street is long and wide, and runs between Fulham Road and the King's Road, west of Beaufort Street. It was named after a village on the Isle of Wight. It is residential with a few restaurants.

No. 41: This was the Odell Arms, and dates from 1856. It was demolished in 1971 and rebuilt in 1974 as the Red Anchor. In 1989, it was renamed the Sporting Page and was given the address 6 Camera Place, despite standing at the corner of Limerston Street.

Lincoln Street

Lincoln Street is north of the King's Road, opposite Duke of York Square. It was named after Stroud Lincoln, who was

an executor of the will of James Colvill, owner of a nearby nursery ground. It has two early pre-1917 road signs.

Lombard Terrace

Lombard Terrace was formerly on the north side of old Lombard Street and Duke Street, and was all that was left when the Chelsea Embankment was built. A surviving remnant of the old village in 1906 was the Rising Sun pub, which was still there in 1925.

Lordship Place

Lordship Place is a small street between Cheyne Row and Lawrence Street that leads west to the Cross Keys public house. There is a pre-1917 black-and-white road sign that reads 'Lordship Place, S.W.'.

CURIOUS CHELSEA

There are so many mulberry trees planted in Chelsea because of a short-lived venture by Henry Barham, who wanted to cultivate raw silk in the borough in the early 1700s. The experiment took place on some land called Sandhills, part of Sir Thomas More's old estate, now bounded by Fulham Road and the King's Road, and by Park Walk and Old Church Street. Huge numbers of silkworms were imported, and mulberry trees were planted, on which they feed. The silkworms soon died off in the English climate. Some of the mulberry trees are still here, and Mulberry Walk commemorates this brief venture.

No.19 Mallord Street, site of the former
Chelsea Telephone Exchange

Carlyle Lodge is here, as is Tennyson Mansions. On the eastern wall of the latter is an old black-and-white road sign that reads 'Tennyson Mansions'.

Lots Road A M

Lots Road runs from the western end of Cheyne Walk along the river and curves north to Fulham Road. It derives its name from about four acres of manorial land in the neighbourhood called The Lots; this land could be used as common grazing land by manorial tenants to pasture their animals, and could be a bleak area in poor weather.

The Thames at that time was particularly dangerous. In the seventeenth century, Sir William Ashburnham was saved from being lost on the river in fog by the sound of the bell in the Old Church. In gratitude, he donated a new bell to the church in 1679, which today is displayed there. By the beginning of the twentieth century, the area was full of terraces of houses, with noisy industries fronting the filthy river.

Entering Lots Road from the east, on the riverside, are the charming Cremorne Gardens. Halfway along the road heading west on the riverside is the Chelsea Wharf.

The old 'Lots Road' sign on a blue background here is probably Victorian.

No.12: This private house has a carving on the east wall of two winged angel children (not wholly accessible).

No.90: This is the 606 Club, which opened in 1976 and presents live music. Artists who have performed there include Eric Clapton and Ronnie Wood.

No.92: The Rolling Stones' London office was here, having moved from Battersea in June 2012.

No.112: This is the Chelsea Academy. The building is headed with the following: 'Anchored in Christ. A Mixed 11−18 Church of England Academy specialising in the Sciences'.

No.114: Lots Road Pub and dining room are on the corner of the northern curve. Opposite is the Chelsea Harbour complex.

Nos. 132–4: The Worlds End Studios.

Swinging around the bend towards Fulham Road, the buildings are as follows:

Nos. 65–9: On the west side are two buildings that look like large barns, one behind the other. The main building that faces the road is titled Fairbank 2 Studios.

No. 71: The Lots Road Auctions has been sited here since 1978, and hosts a weekly auction with 500–600 lots each Sunday. On this building is an old road sign with white lettering over a dark-blue background titled 'Lots Road, S.W.'.

No. 73: The Heatherley School of Fine Art. Artists including Evelyn Waugh, Lady Butler, E.H. Shepard, Emily Mary Osborn and Walter Sickert developed their art here.

No. 101: Westfield Close South building.

No. 107: The Francis Smith Auction rooms are located here.

To the right is Pooles Lane, an attractive gated residential area. Opposite is a sign headed 'Chelsea Reach'.

Lots Road Power Station was built by American Charles Tyson Yerkes (1837–1905), who chose this site because it was cheap, next to the river, and convenient for the deliveries of coal to run it. Most importantly, there was an artesian well beneath that supplied the boilers. The station provided power to the London Underground system. Work began in 1902, but by June 1905 the neighbours were complaining about noise from the turbines and pollution from the chimneys. In 1963, two of its four chimneys were removed, and two years later the use of coal was abandoned. Power for the Underground system was subsequently obtained from the National Grid.

Halfway along the road heading west is a decorated door titled 'Station House'. At the top of the power station is written 'London County Council', and below are four circular decorations featuring oak leaves and acorns.

The end of the power station came in October 2002, when the then Transport Minister, John Spellar, switched off the last working turbine.

Lower Sloane Street

Lower Sloane Street continues north of Chelsea Bridge Road and was originally

named White Lion Street, but was renamed in the 1880s. Lost buildings include the Chelsea Baptist Chapel (1814) and the Coach & Horses public house.

The Chelsea Barracks are here ('A Heritage. A Destiny. A Legacy'). The Rose & Crown public house is on the junction with Turk's Row, and the Lurgan Mansions and Wellesley House are here just before Sloane Square.

The street has an old road sign with a black background and white lettering that reads 'Lower Sloane Street, S.W.' and is almost certainly Victorian.

No.14: On the roof of this house is a gargoyle of a winged dragon.

Nos.24–6: These houses have highly decorated doorways.

No.52: The Sloane Club, a small boutique hotel, is here.

No.94: Gwynn House.

Lucan Place

Lucan Place runs beside Sloane Avenue, north to Fulham Road, and is residential. It is where the former 1930s Metropolitan Police Service was sited. The station closed here in December 2014.

Makins Street

Makins Street is a turning west from Sloane Avenue, below Ixworth Place. It is a residential street with some commercial buildings.

Mallord Street

Mallord Street is north of the King's Road, running parallel. It was named in 1909 after the painter Joseph Mallord William Turner (1775–1851), who lived at 119 Cheyne Walk in his later years. The street has an early 'Chelsea' road sign.

No.1: This house has a highly decorated entrance.

No.2: This is Mallord House and features an insignia of the letters 'CHA' and the date '1911' above the entrance. On the house's eastern wall, facing Old Church Street, is a blue metal sign that reads 'Mallord House'. Once white, it has a four-petaled flower in the right-hand corner.

No.11: Author A.A. Milne (1882–1956) lived here from 1919 to 1925. It was here in 1924 that he wrote *When We Were Very Young*, a series of verses for children, dedicated to his four-year-old son Christopher Robin, who was born in this house. The family moved next door to No.13 in 1925.

No.13: Milne lived here from 1925 to 1929. Here he wrote *Winnie-the-Pooh* (1926), *Now We Are Six* (1927) and *House At Pooh Corner* (1928). There is a blue plaque here to his honour.

No.17: Tryon House.

No.19: Site of the former Chelsea Telephone Exchange.

No.20: The property is highly decorated, with a central statue of a man over the entrance door in the Greek style. Over the lower front left and right windows is a man's face and a woman's face, respectively.

No.21: This is Vale Court, a large apartment block.

No.28: This house was built in 1913/14 as a studio for painter Augustus John (1878–1961), and there is a blue plaque here in his honour. He was the best-known living painter in England, renowned for his portraits, which included those of George Bernard Shaw and David Lloyd George. He lived here from *c.* 1914 until 1933/34, when singer Gracie Fields bought the house.

Manresa Road 🇱 🅰

Manresa Road is an attractive residential street that runs north from the King's Road to the South Carriage, north of Chelsea Square. Although once called Trafalgar Road, it is now named after the town in Spain.

Nos. 1–8: Here was the Wentworth Studios, built in 1885. Comprising eight studio units, it housed various artists that included Frances Darlington in 1934–9 and Dylan Thomas in the 1940s.

No. 2: Henry Moore Court, with a sizeable black sculpture like wood grain in the forecourt by Andrew Sabin. A plaque here reads as follows: 'Andrew Sabin Painting and Sculpture 2013 Bronze'. Commissioned for Henry Moore Court, this sculpture celebrates the artists of Chelsea College of Art which previously occupied this site. It also acknowledges Moore's *Two Piece Reclining Figure No. 1* (1959), located here from 1965 to 2000. Henry Moore O.M., C.H. (1898–1986) taught at Chelsea between 1932 and 1939. Andrew Sabin was a student and teacher at the college from 1979 to 2005.

No. 15: The building housed the original public library, which first opened in two rooms temporarily fitted up in the old Vestry Hall in the King's Road. This site was made available by the 5th Earl Cadogan KG in Manresa Road, together with a gift of £300 to buy technical books. Beatrix Jane, Countess of Cadogan, laid the foundation stone on 8 February 1890, and it was opened in 1891 by Earl Cadogan himself.

The first librarian, John Quinn, created the archive of local historical material and was also the first librarian in London to provide a separate study room for children. The building was severely damaged in an air raid on 29 September 1940, when fifteen incendiary bombs set it and the neighbouring Chelsea Polytechnic alight. Both were repaired and reopened in 1951. Unfortunately, after consultation with many Chelsea residents, the library was transferred to part of Chelsea Old Town Hall after the merger of the borough into the Royal Borough of Kensington and Chelsea in 1965. The Hampshire School Chelsea is now based here. In January 2015,

GREATER LONDON COUNCIL
This house was built for
AUGUSTUS JOHN
1878–1961
Painter

A.A. Milne

Alan Alexander Milne (1882–1956), otherwise known as A.A. Milne, was author of the Winnie-the-Pooh books. He lived at No.11 Mallord Street from 1919 to 1925, at which point they moved next door to No.13. It was during his time in Chelsea that Milne wrote the books of children's verse *When We Were Very Young* and *Now We Are Six*. It was also during this period that he took his son, Christopher Robin, to London Zoo. The young boy loved a Canadian black bear called Winnipeg, or Winnie. Along with a troop of Christopher's toys, including Tigger, Eeyore and Piglet, Winnie-the-Pooh's adventures around the family's country house in Sussex became two of the most enduring children's stories of all time.

the assembly hall ceiling caved in. Fortunately, there were only a few minor injuries to fifteen children aged between 9 and 12 years old.

No.16: Trafalgar Studios, a three-storey, purpose-built artists' studios, built in 1878. Artists who have lived there include Henry James Brooks (1839–

1925), Frank Brangwyn (1867–1956) and Mervyn Peake (1911–68). The sculptor Frank Dobson had a studio between the wars, and Ernest Dade and Nelson Dawson also rented studios.

From 1878, artist William Holman Hunt (1827–1910) had a studio here, where he painted one of his most famous works, *The Triumph of the Innocents.*

No.21: In 1891, the Prince of Wales (later Edward VII) laid the foundation stone for what would become the South West Polytechnic Institute. Opening in 1895, it aimed to provide scientific and technical education in domestic economy, mathematics, engineering, natural science, art and music. It also provided secondary education for girls at the Carlyle School and boys at the Sloane School. Both were later relocated.

The Institute, renamed the Chelsea Polytechnic in 1922, taught a growing number of registered students of the University of London. It was

Vale End, 32 Mallord Street.
Built in 1913 for the artist Arthur C. Mitchell
by architect Charles R.G. Hall

subsequently reconstituted as Chelsea College of Science and Technology, and was admitted as a school of the University in 1966. The renamed Chelsea College of Art was formally incorporated into the University of London in 1971 and later merged with Queen Elizabeth College and King's College London in 1985. In December 2000, it was announced that the disparate parts of the college would be consolidated at the former Royal Army Medical College next to Tate Britain on Millbank. This building is now residential apartments, and Bernie Ecclestone, the billionaire Formula 1 head, bought a four-bedroom first-floor apartment here in June 2006.

Margaretta Terrace

This terrace is a quiet, attractive residential road parallel to Oakley Street to the east. The street, which

was built by Dr John Samuel Phene and was named after his wife Margaretta, is thought to have been built on a medieval plague pit site.

Markham Place

Markham Place is just north of the King's Road. It is a small, private courtyard off Elystan Place.

Markham Square

Markham Square is in the same area as above and was named after the Markham Evans family, who owned Box Farm, which was situated in the King's Road from c. 1580 and demolished c. 1900. This was one of several squares that led off the main road. It is residential, but only has houses on three sides, as the King's Road takes the fourth side.

The Chelsea Congregational Chapel was originally on the opposite side but was demolished in 1953, and new houses were built on the site.

On the west side, just before the King's Road junction, is a statue by Richard Claughton called *Bronze Man and Eagle*.

No.47: A blue plaque on the front wall is in honour of Dame Maud McCarthy, a nursing sister who became matron-in-chief of the British Expeditionary Force in France and Flanders during the First World War.

Markham Street

Markham Street is in the same area as Markham Square and had the Electric Cinema Theatre on the junction with the King's Road. Built in 1913, it provided

a dramatic contrast to the sober, gas-lit façades of the King's Road. Few will remember the cinema, but for many it was the Chelsea Classic Cinema, to which modernisation in 1937 gave it a new frontage. The last film was shown here in August 1973, and the cinema was demolished that same year. It was replaced by a Boots chemist shop.

Nos.33–5: Here is an oval plaque titled 'Christ's Hospital London', with a central red cross on white with flower decorations.

No 39: This is the Nell Gwynn Cottage, with a decorated name sign.

No.50: This house has a metal plaque with a bird flying at its centre. On the left is inscribed 'Pierre Rouve Bulgarian Diplomat & Man of Letters Lived & Worked here 1978–1998'. On the right is the same message in Bulgarian.

This was home to the poet Dylan Thomas in March 1946, who was lodging in a basement flat owned by his brother-in-law, the artist Anthony Devas. A Welshman to the core, Thomas loathed London and called living there 'capital punishment'.

In May 2008, barrister Mark Saunders was shot dead by police here after firing at neighbours and the police.

Marlborough Street

Marlborough Street is north of Cale Street and west of Draycott Avenue. It was named after the 3rd Duke of Marlborough (1706–58), who was living in a house by Chelsea Common towards the end of his life. The street has a very early, plain black-and-white road sign that is possibly Victorian.

No.8: The building has a blue plaque in honour of choreographer Sir Frederick Ashton, who lived here between 1959 and 1984.

No.14: The circular plaque inset in the front wall here features the head of an unknown long-haired, bearded man wearing a flat hat.

Milman's Street

Milman's Street runs from the Chelsea Embankment, west of Beaufort Street to the King's Road. It was named after Sir William Milman, who made a fortune trading stocks. He bought a house titled Priest's House in Chelsea in 1697 and was buried in Chelsea Old Church in 1713. In 1726, his four nieces leased the property for building 'a new row of houses intended to be called Milman's Row'. These buildings are on the east side of Milman's Street. At the north end, there used to be a tablet bearing the inscription 'Millman Row 1726'.

At the south end of the street, on the east side, are three brick cottages of two storeys that appear to date from the middle of the seventeenth century. They are shown on Hamilton's map of 1664, where Milman's Street is a narrow lane inscribed 'Way to Little Chelsea'. They are now numbered 55, 57 and 59.

Milman's House is here, a building of residential apartments, which is faced with a frontage of early cobblestones.

No.47: Elizabeth Court is here, with a coloured circular wall plaque featuring a galleon in full sail and a jet plane that looks like Concorde.

Milner Street

Milner Street is north of Cadogan Street and is named after Colonel Charles Milner. He married Mary Jane Moore, the daughter of Richard Moore, who owned land hereabouts and divided it between his five children. It is residential, with commercial shops and businesses.

No.10: This building is sometimes known as Stanley House and was built in 1855 by John Todd for himself. It later became the home of Sir Courtenay Ilbert. Later, in 1945, his nephew, the interior designer Michael Inchbold, lived there.

No.34: The Joseph Peacock-designed St Simon Zelotes Church, which opened in 1859. There is also a church hall here.

Moore Street

Named after Richard Moore of Hampton Court Palace, Moore Street is residential and runs between Cadogan Street and Milner Street, with stucco-fronted houses.

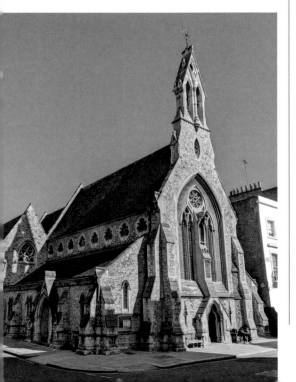

Mossop Street

Mossop Street is a turning north-east of Draycott Avenue. It was initially named Green Lettuce Lane, then Green Street, before it was renamed Mossop Street in 1939. It was named after either Henry Mossop, an eighteenth-century actor who lost most of his money gambling, or Charles Mossop, active in local politics in the nineteenth century. The former was buried in Chelsea Old Church.

No.17: The Admiral Codrington Arms public house was established around 1830.

Mulberry Walk

Mulberry Walk is residential and runs between The Vale and Old Church Street. It's the site where an attempt was made in 1719 to begin a silk-production farm at Chelsea Park. The experiment took place on some land called Sandhills, part of Sir Thomas More's old estate, bounded by Fulham Road and the King's Road, and by Park Walk and Old Church Street. The idea was that of Henry Barham, a surgeon who had practised in Jamaica and had settled in Chelsea around 1716. He persuaded John Appletree to take out a patent in 1718 for the production of raw silk and to issue shares for its exploitation. It was estimated that laying out the gardens and the planting of the trees would cost £25,000. Large numbers of silkworms were imported, and mulberry trees, which they feed on, were grown. The worms did not take to the English climate, and the venture closed after a few years.

There are still mulberry trees in the area, and Mulberry Walk commemorates this brief venture. The street has a pre-1965 'Chelsea' road sign.

No.1a: Rolling Stones founder member Bill Wyman lived here from 1982 to 1987. Other former residents of this street include Mark Knopfler of Dire Straits, ex-Chelsea football club manager Gianluca Vialli, and actor Laurence Olivier. The building has a strange metal doorway with a stone surround and the letter 'V' inscribed above.

No.23: A decorated sundial is set into the wall above the entrance, which is headed with the words 'Sine Sole Silio' ('Without the sun I'm silent').

Houses along Chelsea Embankment

CHELSEA STREETS *N TO Q*

In which you will meet Antarctic explorer Robert Falcon Scott, spy Donald Maclean, the great Northern Irish footballer George Best, poet laureate Sir John Betjeman, Jonathan Swift, the author of Gulliver's Travels, and the artists James Abbott McNeill Whistler and Walter Sickert. You'll visit the pub where George Best used to drink and the hotel where Oscar Wilde was arrested.

Netherton Grove

Netherton Grove is a quiet, tree-lined cul-de-sac that runs south of Fulham Road, parallel with Edith Grove. Buildings of Chelsea and Westminster Hospital take up part of this street.

Oakley Gardens

Oakley Gardens are west of Chelsea Manor Street and was initially named Oakley Crescent. It was developed c. 1850 around a garden square, which was laid out in 1862, and contained terraced houses to the north and south. It was constructed on the site of a former dairy house originally linked with Chelsea Manor. In 1965, the name was changed to Oakley Gardens. The street is residential.

Oakley Street

Oakley Street runs south from the King's Road to the part of Chelsea Embankment facing the Albert Bridge. The name derives from William Cadogan, who was created Baron Cadogan of Oakley

Thomas Hosmer Shepherd, *Winchester House*, c. 1800

in 1718. The street was formed when Winchester House was built by James, Duke of Hamilton, c. 1640, on some of the garden grounds of Henry VIII's manor house. Overlooking the river and sited to the eastern junction with Cheyne Walk, it was bought in 1664 by the bishopric of Winchester as a London home for the bishops of Winchester. Winchester House was demolished in the 1820s and replaced by houses in Cheyne Walk and Oakley Street.

The building of the Albert suspension bridge in 1873 made Oakley Street into

a main road, although its proximity to Chelsea Steamboat Company's Cadogan Pier and the Pier Hotel had already caused it to be of some importance to travellers. The street has an early 'Chelsea' road sign.

No.10: Writer E.F. Benson (1867–1940) lived here in 1923.

Nos.14–25: These houses all have decoration either over the entrances or up high on the front walls.

No.15: The composer Percy Grainger (1882–1961) lived here in 1903, and character actor Richard Goolden lived here from 1967 to *c.* 1972.

No.32: Dr John Samuel Phene (1823–1912) lived here until he died in 1912. He built many houses on Oakley Street, and built and named Margaretta Terrace after his wife. Later, Phene Street and the Phene Arms public house were named after him (*see Cheyne House at No.2 Upper Cheyne Row*).

No.48: This has a rose-painted front doorway with the word 'Love' above.

No.55: The entrance doorway has been changed to a window.

No.56: Antarctic explorer Robert Falcon Scott (1868–1912) lived here with his two sisters and mother from 1904–8 while writing the account of his 1904 expedition to the Antarctic. A blue plaque in his honour is as follows: 'L.C.C. Robert Falcon Scott Antarctic Explorer (1868–1912) Lived Here'.

No.58: This was formerly the home of the distinguished mathematician Charles Sanger (1860–1912). An absent-minded man, he could never remember the number of his house. He used as a mnemonic 'the Septuagint minus the Apostles'.

No.66: This is Adair House, set back from the street and entered through an arched entrance.

No.73: The small Oakley Hotel, where guitarist Albert Lee would sometimes stay in recent times.

No.87: There is a blue plaque in honour of Oscar Wilde's widowed mother, Jane Francesca, Lady Wilde (1821–96), who worked under the pen name Speranza. She moved here in 1876 when it was No.46. The house was later demolished and replaced by the present building.

Nos.92 & 94: These houses have attractive black-and-white tiled stairways from the street to the entrances. There are other houses here with similar tiled doors.

Paradise Walk

No.93: Sculptor Elisabeth Frink (1930–93) lived here from 1954 until 1960.

The Duke of St Albans, a direct descendant of Nell Gwynn (1650–87), also had a house here until recently.

Other famous residents included the spy Donald Maclean and the great Northern Irish international and Manchester United footballer George Best.

The Pier Hotel once stood on the western corner of Oakley Street and Cheyne Walk, but is now a sizeable Mercedes showroom. It was built in 1844 but demolished in 1968 together with the Blue Cockatoo, which stood alongside it. This small restaurant was frequented by many of the literati and artists of the 1930s, 40s and 50s. The modern block, Pier House Flats, has a bronze statue in front of it, facing the approach to the Albert Bridge. The statue called *Boy with a Dolphin*, is dated 1975 and was designed by David Wynne.

Old Chelsea Mews

Old Chelsea Mews is a private cul-de-sac off Danvers Street.

Old Church Street

From its location next to the ancient parish church and its appearance on the earliest maps, it may be assumed that Old Church Street is one of the oldest streets in Chelsea and is definitely one of the longest. Until King Charles II had his private road built (now known as the King's Road), Church Lane (as it was once known) was the only coachway to the riverside village, and that section north of the King's Road was merely called 'the Road to the Cross Tree'.

No.30a: Author and film director Donald Cammel, known primarily for *Performance* (1970), lived here from the late 1960s to the 1970s.

No.34: Although this is now a private dwelling, it still retains the old tobacconist's curved bay window with outer shutters from the past. Thomas Carlyle bought his cigars here in the old days.

No.35: The seventeenth-century Black Lion public house was at the junction with Paultons Street and Old Church Street. It had tea gardens and a bowling green. The present building was erected in 1892 and retains many original features, including elaborate lights and bar fittings. After a series of names, it was renamed The Front Page in 1986, later changed to The Pig's Ear, and is now The Chelsea Pig. The bar is decorated with pictures from the 1960s and 70s, including photographs of George Best, The Rolling Stones and punk memorabilia. Eric Clapton, who lives nearby, was sometimes seen here.

No.46: Here was Wright's Dairy, which was established in 1796 and opened further branches in Kensington, Mayfair and Belgravia. Fifty cows once grazed on

Cook's Ground at the rear of this dairy. Cow heads can still be seen on the front of the building and down the alleyway, high on the redbrick wall of the building. It features several beautifully decorated tiled plaques (*see also No. 69 and No. 352 King's Road*).

Nos. 49–51: The Hereford Buildings, where the sculptor Sir Charles Wheeler (1892–1974) lived. He became a Fellow of the Royal Academy in 1940 and was president from 1956 to 1966. Leaves surround a circular gold-coloured plaque that states: 'Sir Charles Wheeler P.R.A 1892–1975 Lived Here' (although he actually died on 22 August 1974).

No. 53: Poet John Betjeman (1906–84) lived here from 1917–24.

No. 54: Jonathan Swift (1667–1745) was here in 1711, and writer Robert Ross (1869–1918) lived here in 1892.

No. 56: Writer Charles Kingsley (1819–75) lived here from 1836–60. His father was Rector of Chelsea.

No. 64: This is a notable 1930s building.

No. 66: Another 1930s building. Actress Constance Cummings (1910–2005) lived here from 1947 until at least 1967.

No. 77: This small alleyway is named Atlantic Court and is headed 'Leading to Charles II Place SW3'.

No. 107: The entrance to this building is decorated with a two-sided swan extending from the wall. Above that is a white triangular plaque featuring two female figures: one sitting on the left and the other standing on the right pouring her a drink. Above these on either side are two large acorn shapes.

No. 115: This house has a highly decorated and attractive entrance.

No.117: A square stone plaque on the wall beside the front door is inscribed as follows: 'Halsey Ricardo Designed This House 1914 In Memoriam C.P.1928 C.M.P.'.

No.127: The potter and tile-maker William de Morgan (1839–1917) moved here in 1910 with his wife Evelyn de Morgan (artist Evelyn Pickering) (1855–1919). William died here in 1917, and Evelyn was here until she died in 1919. It is mentioned in a book that a blue plaque is here in memory of William de Morgan, but it was not visible to me.

Nos.129–39: This is an outstanding terrace of early nineteenth-century houses.

No.133: The house has a blue plaque to a 'Miss Rose' written in Latin. It is translated: 'She ruled in this house and rules now and forever in our hearts'.

No.137: Artist Anthony Gross (1905–84)

was here from 1948 until at least 1958.

No.139: Architect Edward Maufe (1883–1974) was here from 1962.

No.141a: The author Katherine Mansfield (1888–1923) was here in 1917.

No.143: The Chelsea Arts Club was founded in 1891 by a group of artists led by sculptor Thomas Lee. Members included James Abbott McNeill Whistler, Walter Sickert, George Clausen, Frank Brangwyn, John Singer Sargent, Henry Tonks, Philip Wilson Steer and the scientist Alexander Fleming.

The club moved to its present premises in 1902. Good meals are served among paintings donated by past and present members. It has a splendid garden complete with a fountain sculpted by Henry Pool and there is a simple carved stone plaque at the entrance.

In 1908 the club instigated the renowned

Chelsea Arts Ball, a grand fancy-dress party held on New Year's Eve. It became a very large affair, and in 1949, Ted Heath and Oscar Rabin's bands provided the music, together with the Dagenham Girl Pipers. There were verbal and musical contributions from London art colleges, and more music followed until breakfast was served at 5am. The Ball was prohibited in 1959 then revived in 1984.

No.147: Sculptor Adrian Jones (1845–1938) lived here from 1892 to 1937.

No.149: Sloane House, which used to be an asylum for ladies suffering 'from the milder forms of mental disease'.

No 155: This property has a blue plaque that reads as follows: 'London County Council John F. Sartorius 1775–c. 1830 Sporting Painter lived here from 1807 to 1812'.

Queen drummer Roger Taylor lived in this street with his family for a while.

No.241: Former public house The Queen's Elm stands on the western junction with Fulham Road. It commemorates the spot where Lord Burghley once took shelter from the rain under an elm tree during a walk with Queen Elizabeth I. The building still has the name over the door, but is now a clothes shop.

Ormonde Gardens

Ormonde Gardens is the communal garden for residents of Ormonde Gate, and is accessed from the rear of the houses.

Ormonde Gate

Ormonde Gate is north of the Royal Hospital Road and west of Lower Sloane Street, and is named after Ormonde House, which stood nearby. The house, dating from 1691, was home to Mary, the wife of James, 2nd Duke of Ormonde, who lived there from 1730 to 1733. Minor aristocrats occupied the house until, in 1777, it was taken over by the Maritime

School, founded to train scholars to be naval officers. The proprietor, John Battesworth, taught maths and navigation, but one suspects that the guiding hand was that of the philanthropist Jonas Hanway (who also popularised the invention of the umbrella). The house was demolished around 1890. The street has a pre-1965 'Chelsea' road sign.

Ovington Gardens

Ovington Gardens runs off Brompton Road and into Ovington Square. There is a blue plaque at Ovington Court to singer, actress and entertainer Elisabeth Welch, best known for the song 'Stormy Weather'.

Ovington Square

Ovington Square is located just off Walton Street. It is residential and only moments away from all the fashionable shops and restaurants, including Harrods and Harvey Nichols. It surrounds the Ovington Square Gardens. During the Second World War, a large block was bombed, and eminent producers Michael Powell and Emeric Pressburger were able to use the garden and bombsite

for filming *The Life and Death of Colonel Blimp* (1943). Notable residents included Charles Dickens, socialite and salonist Vera Lombardi (who was arrested in Italy in 1943 under suspicions of spying for the British during the war), as well as Jane and Oscar Wilde.

Ovington Street

Ovington Street runs between Milner Street and Walton Street. It has several Victorian terraces, one of which is the long-time home of the Duke and Duchess of St Albans. Cara Delevingne's 101-year-old grandmother, daughter of the 1st Viscount Greenwood, lived here until recently. Irish novelist Edna O'Brien (born 1930) lives on this street. The entire road is Grade II listed.

No.54: Actor Nigel Patrick (1912–81) lived here from 1979.

Paradise Row

Paradise Row had a much-loved array of rather run-down but picturesque houses and shops dating from the 1690s, and were the last of their kind hereabouts. Historian Reginald Blunt was moved to write a book about Paradise Row, and poignantly sums up the circumstances for destruction in a way that can still be relevant if there are no safeguards.

Paradise Row is now part of Royal Hospital Road, south-west of Smith Street.

Thomas Faulkner lived at what was then No.1 Paradise Row, the site of the later Chelsea Pensioners pub. He kept a bookshop and print shop, and also described on his business card that he was a 'Teacher of the French, Italian and Spanish Languages'. He was a frequent contributor to *The Gentleman's Magazine*. Earlier works included histories of the Royal Hospital and the Royal Military Asylum.

Paradise Walk

Paradise Walk is a plain street east of the Physic Garden and runs south from Royal Hospital Road. Although residential, it benefits from the shops, restaurants and transport facilities the area offers.

Park Walk

Park Walk runs between Fulham Road and the King's Road. It was previously called Lovers Walk and was built at the end of the eighteenth century. The rest, including the northern extension of Beaufort Street, followed piecemeal.

The small chapel, Emmanuel Church, was originally named Park Chapel, a privately owned chapel at the junction with Chelsea Park Gardens. It was built in 1718 at the expense of Sir Richard Massingham. In 1812, its minister was involved in founding the missionary British and Foreign Bible Society. The chapel and its infant school were closed around 1905, and the new St Andrew's church was built here by Sir Arthur Blomfield. The Bishop of London consecrated it in 1913.

Other buildings include Stanley Mansions, Elm Park Mansions, Park Walk Primary School, and Jonathan Cooper Park Walk Gallery.

Paultons Square

Paultons Square is residential and lies between the King's Road and Danvers Street. It was named after George Stanley of Paultons, Hampshire, who married the eldest daughter of Sir Hans Sloane. Built between 1836 and 1840, the square stands on their land and is a Georgian terraced garden square. It is on the site of a former market garden and land previously owned by Sir Thomas More and Sir John Danvers. The houses surrounding it are Grade II listed. The square features a central lawn enclosed by metal railings and is accessible only to local residents.

The street has two early 'Chelsea' road signs and a very old and battered black-and-white road sign that reads: 'Paultons Square Leading To Danvers Street'.

Paultons House is here at the King's Road eastern end (289 King's Road), and there is a blue plaque that reads: 'English Heritage Jean Rhys 1890–1979 Writer lived here in Flat 22 1936–1938'.

No.9: The author Gavin Maxwell lived here, and admirers of his work regularly visit the house. A blue plaque to his honour states: 'Gavin Maxwell 1914–1969 Naturalist and Writer Lived Here 1961–1965'.

No.48: There are blue plaques to Samuel Beckett, the winner of the 1969 Nobel Prize for Literature, who lived at this house from 1933–4. The plaque states:

ENGLISH HERITAGE
JEAN RHYS
1890 - 1979
Writer
lived here
in Flat 22
1936 - 1938

'English Heritage Samuel Beckett 1906–1989 Dramatist and Author Lived Here in 1934'.

A second blue plaque reads: 'English Heritage Patrick Blackett 1897–1974 Physicist and Scientific Advisor live here 1953–1969'.

Paultons Street

Paultons Street is small and joins Paultons Square with Old Church Street. Nos. 1–8 are late-Georgian terraced houses.

Pavilion Road

Pavilion Road is London's longest mews and runs parallel to Sloane Street. Formerly Victorian stable blocks, it has been transformed into a mix of residential, artisan studios and restaurants.

Bellville Sassoon was formerly located along here and served most of the female members of the royal family, as well as many prominent entertainers and socialites over the years. It is now located at 18 Culford Gardens in Chelsea.

No.30: Searcys, one of Britain's top catering firms, is here. This gorgeous townhouse is the venue to hire for all occasions.

A fire station was built here in June 1881.

Holy Trinity Church of England Primary School and Mica Gallery are located

site, adjoining the old churchyard of Chelsea Old Church, had previously contained a house for the parish clerk and the original schoolhouse, which had been built while Dr Richard Ward was Rector of Chelsea (1585–1615). The purpose of the school was defined as 'The Education of Poor Children in the knowledge and practice of the Christian religion'. By 1819, more than a hundred boys and girls were being clothed and educated there for free. The girls later moved to a house in Lordship Lane, and in c. 1825, when new schools were built in the King's Road, the old school building became a fire station and later a mission hall. It was rebuilt in 1890 as a church house but was destroyed by a bomb in 1941. A new parish centre has since been built on the site and is named Petyt House.

at the intersection of Pavilion Road and Cadogan Gardens. Also of note are Marland House, Herbert House and Hans House.

Pavilion Street

Pavilion Street is a short street linking Pavilion Road and Sloane Street. The Cadogan Hotel sits on the corner.

Petyt Place

Petyt Place is on the eastern side of the Chelsea Old Church and is a short row of houses. It was named in 1895 after lawyer and antiquarian William Petyt (1636–1707), who occupied a house nearby. He was Keeper of the Records at the Tower of London. In 1705, he rebuilt the parish school at his own expense. The

Petyward

Petyward is residential and runs west from Sloane Avenue to Elystan Street. It was named after the Pettiward family, who owned land in the vicinity in the seventeenth century. Marlow Court is here.

The Chelsea Police Station that was previously here closed on 1 December 2014.

Phene Street

Phene Street runs east from Oakley Street and was named after the eccentric Dr John Samuel Phene, who was responsible for development of this area. Some houses here have attractively

decorated colour and monochrome tiled entrances. One has an old boot scraper beside the entrance.

The Phene Arms public house is here and now serves as a restaurant. It was the favourite haunt of the great Northern Irish footballer George Best, with occasional visits by Rolling Stone Bill Wyman. A circular white plaque here has a central horned stag surrounded with the words 'Watney Combe Reid 1898'.

No.33: Novelist George Gissing (1857–1903) lived here from 1882–84, and there is a blue plaque affixed here by the Greater London Council to his honour.

The street has an early 'Chelsea' road sign and a much earlier, plain black-and-white sign titled 'Phene Street. S.W.', which is most probably Victorian.

Pond Place

Pond Place runs north to south, parallel with Sydney Street to the east. It marks the original old footpath at the edge of Chelsea Common, where a large pond existed. Apartments now stand on the pond site.

On the wall of the house at the junction of Pond Place and Bury Walk, on the Pond Place side, is a fine circular white Romanesque plaque of a mother and daughter playing flutes.

No.8: A plaster carving of a face is on the entrance here.

No.23: The Kingdom Hall of the Jehovah's Witnesses is here. There are four white plaques inset into the front wall, all of which were laid on 8 January 1908. They read as follows:

Plaque 1: 'Chelsea Temperance Society Founded 1837 To the Memory Of John Henry Brass Esq. President From 1885 to 1894 This Stone Was Laid By The Hon. William Sydney J.P. Mayor.'

Plaque 2: 'Chelsea Temperance Society Founded 1837 This Stone Was Laid by Henry J. Wright Esq. President.'

Plaque 3: 'Chelsea Temperance Society Founded 1837 This Stone Was Laid by

Samuel Henry Dauncey Esq. Vice-President'.

Plaque 4: 'Chelsea Temperance Society Founded 1837 To the Memory Of William Henry Anscombe (For Over 50 Years Secretary). This Stone Was Laid by His Nephew Frederick William Anscombe'.

Pont Street

Pont Street is a fashionable street of magnificent redbrick houses with very ornate entrances built in the 1880s. It is residential with some commercial establishments. It crosses Sloane Street, with Beauchamp Place to the west and Cadogan Place and Chesham Place to the east. There is a pre-1917 blue street sign here with white lettering that just says 'Pont Street, S.W.'

No.51: Politician Harry Crookshank, 1st Viscount Crookshank (1893–1961) lived here from 1937 until his death.

No.54: St Columba's Church was designed in the 1950s by architect Sir Edward Maufe (1883–1974), who also designed the brick Guildford Cathedral. It is one of the two London congregations of the Church of Scotland. The original St Columba's Church building of 1884 was destroyed on the night of 10 May 1941 during the Blitz.

No.57: The 57 Pont Street Hotel.

No.59: The Challoner Club, an exclusively Catholic gentleman's club.

No.75: The Cadogan Hotel, where the actress Lillie Langtry (1852–1929) lived from 1892 to 1897, is honoured by a blue plaque here. The building became part of the Cadogan Hotel in 1895, but Lillie stayed in her old bedroom even after it was taken over. Poet and playwright Oscar Wilde was arrested in room 118 of the hotel on 6 April 1895.

Pont Street Mews

Pont Street Mews is a private cul-de-sac approached through its arch off Walton Street, with no access to the general public. Built in 1879, the two- and three-storey properties are surrounded by a cobbled road surface. The residential properties were used initially as the stable and coach houses for the main homes on Pont Street.

Pooles Lane

Pooles Lane is a gated area of attractive houses on the eastern side of Lots Road that once followed the line of the canal northwards to the King's Road.

Queen's Elm Parade

Queen's Elm Parade is a small strip of road that runs south between Fulham Road and Chelsea Square. There are two road signs here, the highest of which reads 'Chelsea Cross'.

Queen's Elm Square

Queen's Elm Square contains gated residential buildings on the west side of Old Church Street just before it joins Fulham Road. It was built in 1904–06 for the Sloane Stanley Estate on a site behind The Queen's Elm public house. The houses overlook communal gardens and have an access road at the front. Behind are two-and-a-half-storey, neo-Tudor, half-timbered buildings that have remained virtually unchanged since they were built.

CHELSEA IN LITERATURE

Voguish Pont Street became shorthand for haughty views, and features in three works of fiction.

In P.G. Wodehouse's *The Code of the Woosters* (1938), Mrs Wintergreen, widow of the late Colonel H.H. Wintergreen and fiancée of Sir Watkyn Bassett, lives in Pont Street.

In Evelyn Waugh's novel *Brideshead Revisited* (1945), Pont Street is referred to as a place related to typical English snobbery. In the book, the character Julia and her friends say that 'it was "Pont Street" to wear a signet ring and to give chocolates at the theatre; it was "Pont Street" at a dance to say, "Can I forage for you?"'.

In Nancy Mitford's *Love in a Cold Climate* (1949), the heroine's aunt, who is bringing her up to mix in the best society, is said to 'keep her nose firmly to Pont Street'.

Sloane Square

CHELSEA STREETS *R & S*

In which you will meet Sir John Betjeman, Laurence Olivier, and the author of Dracula, *Bram Stoker. You'll also visit the fictional homes of James Bond and Mary Poppins, see a statue of a woman taking off her dress, the church where Charles Dickens married Catherine Hogarth, and see the hub of the 'Swinging Sixties' where The Rolling Stones and Eric Clapton used to watch the fashion parade of the King's Road.*

Radnor Walk

Radnor Walk is a residential street that runs south off the King's Road. The houses here are mid-to-late Victorian and the street is part of the Royal Hospital Conservation Area. The street was named in 1937 after the Earl of Radnor, who had a large mansion here in the seventeenth century called Danvers House. He died in 1685, and his widow, Letitia, remarried Charles, Lord Cheyne, Lord of Chelsea Manor. They lived at Radnor House until Cheyne's death in 1698. The house was demolished in 1888.

No.29: The house here has a blue plaque on the front wall that states: 'Sir John Betjeman 1906–1984 Poet Laureate And Conservationist Lived Here 1973–1984'.

Ralston Street

Ralston Street runs south-east of St Leonard's Terrace and is residential. Bertrand Russell (1872–1970) and his first wife, Alys Pearsall Smith, rented No.4 briefly in the spring of 1905. Russell was a philosopher, logician, mathematician, historian, writer, social critic and political activist. He was elected a Fellow of the Royal Society in 1908, opposed Britain's participation in the First World War, and in 1918 was imprisoned in Brixton jail for six months. In 1921, he married his second wife, Dora, at the Chelsea Registry Office, just six days after his divorce from Alys. In 1934, he was awarded the Sylvester Medal of the Royal Society and the De Morgan Medal from the London Mathematical Society. He was re-elected a Fellow of Trinity College in 1944 and was awarded the Nobel Prize for Literature in 1950.

Ramsay Mews

Ramsay Mews is tucked away between shops on the south side of the King's Road, opposite Dovehouse Green, and is a private, cobbled cul-de-sac. It is located on the site of an original mews but has been redeveloped to a degree that it no longer contains any surviving mews properties. At some point between October 1940 and June 1941, a high-explosive bomb fell just off Bramerton Street, south-west of the mews. No access is permitted to the general public.

Rawlings Street

Rawlings Street is a tree-lined residential street that runs north of Cadogan Street to Milner Street. It is named in memory of Charles Rawlings, who left £400 for the parish poor when he died in 1862. Orford House is here, and there are a few commercial buildings on the Cadogan Street end.

Red Anchor Close

The name Red Anchor Close suggests the nearby location of the Chelsea Porcelain Works in Lawrence Street, which had a red anchor as one of its maker's marks. It is a modern mews-style, gated and part-paved cul-de-sac approached through an entrance under a building on Old Church Street. It contains seven residential properties.

Redburn Street

Redburn Street is residential and runs east to west below Radnor Walk. The street has a very early blue sign with white lettering that is possibly Victorian.

Redesdale Street

Redesdale Street runs east to west below and parallel with Redburn Street, and was named after Lord Redesdale, who lived in Lindsey House on Cheyne Walk. The road name was approved in 1871.

Riley Street – *See Cremorne Estate in the Miscellany.*

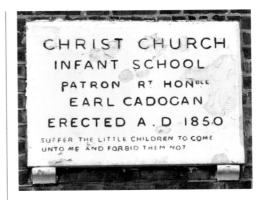

Robinson Street

Robinson Street is a small street east of Flood Street. The Christ Church of England Primary School is on this street and has an old plaque on the wall that says: 'Christ Church Infant School Patron Rt Hon.ble Earl Cadogan Erected A.D. 1850. Suffer the little children to come unto me and forbid them not'. The street has an extended pavement area around the school entrances for the children's safety.

Ropers Gardens A

Ropers Gardens are on the Chelsea Embankment, west of Old Church Street. It was once an orchard. German bombing destroyed the buildings here, and an attractive sunken garden was created on the site featuring sheltered seating and enclosed grass and shrub areas. An ancient cherry tree is the garden's most outstanding feature. It was planted to celebrate the visit of Gunji Koizumi, who introduced judo to the UK.

A foundation stone here states: 'Metropolitan Borough of Chelsea The worshipful The Mayor Councillor Lady Heath laid this stone on 11th March 1964 to commemorate the construction of Roper's Gardens on the site of buildings destroyed by a parachute

mine on 17th April 1941. The site of this garden formed part of the marriage gift of Thomas More to William and Margaret Roper in 1521. Architects Bridgwater Shepherd & Epstein. Contractors Marshall-Andrews & Co'.

There is another plaque here as follows: 'These trees are in memory of Basil Marsden-Smedley 1901–1964 who loved and served Chelsea'.

The gardens also feature a Jacob Epstein stone relief called *Woman Taking Off Her Dress*. It was unveiled in June 1972. Its alternative title is 'A Woman Walking Against the Wind'.

On the back of the stone relief is the following inscription: 'Unveiled by Admiral Sir Caspar John G.C.B. 3rd June 1972. This carving by Jacob Epstein commemorates the years 1909–1914 when he lived and worked in a studio on this site, which was originally Sir Thomas More's orchard. This setting was designed by Stephen Gardiner'.

In 1965, the bronze statue of a naked woman called *The Awakening* by Gilbert Ledward was erected in the centre of the garden. He was an English sculptor born nearby. The plaque here states: '"Awakening" – Gilbert Ledward O.B.E. R.A. 1888–1960'.

Ropers Orchard

Ropers Orchard is a cul-de-sac off of Danvers Street.

Rosemoor Street

Rosemoor Street is a residential street that lies east off Draycott Avenue and parallel with Cadogan Street. It was originally named Little Orford Street. Rosemoor refers to a Cadogan residence in Torrington, Devon.

Royal Avenue

Royal Avenue runs south off the King's Road and west of Duke of York Square.

It was designed by Sir Christopher Wren (1632–1723). The road was never finished but the section that remains was completed in 1694. It was enclosed by a hedge and a small white fence, and by 1748 it was known as White Stile Walk. The central part was filled with gravel and lined with grass verges and horse chestnuts. The terraces were laid out between 1817 and 1848, and a central garden was created giving an unrestricted view of the Royal Hospital. This aspect continues to be protected.

On the junction with the King's Road was the Aylesbury Dairy, one of many small dairies in the area that existed before the First World War. They would deliver milk, butter and many other dairy products as often as two or three times a day.

There is a large, oblong blue plaque that reads as follows: 'Royal Borough of Kensington and Chelsea Royal Avenue was laid out by Sir Christopher Wren in 1682 as a direct route from the Royal Hospital to Kensington Palace. In 1685 King Charles II the Sponsor died, by which time only the first section as far as the King's Road was completed, and the full scheme never materialised. The houses on either side were built in the early part of the nineteenth century'.

In the 1960s, owing to their dilapidated state, demolition was considered, but luckily only Nos.1–15 were removed. As well as being the fictional home of James Bond, several notable people have lived here, as follows:

No.18: The artist Bernard Stern (1920–2002) lived here, followed more recently by the architect Richard Rogers.

No.29: The blue plaque here in honour of film director Joseph Losey (1909–84) states that he lived here between 1966 and 1984.

No.30: Joseph Losey, the American film director, came to England during the McCarthy era to escape the Communist witch-hunt. One of his best-known films, *The Servant* (1963), starring Dirk Bogarde, Susannah York and Edward Fox, was set in an empty house opposite his own.

No.36: This house was rented to Dante Gabriel Rossetti for his mistress Fanny Cornforth.

Royal Hospital Road

Royal Hospital Road runs north-east from the Chelsea Embankment to Chelsea Bridge Road. It was earlier named Queens Road. To the south is the Chelsea Physic Garden, and to the south-west is the Royal Hospital Chelsea, hence the name. The street has a very early, plain black-and-white road sign.

The National Army Museum is located here, having been established in 1961 to display the history of the British Army from the reign of Henry VII to recent wars involving British troops. The first building was completed in 1971 and additional facilities have followed. The museum's collections include uniforms, 40,000 books, 25,000 prints and drawings, and 500,000 photographs.

Just before Tite Street and to the north, there is a plaque inset in a wall off of the pavement area that reads: 'This face of this wall at this position indicates the western boundary line of the property belonging to the Royal Hospital'.

The Chelsea Pensioner public house was on the corner of Smith Street in 1904.

In c. 1862, the artist James Abbott McNeill Whistler took rooms in a house here.

No.19: An amazing five-storey Dutch-style house.

No.66: The Chelsea Physic Garden doorway. However, it is not accessible to the general public.

There is a wall plaque here, headed 'Physic Place 1988'.

Little Cheyne House is here, as is a Grade II listed building dated 1876, with a plaque.

Rysbrack Street

Rysbrack Street is a plain street with a few residential properties. It runs east from Basil Street to Pavilion Road. John Michael Rysbrack (1693–1770) is the sculptor of the statue of Sir Hans Sloane which stands in the Chelsea Physic Garden.

St Leonard's Terrace

St Leonard's Terrace runs parallel to and south of the King's Road, joining Duke of York Square to the east, and is north of Burton Court, part of the Royal Hospital Chelsea. The terrace was built by John Tombs, who came from Upton St Leonards near Cheltenham (hence the name). The houses here were built in 1765. A map of 1769 shows the surrounding land marked in the name of Richard Green and was for many years the property of the Green family. In a map from 1836, this land was known as Green's Row. The new road name was approved in 1845.

In 1856, Richard Redgrave of the Department of Science and Art designed an ornate pillar box for use in London and other large cities. The design was improved in 1859, and this became the

St Leonard's Terrace

First National Standard pillar box. Green was adopted as the standard colour for the early Victorian postboxes. Between 1866 and 1879, the hexagonal Penfold postbox became the standard design for pillar boxes, and it was during this period that red was adopted. There is a good example here.

The street has two early road signs. One is blue with white lettering and is probably Victorian.

Sir Laurence Olivier moved from Cheyne Walk to a house here.

No.14: There is a decorated doorway with an extraordinary door knocker here.

No.18: This house has a blue plaque to the Irish novelist, actor and theatre manager Abraham 'Bram' Stoker (1847–1912). He lived here from 1896 to 1906, having moved from 27 Cheyne Walk. He was the author of the immortal legend of the vampire Count Dracula and a great friend of Sir Arthur Conan Doyle (the author of the Sherlock Holmes stories).

No.21: The singer Joyce Grenfell (1910–79) lived here after her marriage.

No.28: Joyce Grenfell lived here before her marriage in 1929.

St Loo Avenue

St Loo Avenue runs east from Chelsea Manor Street and parallel with the Chelsea Embankment. It was named after Sir William St Loo, Captain of the Guards to Queen Elizabeth I, and the third husband of Elizabeth 'Bess' of Hardwick (1518–1608). Bess' fourth husband was the Earl of Shrewsbury, who owned Shrewsbury House (later renamed Alston House), which stood near Oakley Street. The house was built in 1530 and was gradually demolished after 1813, having stood derelict. The street has two identical pre-1917, plain black-and-white road signs.

St Loo Court is a residential building.

The residential Rossetti Garden Mansions were built in 1898 and have highly decorated entrances.

St Luke's Gardens

St Luke's Gardens is immediately to the south of St Luke's Church in Sydney Street, and has tombs and gravestones bordering it in places. There are many wooden seats here dedicated to various parishioners. Grey squirrels are numerous, to the delight of the children who sometimes picnic here with their parents.

In late 2016, the Gardens were restored to their Georgian splendour after railings removed during the Second World War were replaced. The project was a collaboration between the Royal

Borough of Kensington and Chelsea and Cadogan. It was celebrated with Lady Cadogan unveiling a plaque at the new railings that separate St Luke's Church from the gardens.

St Luke's Street

St Luke's Street is behind St Luke's Church and runs parallel to Sydney Street. At Nos.30–1 is St Luke's House, which incorporates St Luke's Hall, a very popular hall used for children's parties, group meetings and exercise classes. The Ringrose Kindergarten is here too, where, together with other local celebrities' children, Bill Wyman's three daughters were schooled in the late 1990s. The school plaque is on the wall with a central ring of roses and the lettering 'Ringrose Kindergarten Chelsea'.

Shafto Mews

Shafto Mews is a cobbled cul-de-sac approached through its own arch on Cadogan Square, opposite Clabon Mews. It was originally the stable and coach houses for the main houses in Cadogan Square and is now residential.

Shalcomb Street

Shalcomb Street is residential and runs north from the King's Road, parallel with Edith Grove to the west. It is named after a village on the Isle of Wight.

Shawfield Street

Running south from the King's Road, parallel to Flood Street in the west, Shawfield Street is residential apart from a few commercial properties at the entrance to the King's Road. The Barbieri family's renowned coffee shop, the Picasso, was on the junction with the King's Road. In the 'Swinging Sixties', the Picasso's open front made it a good meeting place for regulars, including members of The Rolling Stones, Eric Clapton, and other rock-and-rollers, who could observe the passing parade of Chelsea's fashionably clad bright young things. Many mourned the passing of the Picasso in 2009, when changing times brought about its closure.

Shawfield House is a redeveloped gas engineering works halfway down Shawfield Street.

Slaidburn Street

Slaidburn Street is a cul-de-sac that runs north from the King's Road, parallel with Edith Grove to the west, and is residential. The Chelsea football team's 1970 FA Cup triumph against Leeds

United was celebrated with a street party here. It was the hub for Chelsea's supporters and decked out in blue. Just as the club has enjoyed a transformation, so has the street. In 1899, it was described by social reformer Charles Booth as 'one of the worst streets in London — drunken, rowdy, constant trouble to police: many broken patched windows, open doors, and drink-sodden women at windows'.

Sloane Avenue

Sloane Avenue runs south from Fulham Road to the King's Road. It is a large, busy street full of commercial properties and residential buildings that include the Sloane Avenue Mansions and Nell Gwynn House. The street was named after Sir Hans Sloane, who was Chelsea's Lord of the Manor in 1712 and lived in Chelsea from 1741 until his death.

There is a plaque for Marlborough Road School, which opened in 1878.

The School Board for London was set up under the Public Elementary Education Act of 1870 for the whole of the city. Marlborough Primary School is still on that site. The main entrance is on Draycott Avenue.

Sloane Court East

Sloane Court East is south of Sloane Square and runs parallel with Lower Sloane Street, which is situated just to the east. It is residential, and the mansions here were completed around 1890. The narrow streets of squalid houses that used to stand here were transformed into wide avenues of mansions. The street has an early 'Chelsea' road sign.

In July 1944, a V-1 flying bomb (or Doodlebug) exploded at the north-west end of the road, close to the intersection with Turk's Row. It destroyed the surrounding housing units and started a fire, becoming the single greatest incidence of loss of life for American servicemen and the second worst V-1 incident in London. The exact

death toll from the blast remains unclear, but at least 65 American servicemen and nine civilians lost their lives. Glenn Miller, the U.S. Army bandleader, had been stationed at Sloane Court, but had left the day before the bombing.

Sloane Court West

Sloane Court West is also south of Sloane Square, running parallel with Lower Sloane Street, and is residential. The street has two very early, black road signs with white lettering, which are possibly Victorian.

No. 11: Sloane Court Clinic. It was built on the site of a public house called the Royal Hospital Inn, which stood on the left-hand corner from the mid-eighteenth century until its demolition in the late nineteenth century.

Sloane Gardens

Sloane Gardens is residential and runs south of Sloane Square to Lower Sloane Street. An innovation of the Cadogan Estate management in the 1980s was to instigate external stone and brickwork cleaning of their properties by new leaseholders. This immediately improved the buildings, which are mostly redbrick. They are characterised by a variety of highly decorative entrances, some with winged dragons and heads.

No. 1: The Sloane Gardens Mansions were built *c.* 1880s/90s on Cadogan estate land, replacing many small, overcrowded and run-down houses. There is an early road sign here.

Sloane Square Ⓜ

Sloane Square is at the eastern end of the King's Road, and forms the boundary between the two largest aristocratic estates in London: the Grosvenor and Cadogan estates. It is named after Sir Hans Sloane (1660–1753), whose heirs owned the land at the time. Henry Holland was the eighteenth-century builder and architect who developed Hans Town, the entire area between the King's Road and Brompton Road. Holland leased eighty-five acres of farmlands known as Blacklands from Lord Cadogan in 1771, although building did not begin for another eight or nine years. Holland retained a generous portion for his own house, the Pavilion, and its extensive gardens, most of which later became Cadogan Square. When first laid out, the centre of Sloane Square was no more than a grass patch surrounded by a chain fence, later replaced by railings. The Queen Charlotte's Volunteers were drilled here and boys also played cricket on it. At this time, there were fields almost all the way to the site of Victoria Station.

Sloane Square

On the north-west corner of the square stands a marble drinking fountain, originally erected on Elgin Road in 1882. It was reinstalled here a year later. The plinth facing south states 'Metropolitan Drinking Fountain and Cattle Trough Association' (similar to the one at Chelsea Old Town Hall). The plinth facing north states: 'To a revered husband & father from his loving wife & children'.

The Venus Fountain, which stands in the centre of the square, was designed by sculptor Gilbert Ledward and constructed in 1953. It depicts Venus, and on the basin section of the fountain is a relief that depicts King Charles II and Nell Gwynn by the Thames, a reference to a nearby house that Nell Gwynn had used. The fountain is Grade II listed.

The Royal Court Theatre opened on 24 December 1868. It was rebuilt in 1888, and there were successful runs of plays by George Bernard Shaw, among others. Eventually, however, competition from the movies took its toll, and in 1932 the theatre closed down. From 1935, the building was used as a cinema. It suffered greatly in an air raid on Sloane Square underground station on 12 November 1940, when thirty people were killed and fifty injured.

The theatre was rebuilt and reopened on 2 July 1952 under the management of the London Theatre Guild. It was a considerable success, with productions including *The Threepenny Opera* and *Airs on a Shoestring*. The turning point in the theatre's reputation was in 1956, when George Devine and the English Stage Company took over. Their management saw first performances of John Osborne's *Look Back in Anger* and *The Entertainer*,

as well as new plays by Arnold Wesker, Harold Pinter and Samuel Beckett. Aided by Lottery funding, the Royal Court has had a major overhaul, and the front is highly decorated.

At the south-eastern corner is Sloane Square underground station (District and Circle line), which opened on Christmas Eve 1868. Unfortunately for Chelsea, it was not possible to continue the line along the King's Road due to the nature of the land.

There is a large war memorial here dominated by a Portland stone cross. Below is inscribed 'Invictus Pax In Memory of the men and women of Chelsea who gave their lives in the Great War MDCCCCXIV MDCCCCXVIII and MCMXXXIX MCMXLV'.

Further west is a blue metal plaque set into the pavement that reads: 'The Royal Borough of Kensington & Chelsea Environment Award 1992'.

Nos. 7–12: Sloane Square Hotel, which is said to have been built in 1887 (although there's a plaque high above that states the building was built in 1895). The hotel is in the heart of the city's most affluent district, and offers a choice of bedrooms and suites, as well as access to the private Cadogan Gardens and tennis courts. There is a large black clock hanging above the entrance.

No. 15: A building titled 'Sloane Square' with a highly decorated entrance, featuring child angels and a heraldic plaque. High above there are two separate faces featured.

No.37: This property has a stone carving of a rampant horse dated 1677. I have previously seen this insignia on military badges.

Nos.50–2: This is the very popular Colbert restaurant, regularly frequented by a host of celebrities. It has a highly decorated entrance with the date 1899. Above the entrance is a devil's head.

The Peter Jones department store dominates the west end of the square. It was founded in 1877 by Peter Rees Jones, the son of a Welsh hatmaker, who had arrived in London ten years earlier. In 1900, the business was doing so well that it was floated as a public company. By 1903, the annual profits had risen to £12,000 (£1 million in today's money). Jones sadly fell ill that year and died in 1905. A year later, it was bought by John Lewis. The present building, which

occupies an entire island site on the west side of Sloane Square, was built between 1932 and 1936.

Sloane Street

Sloane Street runs south from the eastern end of Fulham Road to Sloane Square. Spring Gardens dominate the eastern side of the lower half of the street. It is a major shopping street, with the Harvey Nichols department store at the northern end. The street has a number of residential apartment buildings that include Dorchester Court, Durley House, Fordie House, Grosvenor Court, Knowsley House and Sloane House. The Millennium Hotel is also here.

Just north of Sloane Square on the eastern side is the Church of the Holy and Undivided Trinity with Saint Jude (more commonly called Holy Trinity). Built in 1830 in a Gothic Revival style, the building lasted sixty years before it was replaced by the present building in 1890. The interior is based on

fifteenth-century Gothic architecture and is lit by magnificent stained-glass windows designed by Edward Burne-Jones and made by William Morris. The interior is decorated with marble and semi-precious stones. Beloved by John Betjeman, it was saved from extinction some years ago. The front entrance has a highly decorated plaque above the door.

Nos.3–4: The old Swan public house was still here in 1914.

No.42: Haden's House, where in 1847 James Abbott McNeill Whistler spent nearly a year living with his sister and brother-in-law.

No.75: The Cadogan Hotel, which became infamous shortly after opening for the arrest of Oscar Wilde in room 118 on 6 April 1895.

No.76: Charles Wentworth Dilke (1843–1911), Chelsea's member of parliament from 1868 to 1886, was born and lived here, his family home, his entire life. He was anti-monarchist when it was unusual to be so, and criticised Queen Victoria for not paying income tax. His downfall came unexpectedly in August 1885, when Donald Crawford, the MP for Lanark, sued his wife for divorce on the grounds of her adultery with Dilke. He was then forced to withdraw from public life.

No.95: Traveller, archaeologist and diplomat Gertrude Bell (1868–1926) lived here. There is a blue plaque here in her honour.

Nos.187a & 189: Mme Leah Nathalie opened her fan-making shop here in the mid-1880s. She continued in business until 1912, by which time fans were no longer an essential fashion accessory.

Sloane Terrace

The Christian Scientists built a capacious and lavishly furnished church on Sloane Terrace in 1905–7. The building's architect was Robert Chisholm, whose very original style drew on Byzantine, Romanesque, Indian and Islamic influences. The church closed in 1996. It was subsequently acquired by the Cadogan Estate and reopened in 2004 as Cadogan Hall, which stages classical, jazz, folk and world music events, hosts debates and conferences, and serves as the London home of the Royal Philharmonic Orchestra.

Smith Street 🅛

Smith Street runs south from the King's Road and cuts through Royal Hospital Road. It was named after Thomas Smith, a former vintner, who was the builder of this street *c.* 1800. Thomas Faulkner (1777–1855) moved his bookshop, renamed the Cadogan Library, here, advertising 'an extensive and valuable collection of works in history, divinity, topography, antiquities, voyages and travels, lives and memoirs, poetry and drama'. He was the first major historian of Chelsea and a long-time resident. In 1810, he published *An Historical and Topographical Description of Chelsea and its Environs,* which he followed in 1829 with a revised two-volume edition. One historian warned that Faulkner did commit many errors in his work on Chelsea, although he acknowledged the public's debt to him.

No.4: Above the door here is a king's head with a crown.

No.23: The Phoenix public house lies on the junction with Woodfall Street.

No.33: The decorated plaque on the wall here reads: 'The Royal Borough of Kensington & Chelsea Environment Award 1994'.

No.50: This is the house where Pamela Lyndon Travers (1899–1996) lived for seventeen years. She is remembered for creating the world's best-known nanny, Mary Poppins. The house was the inspiration behind the Banks' family house in the Disney adaptation of the book. It was also here that Travers raised her adopted son, Camillus, and where she resided during her infamous film negotiations with Disney. The character Mary Poppins starred in a series of eight books, but it was the Disney film starring Julie Andrews and Dick Van Dyke that skyrocketed the Mary Poppins character, and an unwilling Travers, to international fame. She is celebrated here with a blue plaque.

Smith Terrace

Smith Terrace is a residential street that runs south of the King's Road and parallel between Smith Street and Radnor Walk. The Chelsea Synagogue is on the site of an earlier synagogue that had stood there since 1916. The present synagogue was consecrated in November 1959.

South Parade

South Parade is a street that runs parallel with Fulham Road, between Old Church Street and Dovehouse Street. It is home to the Brompton Hospital Nurses Home and the Trafalgar Chambers. There is a stone

wall plaque that reads: 'This stone was laid by N.W. Hubbard, Chairman of the Fire Brigade Committee of the London County Council November 11th, 1892'.

Sprimont Place

Sprimont Place runs diagonally between Sloane Avenue and Elystan Place. In 1937, it was named after Nicholas Sprimont, the manager of the Chelsea Porcelain Works from 1745–69. The street has an early 'Chelsea' road sign.

No.7: A blue plaque here states: 'George Seferis 1900–1971 Poet Nobel Prizewinner Greek Ambassador Lived Here'.

No.17: This property has an amusing plaque beside the door of a chained dog, headed: 'Cave Canem' ('Beware of the dog').

Stackhouse Street

Stackhouse Street is a small, ugly street named in 1938 to commemorate the Rev. Thomas Stackhouse (1677–52), a Chelsea resident. The only redeeming feature here is the Pavilion car park.

Stadium Street

Stadium Street runs level with Lots Road and is named after part of Cremorne

Oscar Wilde

Oscar Wilde, poet and playwright, spent plenty of time in Chelsea and its environs. It was where he wrote many of his greatest works, but was also the scene of one of the most defining moments in his life.

Oscar Wilde married Constance Lloyd in 1884 and they moved into No.34 Tite Street, a modest house back in the 1880s. It was in this house where he wrote his most famous works, including *The Picture of Dorian Gray* (1891) and the plays *Lady Windermere's Fan* (1892) and *A Woman of No Importance* (1893). He also commuted from the house to the editorial offices of *The Lady's World* magazine, which he edited between 1887 and 1889. During this time, he convinced the publisher to change the name to *The Woman's World*, to immediate success.

On 6 April 1895, in room 118 of the Cadogan Hotel on Sloane Street, Oscar Wilde was arrested on charges of sodomy and gross indecency. The events in the room were immortalised by the poet laureate John Betjeman in his tragic poem 'The Arrest of Oscar Wilde at the Cadogan Hotel'.

The subsequent trials bankrupted Wilde, and the contents of his house on Tite Street were auctioned off to raise money. During the chaos of the auction, the house was virtually ransacked, and many manuscripts were lost. He left Tite Street for Newgate Prison on 25 May 1895, not emerging to freedom until 18 May 1897, when he sailed to France, never to return to Britain.

REMARKABLE RESIDENTS

House gardens, which were developed by Charles Random in the 1830s as the 'National Sporting Club', or 'The Stadium'. (*see also Cremorne Estate in the Miscellany*).

Stewart's Grove

Stewart's Grove is a narrow and plain mews-style through road. It runs between Fulham Road and Cale Street, parallel with Bury Walk, and has a mixture of residential and commercial buildings. It was named after William Stewart, an auctioneer of Piccadilly, who leased land from the Cadogan family in 1810 and began to build on it in 1827. In 1912, two schools were built here. They were amalgamated in 1959, and in 1962 the Daughters of the Cross were withdrawn after almost a century of devoted work. In 1963, the school was classified as a four-form entry grammar school admitting only boys, and in 1970 it was moved to its present site in Brompton.

At some point between October 1940 and June 1941, a number of

high-explosive bombs fell on to Sydney Street, next to Stewart's Grove, and caused damage. The buildings here were built around 1886.

The Royal Marsden School and Stewart's House are here, and there's a plaque on a corner wall headed 'L.D 1886'.

No.1: Artist Dominick Elwes (1931–85) was one of Lord Lucan's closest friends from his Eton schooldays. In September 1975, less than a year after the murder of Lucan's children's nanny, Sandra Rivett, and Lucan's infamous disappearance, Elwes was found dead here. At forty-four, he had been hounded to death – critics said – by some of Lucan's vicious circle of gambling cronies.

No.7: This house has a beautiful black decorated door.

Swan Walk

Swan Walk runs from Chelsea Embankment north to the Royal Hospital Road. The general public's entrance to the Chelsea Physic Garden is here.

Beside the Physic Garden on Swan Walk is the site of the Old Swan Inn, a popular London resort that was visited a number of times by Samuel Pepys. It was also the finishing post for Doggett's Coat and Badge Wager, a race for apprentice boatmen on the river and the oldest rowing race in the world. Here, the Chelsea Society was formed on 1 April 1927 to 'protect and foster' the amenities of Chelsea. It began at a meeting held in a drawing room at Wentworth House, Swan Walk, which was the residence of Mary, Countess of Lovelace. It was the enthusiasm of Reginald Blunt, son of the Rector of Chelsea, that made its formation possible, and he devoted much

ANNO XXIV
GEORGIVS V
REX

The Gateways, Scrimont Place

of the last seventeen years of his long life to the affairs of the Society.

Mary Astell (1668–1731), well-educated by her clergyman uncle, came to London when she was twenty and settled at a house in Swan Walk. In 1694, her book *Serious Proposal to the Ladies for the Advancement of their True and Greatest Interest* was published. She urged women to spend more time in acquiring knowledge rather than spending hours at mirrors. In 1709, she withdrew from public life and founded a charity school for girls in Chelsea. She died of breast cancer in Swan Walk in 1731, and was buried at Chelsea Old Church. Astell is commemorated on a plaque which was unveiled on the east wall of More's Chapel on the South on 27 October 1934.

Elizabeth Blackwell (1688–1758) lived in Swan Walk from 1734, and appears on the plaque dedicated to distinguished Chelsea women affixed to the chapel in 1934. Blackwell is known for her 500-odd depictions of the plants in the Physic Garden, which she engraved and coloured herself, with the encouragement of the Keeper of the Garden and Sir Hans Sloane. These were published in 1737 as *The Curious Herbal*. Her husband, Alexander, whom she had

supported financially by her labours, went off to Sweden, where he was arrested for treason and tortured before being executed. Elizabeth survived him by eleven years and is buried in the churchyard of All Saints Church.

No. 1: The writer Marguerite Radclyffe Hall (1880–1943) lived here in 1916.

Sydney Street

Sydney Street runs north between the King's Road and Fulham Road. It is named after the Rt. Hon. Thomas Townsend, later Viscount Sydney (1733–1800), who was the Paymaster General of the Royal Hospital in 1767. In 1818, a decision was made to erect a new church in Chelsea. The burial ground there seemed appropriate. Building began in 1820 and St Luke's Church was consecrated in 1824, though the projected spire was never built. The Duke of Wellington had been due to lay the foundation stone, but because of indisposition, his brother, Dr Wellesley, the Rector of Chelsea, did the honours. The church, designed by James Savage, is an early exercise in Gothic Revival. The blue church clock is set in a diamond shape on the church tower and has Roman numerals.

View of Swan Walk from the Chelsea Physic Garden

During an air raid in the Second World War, this house and others nearby were destroyed (*see the wall plaque in Dovehouse Green for details*).

Public toilets used to stand on the west side as the street is entered from the King's Road. They're now gone and boarded up, although the stone entrances still exist.

In 1836 Charles Dickens was married here to Catherine Hogarth, whose parents lived on Fulham Road. At that time, the north end of the road was known as Robert Street, and by 1839 it was called Upper Robert Street. By October 1847, however, the whole street had been renamed Sydney Street. Many of the houses here were built during the 1860s and 1870s. Around 1900, in the days of the early motor-buses, bicycles and boaters, St Luke's Infirmary and the workhouse were here.

The main entrance of Royal Brompton Hospital is here, and began life as a single building in Smith Street, Chelsea. It was founded by solicitor Philip Rose and opened in 1842. Two years later, the Prince Consort laid the foundation stone for the mock-Tudor building, designed by F.J. Francis, on the Kensington side of Fulham Road. In recent years, it has been turned into apartments. When the National Health Service was established in 1948, the Royal Brompton Hospital became the centre of expertise for dealing with chest diseases. In 1982, the hospital moved to a large new building in Sydney Street.

No.31: Bertrand Russell and his second wife Dora lived here from November 1921, when he stood as a Labour Party parliamentary candidate.

No.70: The very popular Sydney Arms public house, with its hanging sign of a jockey.

No.125: The main entrance of the Chelsea Gardener, which lies north of Chelsea Farmers Market.

Chelsea Farmers Market consists of shops and restaurants at the north end of Dovehouse Green. To the north is a magnificent market garden that sports a small restaurant.

Symons Street

Symons Street runs east from Cadogan Gardens into Sloane Square. The Peter Jones department store has a side entrance here. The street has a very early, plain black-and-white road sign that could be Victorian.

No.4: This building has an unmarked but highly decorated metal door with a circular plaque reading: 'The Royal Borough of Kensington & Chelsea Environment Award 2002'.

Chelsea Reach and the World's End estate beyond

CHELSEA STREETS T TO Z

In which you will meet the writer Mark Twain, the artists John Singer Sargent, Augustus John, Henry Tonks and James Abbott McNeill Whistler, the author Marguerite Radclyffe Hall, Britain's first de facto prime minister, and the home of Oscar Wilde.

Tadema Road

Tadema Road is west of Lots Road and runs south to Burnaby Street. It was likely named after the Dutch artist Sir Lawrence Alma-Tadema (1836–1912), who settled in England in 1870. It is residential.

St John's Church, consecrated in 1876, stood on the junction of Ashburnham Road and Tadema Road. The Luftwaffe destroyed it, and the site was later used for housing.

No.35: Hob Mews.

Tedworth Square

Residential Tedworth Square is between St Leonard's Terrace and Redburn Street. The Cadogan family acquired the land in 1753 upon the death of Hans Sloane, and the estate was divided between his two daughters, Sarah Stanley and Elizabeth Lady Cadogan. The square was laid out in 1871 on the original market gardens of Durham House. The north side was demolished in 1977 and rebuilt, while the central garden is well-kept and for private residents.

No.1: Tedworth House, which contains rented apartments.

No.15: Lillie Langtry (1853–1929) lived here at some point. Before becoming an actress, she was the mistress of the Prince of Wales, the future Edward VII. Before that, she was a decorous socialite and married to a shipowner. But it was her liaison with the future king that helped her in her stage career. She later sold this house to the famous cricketer Plum Warner. The renowned actress Mrs Patrick Campbell (1865–1940) lived here for a while and was a friend of George Bernard Shaw.

No.23: Mark Twain (born Samuel Langhorne Clemens) (1835–1910) was born in Minnesota, USA. In 1870, he married Olivia Langdon and began his new career as an author with a string of successful books, including *Roughing It* (1872), *The Adventures of Tom Sawyer* (1876), *A Tramp Abroad* (1880), *Life on the Mississippi* (1883) and *Huckleberry Finn* (1884). He went on an extended tour of Europe in 1891 and moved to this house with his family in the autumn of 1896, staying a year. This house was his refuge from his grief over the death of his daughter Susy. He is thought to be the first author to have sent a typed manuscript to a publisher. There is a blue plaque on the front wall in his honour.

LONDON COUNTY COUNCIL
SAMUEL L. CLEMENS
"MARK TWAIN"
1835 – 1910
American Writer
lived here in
1896–7

Tetcott Road

Tetcott Road is residential and runs south from the King's Road. It is parallel with Lots Road and leads to Westfield Park. The large building on the west has a decorated green plaque that states 'AD 1898.'

Thorndike Close

This small cul-de-sac runs south of the King's Road and has the Cheyne Children's Centre at No.10. The road sign here reads: 'Leading to Richard Castillo Day Centre.'

Ⓐ Tite Street

Tite Street is residential, runs north-west of the Embankment, and is crossed by the Royal Hospital Road. It terminates at Tedworth Square. It used to be called Calthorpe Place until 1875, when it was named after Sir William Tite MP (1798–1873), who had earlier been closely concerned with the construction of the Thames Embankment. Its occupants at various times make it one of the best-known thoroughfares.

During the eighteenth century, Gough House stood on the street's eastern side. It became a school in 1830 and then the Victoria Hospital for Children in 1866. The hospital was enlarged in the 1890s but was demolished in the 1960s. Services were transferred to St George's Hospital at Tooting. The site was then used for St Wilfrid's, a residential home for the elderly.

No.3: This is River House, which has a highly decorated entrance.

No.11: American artist John Singer Sargent (1856–1925) lived and died here, but had his studio at No.31 (see below).

No.13: James Abbott McNeill Whistler rented this house in January 1881. He married E.W. Goodwin's widow Beatrix in 1888, but left London in 1892 and briefly moved to Paris.

No.29: St Wilfrid's residential home for the elderly. It was established in 1869 as St Wilfrid's in Cale Street, Chelsea. It moved to Tite Street in 1976 and was registered as a care home.

No.30: A blue plaque on the wall reads as follows: 'Philip Arnold Heseltine Peter Warlock 1894–1930 Composer Lived Here.'

Peter Warlock
Composer
1894–1930
Philip Arnold
Heseltine

lived here

GREATER LONDON COUNCIL

NO.31: This was the studio of John Singer Sargent, who became one of the most important portrait painters of his time. Many famous people came to sit for him in his studio here, including actress Ellen Terry. At his parties in Tite Street, he introduced the music of his friend Gabriel Faure, and later that of Percy Grainger. A plaque is inset on the front wall here that reads: 'John S. Sargent, RA who was born in Florence Jan. 12, MDCCCLVI (1856). Lived and worked 24 years in this house and died here April 15 MCMXXV (1925)'.

NO.32: This house has a plaque between the windows decorated with plants.

NO.33: This house is named The Studios. Artist Augustus John (1878–1961) lived here intermittently from 1940 until 1958.

The interior designer David Milnaric lived here throughout the 1960s and 1980s. He designed interiors for celebrities.

including Lord Rothschild, Mick Jagger, Eric Clapton and Bill Wyman's Gedding Hall in Suffolk.

NO.34: Oscar Wilde, who married Constance Lloyd in 1884, moved to this modest house, where he wrote his most famous works. He commuted daily from the house to the editorial offices of *The Lady's World* magazine in Charing Cross after he took on the editorship. He persuaded the publisher to change the magazine's name to *The Woman's World*, which was an immediate success. In 1891, Wilde's *The Picture of Dorian Gray* was published, followed by a string of successful plays, including *Lady Windermere's Fan* and *A Woman of No Importance*. Before his trial, the contents of Wilde's house were sold to raise money. In the disorder of the auction, the house was virtually ransacked, and many valuable manuscripts were lost or destroyed.

After leaving prison, Wilde moved to the Continent and died in Paris from meningitis on 30 November 1900. His last words were apparently: 'That wallpaper is atrocious, one of us has got to go'.

His writing remains among the cleverest and wittiest in the English language, and there is a blue plaque on the building that states: 'Oscar Wilde 1854–1900 Wit and Dramatist Lived Here'.

A wonderful adaptation of Wilde's play *The Importance of Being Earnest* was released in 1952, directed by Anthony Asquith and starring Michael Redgrave, Edith Evans, Margaret Rutherford and Joan Greenwood. Joan Greenwood was born in Chelsea on 4 March 1921 and

...died of a heart attack in Chelsea on 28 February 1987. However, where she lived in the area is not known to me.

No.38: A blue plaque here states: 'Lord Haden-Guest 1877–1960 Physician Lived Here'.

No.39: An unusual house with decoration.

No.48: James Abbott McNeill Whistler engaged the services of architect E. W. Godwin in the mid-1870s to design a studio. The three-storey house became known as the White House, and was designed with a studio on the top floor and a 'school' on the second. Whistler declared himself bankrupt on 8 May 1879, and the White House and its contents were auctioned on 17 September 1879. There is decoration above the first-floor windows inscribed '1894'.

The White House

No.52: The house has three small sun faces above the entrance.

No.56: Shelley Court. The author Marguerite Radclyffe Hall (1880–1943) lived here at flat 7 from 1909–11.

Tryon Street

A curved and narrow residential street that runs north from the King's Road and parallel to Draycott Avenue to the east. It was previously part of Keppel Street, and was named in 1913 after the luckless seaman Vice Admiral Sir George Tryon. Sir George Tryon drowned in 1893 after his flagship, the *Victoria*, was rammed and sunk during fleet manoeuvres. Tyron and most of his crew perished. It is said that when the ship plummeted to the bottom, his ghost appeared at his house in Eaton Place, 1,500 miles away, where his wife was holding an at-home. Apparently witnessed by several hundred people, it strode with a grim visage and unseeing eyes across the room, then turned and vanished.

Nos.7–9: This was once the Just Men shop, which sold suede and leather suits, sweaters, flared trousers and tailored suits, but is no more.

No.19: There is a circular plaque on the front wall featuring a flying angel carrying two babies.

The Queen's Head public house is at the junction of Tryon Street and Elystan Place, but is now closed and boarded up.

Turk's Row

Turk's Row runs west from Chelsea Bridge Road to Franklin's Row. The residential road dates from around 1746. The name is thought to have derived from a coffee house sign. It became a slum area later. Established in 1951, the independent Garden House School is on Turk's Row.

St Jude's Church, built by George Basevi, was erected here in 1833/34. It closed in 1932 and was demolished in 1934, with the residential York House replacing it.

Upcerne Road

Upcerne Road is residential, and runs parallel and east of the northern end of Lots Road.

No.52: There is a highly decorated doorway here.

Upper Cheyne Row ▲ A

Upper Cheyne Row runs west from Oakley Street to Cheyne Row. The street has two early dark-blue metal road signs with white lettering titled 'Upper Cheyne Row, SW'.

No.2: This was formerly Cheyne House, the original of which was here in 1715. It was built for Elizabeth, Duchess of Hamilton, whose husband, the 4th Duke, was killed in a duel over her inheritance. During her short time here (1715–18), the young widow became intimately acquainted with the American writer Jonathan Swift, who was occupying lodgings locally.

The artist John Collett lived here from 1766–73, and fellow artist C.J. Lewis lived here from 1858–83. It is here where Dr Phene built his extraordinary 'chateau' in 1901–3.

No.14: Composer Percy Grainger (1882–1961) lived here from 1905–7.

No.16: This house has the date 1767 above the front window, although the house appears to be very modern.

No.22: A plaque on the wall here states: 'LCC Leigh Hunt 1784–1859 Essayist & Poet Lived Here'.

No.27: This cute, single-storied house has a pointed roof and a church-like door with a curved pointed top. The main building sits behind.

The street ends to the west with a charming little cul-de-sac of a few houses.

Uverdale Road

Uverdale Road is a pleasant tree-lined residential street that runs north between Lots Road and Ashburnham Road. It contains Westfield Park, a popular, well-designed neighbourhood park

Leigh Hunt

LCC
LEIGH HUNT
1784–1859
Essayist & Poet
Lived Here

Leigh Hunt (1784–1859), who lived at No.22 Upper Cheyne Row, is a largely forgotten writer but was highly regarded and notorious in his time. With his brother, he published a paper called *The Examiner*, which strongly advocated the reform of Parliament. In 1812, they were prosecuted for libelling the Prince Regent and were sentenced to two years in gaol. He was incarcerated at Clerkenwell, and many visitors came to see him.

He was on intimate terms with Lord Byron, Percy Bysshe Shelley and John Keats, and it was Hunt who, in 1816, championed the talents of the latter two poets to the nation. With his wife and their seven children, he sailed to Italy in 1821 to see Shelley and Byron, and he was present when Shelley's body was cremated there in 1822. Hunt wrote the epitaph on his tomb.

In 1833, Hunt returned to England with his family, and the following year he was instrumental in finding the house in Cheyne Row for his friend Thomas Carlyle. In 1844, he moved to Hammersmith, impoverished by a large family and a wife who had taken to drink. Friends came to his rescue, including Charles Dickens, who gave readings for him, and he obtained a royal grant of £200.

The Vale Ⓐ

The Vale is a residential street that runs north from the King's Road to Elm Park Road. It was built partly on a paddock belonging to Vale Grove, a villa in Old Church Street at the time. In 1909, the ceramist and potter William de Morgan gave a party to see the end of the old buildings, which were to be redeveloped the following year. In 1924, the residents attempted to change the name to Vale Avenue, but the application was refused.

There is a circular wall plaque inset here titled 'FMW 1912', and an oval copper door plaque titled 'Vale End'.

No.1: There is a stone plaque on the wall here titled: 'Henry Tonks FRCS 1862–

1937 Painter and Slade Professor in the University of London lived here from 1910 for the remainder of his life'.

No.2: The painter James Abbott McNeill Whistler lived here from 1886 to 1890.

No.4: Cameron Vale school is a co-educational pre-prep and preparatory school for children aged 4–11 years. Among others, Bill Wyman's and Mark Knopfler's daughters were educated here in the 1990s, together with Charlie Watts' granddaughter.

No.11: This house features a white circular plaque of four ladies and children.

No.19: This house has a decorated entrance. High above the window is the carving of a child's head.

No.21: Vale Court is here, which has a circular plaque of two ladies and a child.

between the King's Road and Lots Road. It encompasses grass, trees, shrubs, flowerbeds and a children's play area.

No.16: This is Walpole Street Practice, a dental surgery with a bright-blue door.

No.35: Walpole House. Sir Robert Walpole, Britain's first de facto prime minister, resided here from 1722 to 1745. It was used in August 1729 for a banquet in honour of Queen Caroline, wife of George II, and her children. Later, the house was converted by Sir John Soane into an infirmary for the Royal Hospital.

Walton Street

Walton Street runs parallel with and south of Brompton Road, joining Draycott Avenue in the west. It was named after George Walton Onslow, a trustee of the Henry Smith Charity based in Kensington. This street is partly residential and is filled with beautiful boutiques and galleries. It has an old blue road sign that is probably Victorian. The Marlborough Buildings are also here.

Nos.1–3: The Scalini restaurant, an exposed-brick trattoria hung with photos of celebrity patrons and serving classic Italian cuisine.

Nos.60–2: Opposite Scalini's is the old police station building.

Nos.111–13: The Eclipse Bar opened in 1998 and was at the forefront of the revolution in London's cocktail culture.

Waldron Mews

A small residential gated mews which has been redeveloped in part from an office block to provide residential housing.

Walpole Street

Walpole Street is residential and runs south-east from the King's Road to St Leonard's Terrace. It was named after Sir Robert Walpole (1676–1745), the first de facto prime minister, who lived at No.35 before moving to a house that became the Royal Hospital Infirmary.

No.26: This building has a highly decorated entrance, which has been boarded up. Winged lions holding books with Latin lettering are in the plasterwork.

No.27: The Russian House was initially built for an exhibition at the Crystal Palace between 1890 and 1900, and subsequently moved here. In 2015, it was up for sale for £16 million. There is a coloured oval plaque titled 'The Russian House 27' with various flowers below.

Wellington Square

Wellington Square runs south off of the King's Road and is residential. It was built c. 1852 and was named to commemorate the first Duke of Wellington, whose body lay in state at the Royal Hospital Chelsea in 1852 before his funeral at St Paul's Cathedral. His brother was Rector of Chelsea between 1805 and 1836. The street has an early road sign.

In the central park area is a delightfully decorated marble fountain featuring three children holding hands around the central column and another above the large dish with its arms around the column.

No.22: Wellington Cottage.

No.24: On 9 May 1870, Chelsea witnessed two murders by Walter Miller, a plasterer from Fulham. He murdered the Reverend Elias Huelin at this house (the clergyman owned several properties in Chelsea), robbing the victim of cash and valuables. He then went to the clergyman's main house at No.15 Paultons Square and murdered the housekeeper, Ann Boss. After spending several days drinking in the company of a woman, he was caught, tried and hanged.

No.25: This is thought to be the fictional home of James Bond, based on Ian Fleming's 1955 thriller *Moonraker:* 'A comfortable flat in a plane tree'd square off the King's Road,' is how Fleming described it. Author William Boyd deduced it was No.25 because it fitted the description and was the flat of Desmond MacCarthy, a literary critic and friend of Fleming's.

Westfield Park – *see Tetcott Road and Uverdale Road.*

Whitehead's Grove

A tree-lined residential street, including Cranmer Court. It runs west from Draycott Avenue and is parallel and north of the King's Road. It was named after William Whitehead, who leased Chelsea Common in 1810 from the Cadogan family and promptly built this street.

Winterton Place

This small cul-de-sac south of Fulham Road is entered from Park Walk and runs west. It contains a few residential buildings, one of which is Fleming Close (No.3).

Woodfall Street

Woodfall Street is a cul-de-sac south of the King's Road that runs east off of Smith Street. It was initially used as the stable and coach houses for the main houses on St Leonard's Terrace. It was named after Henry Sampson Woodfall (1739–1805), a famous printer of his time and a Cheyne Walk resident. The

mews properties are now residential, though some commercial activity remains. The popular Phoenix pub is on the corner with Smith Street.

During the Second World War, a high-explosive bomb fell on to Smith Street, just outside the mews, causing damage to the properties. The street has a very early black-and-white road sign, which is probably Victorian.

World's End Place

World's End Place has a long and varied history – from being part of Chelsea Farm in the early eighteenth century to an open-air brothel in 1845, in the 1900s, it was a public space, and then a council housing estate was started there in 1967, which completed in 1976.

Today, it stands as one of the most impressive of the high-rise, high-density developments of its time and perhaps one of the most likeable.

Yeoman's Row

A cul-de-sac running south from Brompton Road to Walton Street. At No.18 is a blue plaque to Wells Coates, a modernist architect and designer. He is probably most famous for London's Isokon building and sister building, Embassy Court in Brighton.

HISTORICAL CHELSEA

Spies Like Them

Before Chelsea was the home and playground of the rich and wealthy, it was bohemian, attracting musicians, intellectuals, artists, writers and other sub-cultures. Having been extensively bombed during the Blitz, the neighbourhood wasn't expensive. It was also a great place to hide. The number of those involved in espionage seems significant.

We've already met double agent Kim Philby at No.18 Camera Square. The writer Erskine Childers lived in Carlyle Mansions. He was an RAF intelligence officer who wrote *The Riddle of the Sands: A Record of Secret Service*, an espionage novel published in 1903. Remarkably, Ian Fleming lived in the same block of flats. Fleming was recruited into the secret service by Maxwell Knight, reputedly the inspiration behind 'M' in the James Bond books. Knight ran a section of MI5 from his flat in Sloane Square before it moved to Dolphin Square in Pimlico.

William Boyd said that the location of James Bond's flat, as described in Fleming's 1955 thriller *Moonraker*, was 25 Wellington Square. It fits the book's description and was the home of Fleming's friend, the literary critic Desmond MacCarthy.

Published in 2023 by Unicorn
an imprint of Unicorn Publishing Group
Charleston Studio, Meadow Business Centre, Lewes BN8 5RW
www.unicornpublishing.org

Text © Ripple Productions Limited
Images – see picture credits below

ISBN 978-1-911397-35-9

10 9 8 7 6 5 4 3 2 1

Editor: Daniel Neilson
Designer: Felicity Price-Smith
Printed by Fine Tone Ltd

All images are courtesy of Ripple Productions Limited, with the following exceptions:

Allan Cash Picture Library/Alamy Stock Photo: p.62–3; Alpha Stock/Alamy Stock Photo: p.60; Bailey-Cooper Photography/Alamy Stock Photo: p.190–1; Ben Brooksbank: pp.147b, 158; Biodiversity Heritage Library: p.69r; British Library: pp.18, 29l, 73; Courtesy of Cadogan: pp.4, 19br, 25, 148–9; Courtesy of Chelsea Old Church Library: p.39; Chronicle/Alamy Stock Photo: pp.2–3; David Hawgood: p.201b; David Iliff: pp.19bl, 221; Elisa Rolle: pp.50, 226; Flickr/Alison Day: p.104t; Flickr/Amanda Slater: pp.56t, 146b; Flickr/Jim Linwood: pp.26t, 79b, 135b, 227; Flickr/Maggie Jones: p.212t; Flickr/Scio Central School Website: p. 238; Flickr/Tony Hisgett: p.83b; Fortepan/ Közösségi Szocialis Szövetkezet: p.100; George P. Landow, Victorian Web: p.144, Harold Chapman/ TopFoto: p.90t; Harvard Art Museums/Fogg Museum, Bequest of Grenville L. Winthrop: p.79r; horst friedrichs/Alamy Stock Photo: p.102, istock/Chunyip Wong: p.43; istock/Serts: pp.213, 239, John Hendy: p.90br; John Michaels/Alamy Stock Photo: pp.6–7; © Julia Page: p.29br; © Laura Stoner New: p.51t; Library of Congress: p.233f; Maurice Savage/Alamy Stock Photo: p.214; Metropolitan Museum of Art, purchase, Edward C. Moore Jr. Gift, 1923: p.80; Mirrorpix/Alamy Stock Photo: p.92; Paul Museum of New Zealand Te Papa Tongarewa: p.83t; PA Images/Alamy Stock Photo: p.87; Paul Leonard: p.107b; Photo collection Anefo: p.89; Photo-Loci/Alamy Stock Photo: p.12; Pictorial Press/ Alamy Stock Photo: pp.88, 90bl, 91, 93, 94; RHS / Georgi Mabee: p.57; Robert Anton Reese: p.228; Robert Rimell: p.226; Royal Borough of Kensington & Chelsea Local Studies & Archives: p.34; Ryan Gearing: pp.32bl, 67, 110r, 118, 121, 123, 137, 143t, 145, 150r, 151l, 152t,bl, 156b, 160b, 163b, 166b, 171, 177l, 178, 179bl, br, 180b, 183t, 185, 187tl, 194, 196t, 204t,b, 205, 216t,br,bl, 218, 219, 220r, 225, 236t; Shutterstock/Joe Dunckley: pp.128–9; Shutterstock/William Barton: pp.206–7; Shutterstock/Ron Ellis: pp.8b, 154, 198–9; © Tate: p.79; The Cleveland Museum of Art, Nancy F. and Joseph P. Keithley Collection Gift: p.16–17; The Metropolitan Museum of Art, Bequest of Julia H. Manges, in memory of her husband, Dr. Morris Manges, 1960: p.42; The Print Collector/ Alamy Stock Photo: p.8t; The Yorck Project: pp.32, 78; Tony French/Alamy Stock Photo: p.173; Courtesy of the Wellcome Collection: pp.13, 14, 22, 49, 50b; Wikimedia commons/No Swan So Fine: p.140bl; Wikimedia commons/spudgun67: pp.126t, 170; Yale Center for British Art, Paul Mellon Collection: pp.10–11, 19t, 29tr, 35, 70; Yale University Library: p.56b.